Shipwrecks
and Archaeology

Shipwrecks and Archaeology

The Unharvested Sea

~~~~~~

BY Peter Throckmorton

LONDON
VICTOR GOLLANCZ LTD
1970

Chapter IV appeared originally in the *Atlantic*. Facsimiles of Crown-copyright records in the Public Record Office appear by permission of H.M. Stationery Office.

PRINTED IN GREAT BRITAIN BY
LOWE AND BRYDONE (PRINTERS) LTD., LONDON

For All the Ephors

Preface

∽∽∽∽∽

In the spring of 1958 a Turk named Mustafa Kapkin and
I persuaded a boatman from Bodrum, a town on the
south coast of Turkey, to take us out to Yassi Ada, a tiny
island which protrudes into one side of the channel between the Turkish mainland and the Greek islands of
Kalymnos and Kos. After several dives we understood
that Yassi Ada was a graveyard of ships wrecked from
Hellenistic times to the year before I was born.

At Yassi Ada I began thinking seriously about shipwrecks, and started the slow change from being an enthusiastic amateur archaeologist who happened to be a
diver, to becoming a specialist in the marvelous new field
of marine archaeology. In another book, *The Lost Ships*,
I have described how Mustafa and I went on to discover,
at Cape Gelidonya in south Turkey, the oldest shipwreck
ever recorded, and how George Bass and I, with a team
from the University of Pennsylvania Museum, made it the
object of what we believe was the most scientific excavation of a shipwreck site done up to that time.

The Cape Gelidonya excavation was the beginning, you
might say, of my professional career as a marine archaeologist, and the end of my career in Turkey. It was there that
I made the mistake of firing a Turk whose uncle later
became a high government official. I was "tried" in absentia

by a secret committee of inquiry, who found me to have been an antiquities smuggler all along. No formal accusations were ever made; press releases were more than enough. Like James Mellaart, the young British archaeologist recently in trouble over the same sort of charges, I struggled along for a couple of years, trying to clear myself. But I never managed to do so, and slowly gave up hope of working again in Turkey.

George Bass stayed on, and carried out a wonderfully organized excavation of a Byzantine ship at Yassi Ada, one of the group Mustafa and I had found in 1958.

I went west to Greece. There I spent three years trying to convince a series of governments that organized underwater exploration would be useful. Little was accomplished. We were opposed by archaeological administrators suffering from all or some of a variety of impediments: lack of imagination to believe that wrecks actually existed and could be correctly excavated; jealousy of the large sums we raised for underwater work; the idea that an expedition would be a cover for a fancier-than-usual smuggling operation. Above all, we were stopped by the confused political situation, which let no minister or departmental director feel secure in his post, thus discouraging anything even mildly experimental.

The prejudice in Greece against foreign involvement with local antiquities began with Lord Elgin, during the Turkish occupation at the end of the eighteenth century. He bought whole shiploads of ancient art from the Turks and shipped them to England, thinking, perhaps correctly, that he was rescuing statues which would otherwise likely be burned into lime.

The Greeks disagreed, and journalists still quarrel irritably about the Elgin marbles. Angry editorials demanding the return of the marbles are a standard dog day feature of the Greek press, with every season producing another headline "Elgin," or two or three. The English say, when they say anything at all, that the Greeks ought to look after the friezes still on the Parthenon, neglected and suffering from industrial gases blown up from the Piraeus, before there can be talk of returning the Elgin marbles. This doesn't impress the Greeks, any more than the English liked Duveen's remark that Gainsboroughs are better off in American air-conditioned galleries than in damp and drafty English country houses. (In any case, Lord Duveen made a fortune exporting European art to America, and spent part of it on an air-conditioned gallery in the British Museum, to house the Elgin marbles.)

Compounding resentment at the loss of ancient sculptures to foreign museums is the conviction that the sea is littered with priceless treasures which foreigners are dead set on stealing. (Here, digressing for a moment, it is instructive to observe that the Greek for "guest" and for "stranger" is the same word. Tourist guides make much of this, touting peasant hospitality, but others point out correctly that the inspiration of the proud and delightful hospitality offered guests is a fear of that guest, the stranger, and the damage he might do his host if not placated.)

Like most obsessions, there is just enough truth in this one to make it impossible to cure with reasonable argument. There have indeed been fabulous finds in Greek waters, the most interesting of them being the Antikythera wreck which had a cargo of life-size and colossal bronze and marble sculptures. Another wreck, off Cape Artemesion, produced the famous bronze Poseidon, or Zeus, that is now in the Athens Museum. A copy stands in the lobby of the United Nations building in New York.

It is a frustrating and fairly useless proposition to argue

to the Greeks and Turks and the diminishing group of western land archaeologists still against "going under-water" that a huge national and international effort is needed if ancient shipwrecks are to be saved. I now have nearly a thousand Aegean shipwrecks in my files. Most of these are steadily being robbed. It is generally conceded that all ancient wrecks in the south of France, down to a depth of fifty meters, have been looted and destroyed by skin divers. It is as bad in Italy and Spain. Although marine archaeology has been developing as a subdiscipline of land archaeology for twenty years, and hundreds of shipwrecks have been "excavated" by skin divers, sponge divers, and conventional archaeologists, I am hard put to think of ten correctly excavated and published marine excavations. Ancient shipwrecks in the Mediterranean, like the buffalo of the great western American plains a hundred years ago, are disappearing.

There is a lack of trained underwater excavators to use the means which navies, foundations, and governments are often willing to put at their disposal, and it is the archaeologists' fault that this is so. There are few incentives for young people to go into marine archaeology, and many difficulties put in their path. As a result, there are not more than five trained marine archaeologists in the world.

In contrast, the world of marine archaeology is overrun with amateurs and adventurers who can be compared with the treasure hunters who ruined so many land sites at the beginning of the development of modern archaeology in the early 1900's. As then, there is a time gap between in-terest and technique, technique and its inclusion in re-spectable curricula of universities. The gap is presently filled by sticky-fingered sportsmen, the subject itself dis-persed to the mantelpieces and coffee tables of the world.

Recently the French government gave permission to a

skin diving club to excavate an Iron Age shipwreck with a cargo of bronze tools. In Turkey, treasure hunting concessions are sold. Although responsible exploration of sites known to be undergoing pillage is often forbidden or made very difficult by the department of antiquities, material from these sites is on public sale in every small port along the Turkish coast. The Greek government has never given a permit directly to a recognized marine archaeologist, but it has authorized a retired Greek-American restaurant owner to search for the mythical arms of the Venus de Milo. Amphoras stolen from wrecks are for sale in dozens of tourist shops, and the government authorizes export from Greece of this material because amphoras add little to the interest of the already vast collections of the National Museum.

This unhappy situation exists because most of the people concerned have no idea of what marine archaeology is all about. What are wrecks like? Is it worthwhile to work on them? What can we find out from them?

In 1925 Soloman Reinach wrote that "the richest museum of underwater antiquities in the whole world is still inaccessible. I mean the sea bed of the Mediterranean." It is not inaccessible any longer. Thus this book.

* * *

Anyone writing a general book about underwater archaeology finds himself in danger of being either too technical or not technical enough. There are several books about it, and many articles have been published in recent years. But there is as yet no general technical handbook, and if there were it would be outdated at the end of every major expedition, so quickly is this new subdiscipline developing.

There are many good handbooks of diving. I have therefore avoided giving a lot of diving data that is simply copied, in many places, from the U.S. Navy diving manual. I have tried to keep rewrites of other people's diving books to a minimum, and simply give the gist of what happened, referring the reader to the original sources. I have given longer accounts of projects which are not well known, and which have not been published before.

Archaeologists will find that I do not give some problems the space and annotation they deserve, and divers and technicians will find the same lack in material of particular interest to them. I've tried to remedy this by putting references and technical comments in an appendix and selected bibliography at the end of the book.

I believe it is more unkind to a dead or retired colleague's memory to gloss over his failings than to discuss his place in the history of what the Italians call "our mystery." Everyone who gets involved in marine archaeology today soon discovers that he is struggling to learn more things than he ever imagined existed. None of us knows enough. The jungle of classical scholarship is full of paths perilous for the nonprofessional, and classicists tend to stumble when they deal with the sea. It is very difficult today for one individual to acquire the experience needed to become an effective leader of underwater excavations in time to be young enough to stand up to the job. Few have, which is why so few underwater expeditions produce published reports which are useful to students of the past.

I want to thank Professor Nino Lamboglia for allowing me to visit the *Daino* and the storerooms of the nautical museum at Albenga, and for allowing me to dive on the Albenga wreck; Professor Fernand Benoit for allowing me to see unpublished material in the Musée Borely; Captain Philippe Taillez, Mrs. Gil Faure, Captain Jacques-Yves Cousteau; Henri Broussard and Honor Frost for their information on the early days in the south of France; Gerhard Kapitän for making his voluminous research in marine archaeology available to me; Virginia Grace, Gladys Weinberg, Mike Valtinos, Niki Konstas, Captain John Lyndiakos and the authorities of the Greek National Museum and Library for their help on Antikythera; Benkt Borjesson for his information on the *Vasa;* Joan St. George Saunders, who found much of the *Nautilus* material in the Public Records Office; and to the authorities of the National Maritime Museum and the Public Records Office for their generous help and for permission to reproduce the *Nautilus* material; Dr. George Crile for permission to quote from *Treasure-diving Holidays;* Sam Barclay, Jon Smith and Roger Stafford for their help with navigational problems concerning the *Nautilus;* Ora Patoharju for information on the Baltic; Hugh Edwards for information on Australia; and Alexander McKee for information about England.

I owe a debt to the late James Dugan for writing *Man Under the Sea,* the classic book about the history of diving, on which I have drawn heavily; and to Lionel Casson for writing another classic, *The Ancient Mariners.*

Translations from Greek which occur in this book were done with the help of Peter Green, Niki Konstas, and Mike Valtinos. Swedish articles were translated by Niki Konstas.

I am indebted to James Dugan and to Peter Green, Peter Davison and John Bullitt for reading the manuscript and making valuable suggestions, and to Henry Chapin, without whose encouragement I should not have written the book.

I could not have written this book without the help generously given by my wife, Joan Henley Throckmorton, who edited and typed the manuscript as well as rewriting so many parts of it that I am tempted to call her Colette.

Piraeus   PETER THROCKMORTON

Contents

〜〜〜〜〜

Illustrations

∾∾∾∾∾

ILLUSTRATIONS

PART I

I

~~~~~

The Sea Change

What a Shipwreck Is

He strack the top-mast wi' his hand,
The fore-mast wi' his knee,
And he brake that gallant ship in twain,
And sank her in the sea.

— *The Daemon Lover,*
Anonymous ballad

A FILM of oil, almost invisible in the slight chop that ruffled the surface of Melos bay, glistened on the water.

"Here she is."

We dragged the anchor line till it hooked, and were swimming down it in five minutes. We could see about thirty feet. A great bulk loomed out of the murk: the *Artemis*. An anchor hung on the stern rail. The sterncastle swarmed with little fish which poured out of the inner recesses of the wreck and swarmed round us like butterflies. I hung for a minute on the emergency steering wheel on the poop while someone took my picture, the standard wreck picture of the diver at the wheel on a voyage to nowhere.

We swam forward, staying well over the shattered after holds with their fangs of iron. *Artemis*, once a sturdy well-

S.S. Artemis.

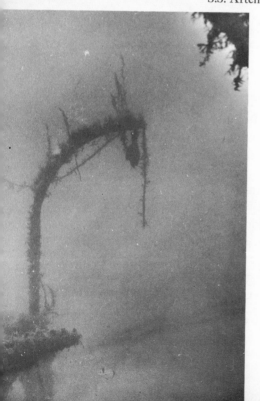

A davit of S.S. Artemis.

The engine room of the Artemis *with human bones laid out on the engine.*

Another view of the Artemis's *engine room.*

decked cargo ship of 4,200 tons, lay on the bottom like an old lady struck down by a runaway car, spread-eagled on a mean street with her skirts over her head.

The foremast swam out of the murk, the wire shrouds overgrown with long tendrils of weed. The booms were still rigged over hatches that had been open for twenty years.

In the spring of 1942 she had been in Melos harbor with a mixed cargo of gasoline in drums, ammunition, land mines, tank tracks, lampshades in cases, and kerosene in two-gallon cans. She was on her way to Egypt, to Rommel's Afrika Corps; the Germans had taken her over with her crew from her Greek owners. Three black torpedo bombers had come out of the sun early one morning while the people of Melos were going to work. A torpedo smashed into her number three hold behind the engine room, and *Artemis* blew up with a crash that broke nearly every window in town and sent a column of smoke more than a thousand feet high, engulfing the plane which had dropped the torpedo and spreading, thick and greasy, across the bay. When the cloud cleared ten minutes later the ship had disappeared, leaving a few heads bobbing in the water along with scattered debris. Fourteen men died.

We swam around her. The wooden bridge had almost disappeared, as well as her planked decks. The sea was taking over. Here at 150 feet the wreck was not affected by what happened on the surface. The only movement was of sea animals who were quietly and efficiently reducing *Artemis* to her original elements. The engine room, into which we swam uneasily and then returned to with morbid curiosity, was very cold from the winter water trapped in it. There was little growth. The copper pipes around the old-fashioned triple-expansion engine had, as they corroded, contaminated the water so that marine organisms grew slowly. An ordinary leather work shoe lay on the upper grating which surrounded the great cylinders. I picked it up, and the bones of a man's foot poured out, rustling through the grating. His long bones and skull lay beside the third-stage cylinder. A chain hoist hung overhead, its hook still tucked into a wire strop which was wrapped around the cylinder of an auxiliary pump. The brass plate on the pump was still clean. It read *Hamburg* — 1908. The glass of the pressure gauge was cracked.

We swam up and out of the morgue-like engine room and headed for the foremast, over what had once been the boat deck, past davits from which heavy blocks still hung, held by ropes which broke from the current of our passing. One of the divers picked up a German coal-scuttle helmet which stuck out of the mud overlying the deck. As we swam up the foremast, where we had attached the mooring line which led to the small boat high above, a school of *liche*, great silver pelagic fish, swooped close for a look at us and sped away into the murk after circling the huge smokestack. We hung for a moment, like gulls, on the crosstrees. Shrouds ran down to the loom of the now invisible ship, fifty feet below us. The man with the helmet gestured and, clowning, tried to put it on. As he turned it over, the upper part of the dead German's skull fell out and fluttered down to the corroding deck below.

Artemis is a good example of the sea change that takes place in wrecks, as well as in the Hollywood picture, ghoulish but strangely beautiful, of a dead ship under the sea. When Logan Smith, the diver who was with us that day, had first seen the wreck three years before, the pine decks and wheelhouse still stood, and lifeboats still swung in the davits. Now the teak binnacle was there, but the pine wheelhouse around it had collapsed. In twenty years only her bare iron bones will stand, a dangerous skeleton ready to collapse, and in thirty more she will be nothing but an overgrown heap of scrap iron on the bottom.

What is a shipwreck, then, and how does it happen? Scenes of shipwreck, like those of love and man-to-man combat, cannot have changed much in all these thousands of years, and as usual Shakespeare and the Bible have the situation pretty well surrounded. *The Tempest* has all the fear, the terror, of once friendly elements now turned hostile, the desperate last-minute joking ("I have great comfort from this fellow: methinks he hath no drowning mark upon him; his complexion is perfect gallows") known to every frightened mariner losing his ship beneath him. "The direful spectacle of the wreck, which touch'd/ The very virtue of compassion in thee" is described with a lot less emotion and more technical information, as if for evidence at a court-martial, by the chronicler of St. Paul.

On his way to Rome with a military escort in a grain ship, Paul's ship was caught in one of those winter southeasterly gales which play so large a part in the history of Mediterranean shipwrecks.

And when the ship was caught, and could not bear up into the wind, we let her drive. . . . But when the fourteenth night was come . . . about midnight the shipmen deemed that they drew near to some country; And sounded, and found it twenty fathoms: and when they had gone a little further, they sounded again, and found it fifteen fathoms. Then fearing lest we should have fallen upon rocks, they cast four anchors out of the stern, and wished for the day. [*Acts 27:15, 27–29*]

The only unusual thing here is the act of dropping anchors out of the stern. This is understandable if one looks at the traditional ship types which are still working in the Mediterranean. They are mostly built to run with the sea aft, rather than heave to in bad weather. St. Paul's ship can well have been built like most of the big ships shown on Roman mosaics and wall paintings, and the modern *perama* or *trechendiri* that sails the Aegean today.

Such a ship would be well off anchored stern to the weather, especially as she could lift her steering oars clean out of the water.

Other questions in the rest of the account were resolved when I understood, as Bible scholars had done long before me, that the King James version was superb literature but not all it might be as a precise translation. The original Greek had not said that the anchors were *taken up*, but most probably meant that the anchor ropes were cut. Nor did they hoist the mainsail, but the *artemona* or foresail. Nor, finally, did they *wish* for day. They prayed.

They had anchored when they heard breakers. One or more anchor cables had chafed. Others were let go. Crew and passengers shivered in the dark from fright and chill until the dawn. With an anchor or anchors still holding, faced with the risk of driving ashore the next night in a place not of his own choosing, the ship's master then decided to drive the ship ashore in daylight and save the people. From a nautical point of view, his decision was impeccable. From a theological point of view, a lot of people learned a lot more about sin than they might have done had St. Paul drowned in the breakers, but here we retreat from questions happily outside the province of this book.

And so, when the last anchor cable was about to chafe through, the master cut it, loosed the rudder yokes, hoisted the foresail, and let the ship drive. That way she was under control to the very end, and he could put her ashore in the safest possible place. Paul takes a sour view of all this unpleasantness, refrains from any expression of gratitude to the captain, with whom he had anyhow earlier quarreled, and assumes credit himself for the saving of the people. Companions in shipwrecks are seldom of one's own choosing, but chances are the captain went light on saints in the passenger lists of his later commands.

In 1964, near Taranto in southern Italy, we found the pitiful relics of just such a story, the outline in lead and clay of the same disaster fallen upon a similar ship caught in a similar gale, *sirocco* or *euryclydon*. Five enormous lead anchor stocks, each weighing almost exactly 1,300 pounds, lay in a nearly straight line which began a mile offshore, following the direction of these seasonal southerly gales. A line drawn on a chart through the position of the anchors led to a point on shore where we found the shattered bits of many hundreds of first century A.D. amphoras and roof tiles. The ship itself must have been driven ashore, like St. Paul's, the captain preferring to trust his person, his crew, his passengers, and what could be salvaged of his cargo to the uncertain mercies of a foreign coast in daylight, than to take a chance on still another terrifying night at sea, with the risk of foundering in deep water in darkness.

That is how one kind of shipwreck happens, in the kind of storm that plays so large a part in many of the stories below. Ships lost in these circumstances would likely have smashed to bits within days, as will a ship hammered and ground to pieces on a shallow reef. Given slightly different circumstances, the ship might survive.

There are many other sorts of wrecks, of course — the occasional drama of fire on the high seas, ships sunk by enemy in battle or by sabotage, the rotten ship unwisely sailed which suddenly gives up and dies, ghost ships abandoned for who knows what reasons. There are as many stories of wrecks as there are ships under the sea, but many of these we leave to other sorts of chroniclers. My peculiar job as ship archaeologist ("You do *what?*" I am often asked after stumbled introductions among strangers) is to read, from the wrecks of those which sank, the story — long or short — of the ships which sailed safe to port.

Our theoretical ship having sunk, what then will happen? Perhaps surprisingly, the chances are that this question can be answered with some fair amount of precision. If we know what the ship was made of, what kind of water she sank in, and what kind of bed awaited her at the bottom of the sea, we can more or less predict the course of her life-in-death from the moment of her last agony till her "resurrection," if ever, at the hands of human searchers and observers.

Assuming the ship had not smashed to bits, the survival of the ship as wreck is principally dependent on the nature of the water which surrounds her. Life destroys, and here we speak of the microorganisms which eat slowly and invisibly at the organic material of the ship; of the teredo worm which is said in the Far East to be edible, but certainly not enough to compensate for the terrific damage it inflicts on wooden hulls in salt seas; and of the skin diver's rape of the exotic treasures of his strange new element.

Heat destroys. Richard Russell, the chemist who worked on material from a silver cargo wreck at the Great Basses, estimated that the rate of corrosion increased by something close to one hundred percent for each centigrade degree above zero. Since moderate heat makes abundant life, geography and depth matter a great deal in the natural preservation of a wreck. The Basses ship, sunk on a shallow tropical reef in A.D. 1704, was in about the same condition as a Phoenician ship of 1300 B.C., ninety feet down in the Aegean, which a University of Pennsylvania Museum group excavated in 1960.

The salt sea destroys. The index of known shipwrecks and their state of preservation varies according to many factors, but as a whole material in fresh water is much better preserved than that in salt water. The wreck of the United States gundalow *Philadelphia*, for example, was raised intact from Lake Champlain in 1935, after more than one hundred fifty years under water. She was in good condition down to the splinters around the hole made by the cannonball that sank her, except for a slight surface checking of her oak timbers which occurred when they dried out. There are a great number of similar wrecks in the Great Lakes, said to be shrinking steadily these years at the hands of souvenir strippers.

At Lake Bolsena in Italy, fresh water has covered a village last inhabited by the forerunners of the Etruscans some nine hundred years before Christ. We surveyed and excavated a good part of this village, and found posts of the houses destroyed in whatever calamity accounted for the sudden flooding of the village. We held in our hands not only the broken cooking pots of the villagers but the remains of the fire they were cooking on, tiny nails, still tinier leaves from some new seedling, and the sheep bones, olive pits, and cherrystones that must have littered their earthen paths as they did ours at our camp on the shore. It was pathetic and in a way ridiculous, the gathering together of archaeologists and technicians from a dozen countries to study this rare Villanovan village, to learn, aside from the house plan of the village, that their housekeeping problems were much the same as ours.

After fresh water, brackish water as in the Baltic does the most remarkable job of ship preservation. Finnish and Swedish divers have found shipwrecks which fit the wildest imaginings of scriptwriters. One of these lies 120 feet deep just south of the Borstö Islands. The wreck of a small galliot of 1700 to 1710, she sits intact on the murky bottom, almost upright, her lower masts still standing. She appears to have been carrying a dignitary to St. Petersburg. In the icy mud of the cabin floor, divers groping in darkness found the bones of a tall old man; a wooden tag on which was written *Monsieur–Madame*, and a name that was hard to read but might have been *Baenikoff;* enameled snuffboxes; pocket watches; a bundle of textiles which proved to be a rococo petticoat; men's stockings; a whetstone, bottles, soup tureens, all things one might expect to find in the luggage of eighteenth-century gentlefolk. Lashed to the deck was an ornate carriage.

The ship was small, and appears to have been overwhelmed almost immediately. It might someday be possible to tell what sails were set when she sank, for the rotten ends of sheets and halyards are still hitched to the cleats inside the bulwarks.

A second splendidly preserved wreck in the brackish Baltic dates from the ninth of July, 1790, when the archipelago fleet of Sweden's King Gustav Adolphus III fought and defeated a Russian fleet off Ruotsalmi in Svensund. About fifty ships went to the bottom, including the Russian frigate *Sankte Nikolai*, which was explored in the 1950's by Finnish sport divers. She is upright on the bottom and almost intact except for her great stern cabin, which was smashed by helmet divers salvaging cannon in the 1930's. The water was so dark and dirty that the divers never saw more than a few feet of the ship at a time, and even less when they touched the wreck and stirred up clouds of mud. They took thousands of measurements and were able to make a model which shows what the wreck must look like were it possible to see her.

The *Vasa* project was and is a fantastic exhibition of Swedish ingenuity and historical interest. A big warship, she lay 120 feet deep in the bottom of Stockholm harbor, having capsized on her maiden voyage in 1628. Except for

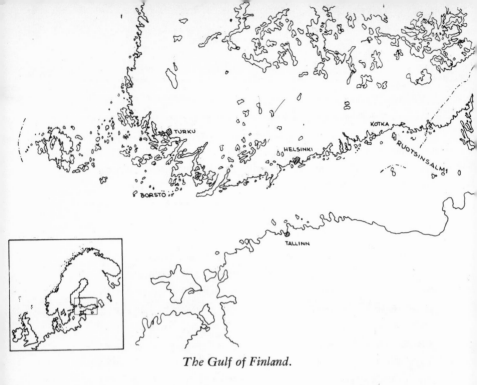

The Gulf of Finland.

The model made by the Finnish divers who worked on the wreck
of the Sankte Nikolai. (P. O. Jansson)

her upper decks and great cabin, which had been damaged when the bronze cannon were salvaged soon after the sinking, she was preserved as if in an icebox by the chill brackish harbor waters. Swedish navy divers, working in helmet gear in what amounted to total darkness, refastened her by driving thousands of wooden pegs into the holes which had held iron nails, now rusted away. They tunneled under the wreck with water jets so that slings could be gotten under her and she could be moved to shallow water, where she was made watertight, pumped out, and floated into dry dock.

There she was "excavated" by teams of archaeologists, who found nearly everything that had been in the ship in a good state of preservation. Many of the professional divers in Sweden worked on the *Vasa*. Some tell of having eaten butter from her stores, and tasted her beer. ("Not much good" was the general opinion.)

Today the *Vasa* is in a specially built museum, continually sprayed by jets of steam and chemicals which, it is hoped, will gradually soak into the great timbers and keep them from warping when she is finally exposed to fresh air.

In very different geographical circumstances, one of the salty marshes in Sicily which neither Mussolini nor the occupying Allies got around to draining, the after thirty feet of a late Roman (seventh-century) ship was found in 1964. A bulldozer digging a drainage ditch struck heavy timbers the width of a large man's forearm. Gerhard Kapitän, passionate student of marine archaeology, heard the news when one of the workmen tried to sell the heavy cypress timbers to the local shipyard!

We excavated and drew the ship in 1965 and found the wood in good enough condition for our draftsmen and gang of Sicilian workmen to walk on, taking reasonable care, without hurting the sodden timbers. Bones of a little sea bird, caught in the storm that sank the ship or having fallen there later, before the ship was covered with sand and mud, lay tucked in tidy order between two frames.

The Black Sea, where salinity at diving depths is about half that of the Mediterranean, must have splendid wrecks. We know that men in ships have traded there since at least the second millennium before Christ, and according to the nature of ships and men and the sea, some of them sank. Certainly wrecks lying below six hundred feet will be in wonderful condition, since there is almost no oxygen at such a depth and renewal of all the bottom water would take, it is estimated, about twenty-five hundred years. This sort of wreck research concerns us only theoretically now, but the theory is encouraging. Several years ago the American research ship *Pillsbury* made core samples in the depths of the Black Sea, and learned that surface animals had died and sunk to the bottom without decomposing in the usual manner. Since some of these marine forms remained intact on the bottom, we might expect to find ships there as well.

Unfortunately for students of Greek and Roman ships, the Mediterranean is not a very good place for conservation of ships, compared to the Baltic or Black Sea. The worst enemy of a wooden ship, sunk or afloat, is the teredo worm, tiny, efficient, voracious, which in the Mediterranean will in very few years tunnel so effectively through a piece of wood that it looks as if it has been riddled by buckshot. Its small pincer beak, less brittle than bone, tougher and sharper than a human fingernail, bites slowly through the wood, digesting whole ships with the quiet speed known to anyone who ever left so much as a dinghy afloat too long in dirty harbor waters. Like the Texas boll weevil, the teredo is an insatiable and clever enemy, ingesting expensive brands of antifouling paint with apparent enthusiasm, crawling over every centimeter of protective copper paint to find the single spot where the painter's brush was dry, where paint ran short, or a careless workman skipped a nearly invisible spot.

There are other ship eaters as well, from tiny organisms not visible to the naked eye to the human scavengers out for a day's sportive plunder: "If it moves, spear it; if it doesn't, put it on the mantelpiece."

The kind of sea bottom a ship falls onto is the most important factor in preservation of Mediterranean ships. This becomes of great importance once one moves back past late medieval ships, back before plans of ships were drawn by or for shipwrights. We could reconstruct ships like the Borstö wreck or the *Vasa* from existing plans more cheaply than raising the sunken ship itself, but nobody yet knows much about the ships built by the ancient Greeks and Romans.

The first obvious, and correct, point is that the deeper wreck has a much better chance of "survival." Deeper and colder water discourages both sea organism and human plunderers, and if the wreck is covered by sand or mud it will last, we may assume, indefinitely. A wooden ship fallen onto a hard bottom will last perhaps seventy-five years as a recognizable ship, at the very outside. But if the ship falls onto sand or mud, particularly when it falls below the depth affected by wave action, generally forty or fifty feet in the Mediterranean, it will probably stay intact long enough for part of it at least to become a sort of natural reef or hillock in the landscape of the bottom of the sea, the current gently sweeping mud and sand onto it as marine organisms live and die, depositing their refuse and shells along with the mud and sand.

The remains of the ship will be surprisingly undisturbed, particularly if she carried a cargo which had not much weight when immersed in water, like the common cargo of amphoras filled with oil or wine. She will have settled slowly, some damage and displacement of cargo occurring, but not much in a ship secured for sea. If she had hatches, the pressure of air forced out of her holds as water rushed in would smash those hatches open. Her cabin might be smashed or damaged by waves as it went under. If she hung at an angle for some time before going down, one could expect that heavy objects would break loose, smashing themselves and anything in their way. In this case, and even when the worst imaginable damage has occurred, say that of a ship thrown on her beam ends and lying with decks swept by great waves until she flooded and sank, one could still expect to find the ship almost intact immediately after sinking.

For a while she would lie there like a child's ship model at the bottom of the bathtub. Soon the sea would begin to bring about its inevitable change. The rigging and sails would be the first to go. The great mainsail would hang swaying in the current for three, four, or five months, then the cloth would rot. The lead sail rings would fall off to be scattered on the deck, which would already be full of mud. If the ship had a cargo of oil or wine, the pressure would probably have driven in the plugs and the water in and around the wreck would be for a few years slightly discolored. If oil had been in the cargo, a slight oil slick would mark the grave for years.

Teredos and other marine organisms would have begun feasting on the hull the day the ship sank. In a very few years it would have been so weakened that a diver might have seen whole sections of it swaying in the current. If the wreck had a tiled cabin roof, the weakened walls and beams would collapse under the weight of the tiles and fall to lodge on the shaky deck.

If the wreck lands broadside to a gentle current on a muddy bottom, she forms an obstruction. Like a natural reef, she will be "homesteaded" by all manner of reef-dwelling life. The mud piles up against the hull, and if the ship fell steeply listed, with one side down and the open hull facing the direction of the mud fall, the lower side of the ship would very rapidly fill with mud or sand. Anything which lay beneath this would be preserved.

In twenty or thirty years the high side of the ship, exposed to attacks by teredos, will have collapsed from its own weight. Then the wreck will have disappeared into the bottom, buried deeper every year by the continual accretion of sand and mud and sea growth.

This is our ideal deep-water Mediterranean wreck. Age makes comparatively little difference. At Cape Gelidonya ("Cape of the Swallows") in southern Turkey, the Bronze Age wreck excavated by the University Museum in 1960 had fragments of the ship itself, together with bits of basket and beads, and its principal cargo of copper ingots and scrap metal. George Bass's group in Turkey has recently finished the excavation of a Byzantine ship so well preserved that, from its fragments, the lines of the ship itself have been tentatively reconstructed.

Making a long jump in time and imagination, one arrives at the Bay of Navarino, off King Nestor's "sandy Pylos" in southern Greece. Here a similar situation probably obtains, with the remains of the Turkish fleet lost there during the Greek War of Independence in 1827. Burned by Admiral Codrington, perhaps the only admiral in modern history who suffered a reprimand from his government on the occasion of winning a major naval battle, the Turkish flagship sank in 175 feet of water in the bay. In the early 1900's rumors of gold aboard the flagship excited Greek sponge divers to attempt a rough salvage job. Frightened by her rotten, shaky upper works still protruding from the mud, the divers set off dynamite on the site. The explosion produced no gold, but it did free some of the huge ship's timbers, which were dragged into shallow water where they still remain, a dubious offering by local boatmen to tourists.

So much for the flagship. But the rest of the fleet is there, under the soft mud of the bottom of the bay. I dived there briefly in 1961, and found one of the other wrecks 180 feet deep. All I saw was the overgrown ribs of the ship protruding six or eight inches from the mud, forming the outline of what might have been a frigate. In the middle was a heap of heavily overgrown iron guns.

Deep water will protect a wreck from wave action, but it will be destroyed anyhow in the Mediterranean unless it is shortly covered over with sand or mud. If there is sufficient oxygen in circulating water, the wreck even at great depths stands no chance of survival. (Recent research has shown that water circulates at even very great depths, bringing the possibility of life down even to the seven-mile depth of the Marianas Trench, the deepest part of the oceans.)

The converse can, however, be true. Until very recently, it had been believed that only deep water would preserve fairly intact shipwrecks. But now we know that, though the odds are against it, shallow water wrecks do sometimes get covered over rapidly enough to allow sand or mud to work its magic of preservation. We have worked on a number of these, in very diverse circumstances.

In 1963 we were in the little harbor called Porto Longo

in the southwestern Greek Peloponnesus. We were looking for the wreck of H.M.S. *Columbine*, sunk in 1824, to
salvage a few scraps of copper and bronze for chemical
experiments, and to learn what we could about deteriora-
tion processes of a wooden ship. We had copies of her
builder's specifications, the captain's court-martial, and of
the log on the day she sank, so arriving at the specific site
didn't seem like much of a job.

With a certain amount of poking around, we did find a
wooden wreck under the mud. After airlifting a section
through it, we arrived on paper at a fairly good reconstruction of the ship. But no matter how many times we
remeasured, forced our several imaginations, or allowed
for the wildest possible error, the wreck refused to measure up to *Columbine*.

Some more research, this time in the Public Records Office in Pylos, told us that it was indeed another wreck,
that of an Austrian brig sunk in 1860. The two ships had
been moored in almost the same position, at the same time
of year, thirty-six years apart from one another. The
mooring was safe except during a southerly gale. Two
captains lost their ships in two different Januarys, from
misjudging the place.

Fifty yards away from the Austrian brig, the *Columbine* had landed on a rocky bottom and been completely
destroyed except for a bit of copper sheathing, a few ship
nails, some scraps of bronze, and fragments of dishes from
the captain's cabin.

That same summer we cleared and drew a section
through still a third modern wreck. This one, called the
Heraclea, had been sunk by German bombers in 1940.
The drawings of these three wrecks together give a sound
idea of the several processes of disintegration we may expect from wooden ships falling on different sorts of bot-

toms in otherwise nearly identical circumstances. Once covered over, it makes little difference whether the ship was sunk a hundred or a thousand years ago, from the point of view of preservation.

We saw this once again in the summer of 1967, excavating the wreck of a Roman ship which had carried a cargo of sarcophagi and other marble pieces and had sunk near Taranto in Italy. The pine planking was yellow and beautiful when we first uncovered it, the frames either in place or clearly indicated by nail holes, nail casts (the chemical increment of the sea forming around oxidizing iron), or the discoloration left by destroyed timbers. This wreck was also in shallow water, some thirty feet deep before excavation.

Given reasonably secure surroundings, then, a remarkable variety of material can be expected to remain in remarkably good condition.

The preservation of this ship material is a completely new problem which is little understood. Iron cannon, raised from a coral reef, can be cleaned of coral and seem in good condition, then in a few weeks fall completely apart. Iron from Roman times in the Mediterranean has almost always completely disappeared, turned to mush. Iron objects exist as negative casts, like plaster of uneven quality or blackened, solidified sand. These molds can be cut apart and cleaned out to take molding compounds which reproduce the form of the original iron object.

A shipwreck, says Mendel Peterson of the Smithsonian Institution, resembles nothing so much as a giant galvanic battery, with the salt water acting as an electrolyte. Copper, bronze, and brass are often perfectly preserved if they have not gotten involved in the electrolytic process. Gold is always incorruptible. Silver has a great affinity for sulfur, an element common in rotting shipwrecks, and usually

The Austrian brig.
The level of the bottom
shows over the diver's head.

The Heraclea *in 1939.*

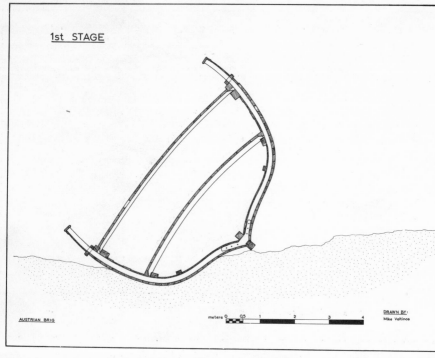

AUSTRIAN BRIG

meters 0   0.5   1   2   3   4

DRAWN BY:
Mike Valtinos

*A section thirty feet forward of the transom
after the ship sank in 1860.*

1870: the wreck begins to break up.

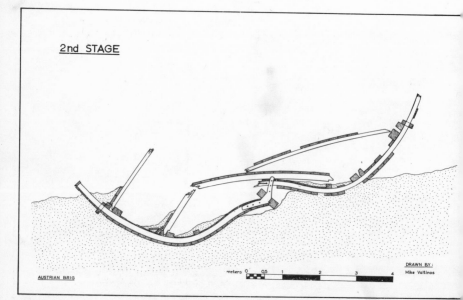

2nd STAGE

AUSTRIAN BRIG

meters 0   0.5   1   2   3   4

DRAWN BY:
Mike Valtinos

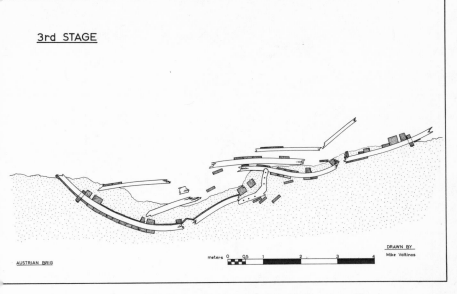

3rd STAGE

meters 0   0,5   1   2   3   4

DRAWN BY
Mike Valtinos

AUSTRIAN BRIG

*1890–1895: the wreck is completely broken up and
is beginning to be silted in.*

1963: the wreck, protected by the mud, will last indefinitely.

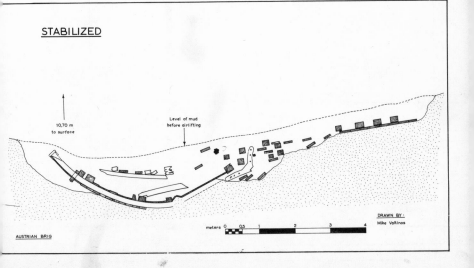

STABILIZED

10,70 m
to surface

Level of mud
before airlifting

meters 0   0,5   1   2   3   4

DRAWN BY:
Mike Valtinos

AUSTRIAN BRIG

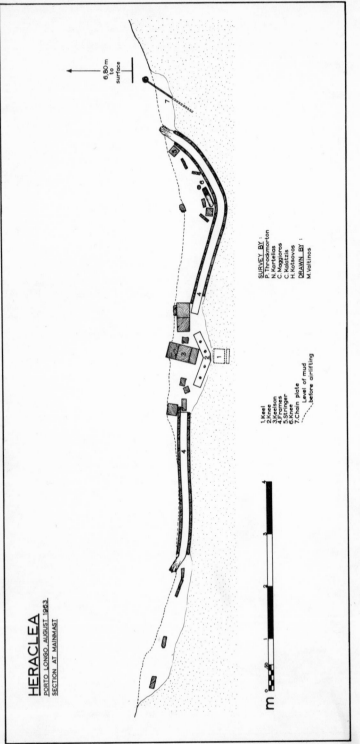

HERACLEA
PORTO LONGO, AUGUST 1963
SECTION AT MAINMAST

6,80 m
to
surface

SURVEY BY :
P. Throckmorton
N. Kartelias
C. Maggioros
C. Kalaitzis
H. Kotsovos
DRAWN BY :
M. Valtinos

1. Keel
2. Knee
3. Keelson
4. Frames
5. Stringer
6. Knee
7. Chain plate
Level of mud
before airlifting

m 0   4

*The wreck of the Heraclea, a 300-ton schooner sunk in 1941, was
found 150 yards from the wreck of the 1860 brig. This shows
a cross-section.*

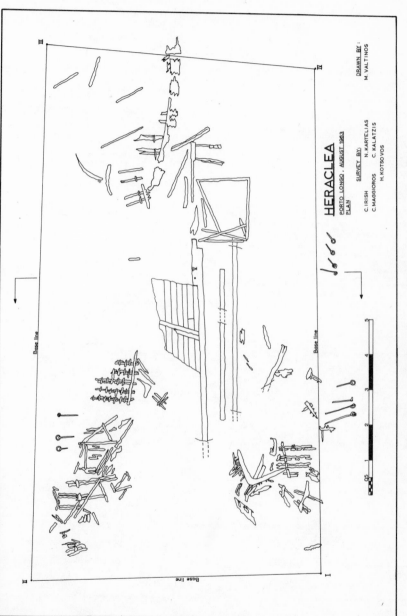

HERACLEA

PORTO LONGO . AUGUST 1963
PLAN

SURVEY BY:

C. IRISH   N. KARTELIAS
C. MAGGIOROS   C. KALATZIS
          H. KOTSOVOS

DRAWN BY :
M. VALTINOS

Base line

Base line

Base line

The Heraclea wreck from above in 1963. Roman numerals show points laid out for a base line survey. Point V is on the ship's keelson. The squarish shape near point V was the main hatch, which fell there when the deck collapsed.

Raising one of the Taranto anchors.

Drawing up one of the five Taranto anchors.

suffers severe damage unless it is near iron, which gives cathodic protection.

Pottery lasts forever under the sea. Marble is often attacked and can be completely destroyed by seaworms. Marble from Antikythera and Mahdia is like new on the side that was protected, and pockmarked beyond recognition on the sides that were exposed to the sea.

The wood of ancient wrecks suffers a sea change as well. When uncovered it seems strong, but something has happened: the cellulose has been replaced by seawater in the course of hundreds or thousands of years. Once exposed to air, this seawater must in turn be replaced by some suitable chemical compound, or the wood will shrink and disintegrate as it dries out.

The problem of what happens to undersea material promises to open a new subfield of chemistry; wood preservation is one of the major problems which confront the marine archaeologist. It is now possible to preserve small pieces of wood, but to preserve whole ships or large parts of ships is very difficult indeed. A solution both satisfactory and economical has not yet been found. The expensive preservation of the *Vasa* (described above), had the technology and the economic and emotional support of a whole nation behind it; materials from ancient wrecks in the south of France have shriveled to pitiful remnants of the originals.

Different kinds of wood absorb and give off moisture in different ways. Oak which has lain long under the sea seems to fare the worst upon drying out. Pine, elm, and cedar do better.

Glass varies in chemical composition. Studies at the Corning Glass Institute indicate a possible connection between annual cycles of temperature and the formation of distinct layers in glass under earth or sea. It may soon be possible to date glass from ancient shipwrecks by this method. The sea change suffered by glass also varies according to the chemical composition of the glass.

Various interesting chemical reactions have been observed in ancient wrecks. At the Grand Congloué, for example, the lead sheathing which had originally covered the ship beneath the waterline was almost completely transformed into sulfate of lead. Phoenician beads from Cape Gelidonya were of soft glass which seemed strong under water and just after they were raised, but then exploded into particles of dust when left to dry out. A basket from the same wreck was preserved because it lay between two copper ingots. The chemical by-products of the slow corrosion of the copper protected the soft matting.

Like the jewels taken by Cinderella's wicked stepsisters, shipwrecks are liable to turn into meaningless junk unless the magic of modern chemistry can be applied to them.

The final question, rudely put, is of course, so what? Who cares if a bit of planking is less rotten than one might have thought after a couple of thousand years underwater? What difference does it make to our tired planet, other than giving pleasure to a few harmless eccentrics who might otherwise be developing the pitless peach or observing wildfowl?

The answer, equally rudely put, is, probably not much. Archaeology is, after all, only the raw material of history. And for all the good the study of history has done in terms of preventing Man's foolishness, we had just as well burn the libraries down. And yet Man still craves knowledge of his own past. Few would condemn archaeology as useless. And if archaeology is justifiable, then the study of ships and their cargoes, the sea paths they sailed and the men who sailed them, is surely worthwhile.

A sailing ship, seen as artifact, is one of the most interesting and beautiful of human creations. In it is concentrated the accumulated knowledge of half a dozen crafts through many generations. Like public buildings, ships are expressions of the societies that create them.

No tradition of studies of ancient ships has grown to parallel rules of method laid down by the scholars who began in the nineteenth century to study and classify temples, vases, statues, and coins, because the ships did not then exist. Now we have found the ships; a discipline for studying them must develop.

An argument can be made for ship excavations from a technical point of view. A shipwreck site in good condition is a better closed archaeological site than most sites found on land. All the material in a ship was in use on the day the ship sank. And if it is undisturbed, as is usual in deep-water sites, it has remained intact as a dated group since the day the ship sank.

The whole argument for marine archaeology might be more simply put. If archaeology is worthwhile, then ship archeology has value. The only reward of all archaeology is that we are learning things which we did not know before. The bottom of the sea is full of junk — seafaring Man's lost tracks. Some of the junk is precious; most of it is meaningful. In the last twenty years men have acquired the technology to explore the first few hundred feet of the continental shelf, where literally hundreds of thousands of shipwrecks lie. What is actually there, in Davy Jones' open locker? And what can we learn from it?

II

~~~~~

Reefs, Archives, and the Age
of Exploration

Rocks and shoals are always dangerous to the mariner,
even where their situation has been ascertained; they are
more dangerous in seas which have never before been navigated, and in this part of the globe, for here they are reefs
of coral rock, rising like a wall almost perpendicular out of
the unfathomable deep . . .

Captain James Cook, writing in
August, 1770, aboard H.M.S. *Endeavor*,
in the Barrier Reef

B EFORE trying to understand shipwrecks which are going
to tell us about things that happened in historical peri-
ods whose written records of maritime history are unknown to us, we should first have a look at a few shipwrecks which are well documented. Ships get wrecked for
good reasons, and they get wrecked in certain places for
reasons which apply as much to the captain of a Royal
Navy sloop of war as to his Roman counterpart.

The Public Records Office off Chancery Lane in London contains most of the records of the Royal Navy from
the early eighteenth century onwards. These logs, court-
martial proceedings of ship losses, and other documents
give a vivid picture of the period, and of the hazards of
seafaring under sail. They also help to explain losses of

ships which are not recorded. Every Mediterranean rock which knocked out the bottom of a ship whose loss is recorded sank several others for which the only evidence is the shattered remains of the wrecks themselves.

A good example of this is at Yassi Ada, a small island between Kos and Kalymnos and Bodrum on the Turkish mainland, where we found more than fifteen wrecks. The earliest was a ship of the third century B.C. The collection of wrecks on the reef includes a Byzantine coastal trader, a big cargo ship from Rhodes of the first century A.D., a nineteenth-century warship, and a local sailing caïque that sank in the 1930's. All of these ships sank for the same reason: a reef 150 yards west of the island is not where a reef should logically be.

In these times of steel ships and safe travel, we have less concern with shipwrecks, although almost any wreck is good for extensive newspaper coverage and the loss of a liner like the *Andrea Doria* becomes a classic. In the days of the sailing ships there was a whole literature of shipwrecks. Penny dreadfuls with fine titles like "The Disastrous Loss of the So and So and Dreadful SOJOURN of her Crew among CANNIBALS" sold like today's spy thrillers all over Europe but especially in England.

One of the best shipwreck story collections was assembled by a nineteenth-century parson named William O. S. Gilley, who was vicar of Norham and canon of Durham. He loves phrases like "Once more they bade god speed to the frail bark," and "The scene of horror and confusion was one that baffles all description."

Some of Gilley's stories really do baffle all description. During the twenty-two years of the Napoleonic wars, the Royal Navy lost over three hundred ships by mishap, and less than a dozen by enemy action. The total establishment of the navy in 1810 was only about two hundred and fifty ships.

Gilley's *Narratives of Shipwrecks of the Royal Navy* went through many editions in the first half of the nineteenth century. He covers the period between 1793 and 1850, listing 372 naval ships lost by mishap, of which he describes 38. Of the total, nearly half were lost by running onto unmarked shoals or rocks. Another 78 foundered at sea, usually with all hands, in gales in the North Atlantic, Caribbean hurricanes, or Pacific typhoons. A dozen were lost by fire, always a danger in the days of wooden warships. Lanterns, candles, and gunpowder or rum made a lethal combination. Navies less disciplined than the British lost proportionately more ships by fire. The Turks were notorious for their carelessness aboard ship, and entire fleets of them took fire and blew up during the eighteenth and nineteenth centuries, with and without help from their enemies.

Any generalizations about ship losses made with naval statistics must be taken with a grain of salt, since naval ships are generally larger, more seaworthy, and in better condition than merchantmen. But it is possible to draw analogies from the smaller classes of warships, which resembled merchant ships of the day, such as the Columbine class of sloops of war. Over a hundred were built. They were as ubiquitous in the Royal Navy of the day as the standard wooden minesweepers and patrol boats of the Second World War have been in our time.

Ships of the Columbine class were rigged as brigs. They were 100 feet long on the deck and 77-plus on the keel. They carried a complement of 121 men and 18 guns. They were mostly built of oak with copper fastenings, and were copper sheathed. A merchantman of that size in the early 1800's seldom had a crew of more than twenty-five men, and often sailed with less. We might expect a naval ship to be better kept up and have stronger gear than the average merchantman. Yet of seventy Columbine-class brigs built between 1803 and 1809, nineteen were lost by mishap. Of these, six foundered with all hands, three in hurricanes in the West Indies, one in the North Atlantic, one off Africa, and another in the East Indies.

Of the remaining thirteen, six were lost by running on reefs or shoals. Three of these were in northern Europe in the wintertime, and two out of the three were lost with all hands. Two more ran on reefs in calmer waters with small loss of life, one in the Adriatic and the other on a Caribbean coral reef. Seven went ashore with small loss of life, two in the Mediterranean, four in the British Isles, another in Nova Scotia.

By going through Gilley, it is possible to extract another nineteen lost 18-gun brigs similar to *Columbine*. Of these, eight foundered with all hands, three in the Caribbean, two on the Halifax Station, two in the Channel and another in the Mediterranean. Four more went onto Caribbean reefs with small loss of life, another two foundered in the Caribbean, and five more were driven ashore in various parts of the world.

There are good statistics on how many merchant ships sank during the last days of sail, when ships were probably better designed, sailed better, and were safer than they had ever been before. In the five years from 1864 to 1869, ten thousand sailing ships insured in England were lost in various parts of the world, nearly a thousand of them without trace. A British merchant seaman in 1867 stood about the same statistical chance of being drowned at sea as an American soldier serving in Vietnam in 1967 stood of being killed by the Viet Cong — 300,000 afloat and 1,500 drowned versus 600,000 in Vietnam and 3,000 killed.

A very large percentage of all working sailing ships were eventually lost. The question that interests the marine archaeologist is not how many were lost, but how many can be found and studied, and which are worth studying. Our sample of thirty-nine Royal Naval 18-gun brigs gives a good idea of the possibilities. Assuming we wanted to find one of these brigs in reasonably intact condition, which should we choose?

The sixteen brigs which foundered at sea are undoubtedly the best preserved. These, however, will not be found in our time, as they lie too deep. Ten ran on reefs. Of those, four were smashed immediately and it is unlikely that anything remains of them except their cannon and anchors. One went on a reef in the Adriatic, sank in deep water, and might retain her archaeological integrity. Five more went on Caribbean reefs. Twelve more ran or were driven ashore. Of these twelve, two are of possible interest but are possibly destroyed.

In short, out of thirty-nine ships it might be possible to find remnants of seven, and of those seven, five are on tropical coral reefs.

It would be wearisome to include even a partial list of the possible coral reef wrecks here, but surely there must be thousands. The Portuguese alone lost 130 ships between 1555 and 1650 on the route to the Indies. The reef areas that flank the trade routes of sailing ship days are, as Mendel Peterson puts it, "littered with underwater sites, particularly when swift currents flow by them and the wind is on shore."

The strange new world of the coral reefs has become familiar to many since the invention of the Aqua-lung and the universal use of masks and fins. One's first encounter with a reef is a moving experience. The reef swarms with thousands of different kinds of fish, many gaily colored. The coral itself is strange and beautiful. The tiny coral animal with its limestone skeleton builds its descendants' houses of fantastic shapes, according to mysterious natural laws. Some coral colonies resemble giant brains, others the antlers of huge deer, others trees, and so forth. Generally speaking, the coral polyps cannot grow below about thirty feet, since they require fairly strong sunlight. Only the surface of the reef is alive, built on top of the limestone skeletons which sometimes continue a thousand feet deep.

For seamen, reefs are traps, because the coral so often rises sheer without breaking the surface. The standard charts used by mariners are often based on surveys the Royal Navy carried out in the eighteenth and nineteenth centuries. Hundreds of reefs bear the names of ships that were wrecked on them. The names on the charts hint at fantastic stories of shipwreck and wild adventure, often in open boats and among hostile natives. Through surviving records we have fascinating glimpses of what happened when a big ship baptized a big reef. For example:

Passed Dondra Head at sunset and then steered E by North during the night to pass well outside the Basses . . . which . . . on the morning of the 2nd [of July, 1813] . . . both the Master and myself felt assured we had done . . . steered north to get in with the land again, keeping a good look out from both the deck and masthead for rocks and breakers . . .

From the Court-martial on H.M.S. *Daedalus*,
August 11, 1813

The chatter in the rigging must have hushed as the captain came on deck and stood by the temporary chart table just forward of the binnacle with the master, Mr. Webster. They leaned over the chart, occasionally peering at the island of Ceylon, which was now clearly visible through their spyglasses.

Then there was a tremor, and a slight bump which most on board did not even feel. H.M.S. *Daedalus* had scraped the reef. There was a flurry of orders from the quarter-deck. One command was to the ship's carpenter, Robert Blackmore, who got all the pumps rigged, the gunports closed, and the hatches battened. He hastily sounded the well and reported to the captain that the ship did not seem to be making water. Then the carpenter's mate inter-rupted with the news that the ship had made three inches in the fifteen minutes that had passed since Blackmore had checked. The master's mate then hurried onto the quarter-deck with the dismal news that the after cockpit was "all afloat."

Captain Murray Maxwell must have cursed the bad luck that had gotten him transferred from his old ship, the *Al-ceste*, which he had commanded for the past four years. The *Daedalus* was handsome and sailed well, but was Ital-ian-built and very light. She had been captured from the French off Lissa two years before by a squadron of four ships commanded by Captain William Hoste, and her name changed from *Corona*, the name she had borne in the French navy. At this distance it is impossible to say just why the frigate was rotten, and why Murray Max-well had not demanded that she be opened out and re-paired. According to Maxwell, she had been in dock in Deptford the year before and had been found to "possess the timbers and scantlings of an 18-gun ship [i.e., of a ship only two-thirds her size] and though found rotten in sev-eral places forward, had not been opened abaft where she showed great symptoms of debility by unusual working and straining whenever it blew fresh, when she also made a considerable quantity of water. The weight of the upper works and guns when she touched crushed her slender frame to pieces."

Perhaps Maxwell did not want to make too much of a fuss if the ship were not hopelessly rotten. There were more captains than ships, and a squeamish commander would not endear himself to their lordships of the Admiralty.

Sails still set, *Daedalus* pulled away from the reef. When Maxwell gave the order to bring her up to the wind, it was found that her rudder was carried away. When she finally rode head to wind Maxwell signaled to the convoy to send all their carpenters. There was still a good chance of keeping her afloat until she could be sailed to Trincomalee, over one hundred miles to the north. She seemed all right, except for a list to port. By this time all hands were at the pumps in the waist, or bailing from the rapidly flooding bread room and cockpit in the after end of the ship.

As the sun rose, so did the wind. It was still calm, but the long swells increased as the big ship drifted to the east and she came out from under the shelter of the shoals where she had struck.

After a whispered conference with Maxwell, the first lieutenant went round the ship with the gunner and boatswain and collected a working party. The ship soon rang with the squeal of gun trucks and shouted orders as squads of sweating seamen tailed onto tackles and handspikes and rolled the after guns forward so as to lighten the ship aft, their bare feet splashing in the clear water that spurted from the pumps, rolling round the deck in little waves before it ran out the scuppers. Other parties sweated in the after storerooms. Tons of barrels and bags followed the guns forward.

The carpenter and his mates, assisted by the carpenters

who were beginning to arrive from the convoy, unshipped
the broken rudder. They found the stern post under it
broken too, to the third rudder pintle. Normally just
above the waterline, it was now ominously deep. When
Blackmore, with a bowline around his waist and three seamen holding the rope that held him by bracing onto the
stern windows, got down to the water, he saw that the
whole stern post was gone. It and the deadwood, the solid
structure of wood which was built up where the ship's
bottom narrowed as it met the rudder, had been completely rotten. No one has recorded what Blackmore said,
swinging on his bowline with his toes in the warm water as
he picked at rotten timbers, but if it concerned the captain
of the Deptford dock, it must surely have been unprint-
able.

Maxwell gave the order that sent thirty-eight guns, four
great anchors and hundreds of iron cannonballs tumbling
overboard, to lighten the ship by over a hundred tons. Another hundred tons of stores from the after hold followed
them, as fifty men under the sailmaker laid a heavy storm
sail out on the after gratings and "thrummed" it by sewing
it full of old rope chopped up for the purpose. A barrel of
tar was smeared over the sail and the sail gotten overboard
around the stern. It had little effect. The ship sank lower
in the water.

Finally, Maxwell wrote:

. . . by four in the afternoon, not withstanding the inde-
fatigable exertions of every officer and man on board, the
water had gained so much as to be two feet above the orlop
decks . . . the carpenters reported that the ship could not
swim much longer: It then became my painfull duty to preserve the valuable lives of the crew and the painfull order for
abandoning his majesty's ship was given . . . two divisions of
the seamen and marines (the others being kept at the pumps)

were put into East India Ships boats and our own, and to their great credit, with as much order and regularity as if moving from one ship to another in any of the king's ports . . . and when the boats returned the remaining divisions and officers quitted the pumps and took with them the hammocks and clothes of the whole ship's company, and when I had ascertained that every soul was removed from the ship I quitted her, with feelings, however painfull, that were well supported by a sense of having done my duty, and five minutes afterwards her mastheads were below the surface of the water.

Maxwell had nothing to fear from the court-martial, which recommended him to be more cautious in the future, but severely reprimanded Webster, the master, declaring him guilty of gross neglect of duty.

Somewhere, a few miles to the east of the reef off the south coast of Ceylon that bears her name, is all that is left of H.M.S. *Daedalus*, a long line of guns pointing to a heap of iron ballast blocks surrounded by copper nails. Scattered around will be those imperishable parts of the ship which have not been affected by the ravenous organic growth of those tropical waters.

Maxwell returned to England after the court-martial, and was posted back to his old ship, the *Alceste*, in 1815. He sailed back to the tropics in February, 1816, with Lord Amherst and his suite on a special embassy to Peking. His lordship's mission accomplished, they sailed for England by way of Manila. Captain Maxwell chose to pass from the China seas to the Indian Ocean and thence to England around the Cape of Good Hope by way of the Gaspar Straits. They sighted the island of Gaspar early on the eighteenth of February, 1817. It was almost flat calm, but the sea was a dirty gray color, making it difficult to spot shallows. In spite of three alert lookouts, *Alceste* struck a coral pinnacle with a crash at 7:30 in the morning. The holds were flooded in five minutes.

"What my feelings were," says Captain Maxwell, "at this momentary transition from a state of security to all the horror of a shipwreck, I do not venture to depict; but I must acknowledge, it required whatever mental energy I possessed to control them, and to enable me to give with coolness and firmness the necessary orders preparatory to abandoning the ship, which a very short period of hard working at the pumps showed the impracticability of saving."

Maxwell got Lord Amherst and his suite ashore along with most of the ship's company and a fair amount of food and gear. After a series of adventures which included being besieged by Malay pirates who drove the British salvage party off the wreck and then burned it, they reached Batavia and found passage to England.

On the way home, Maxwell's ship touched at St. Helena and he met Napoleon, who, remembering the part of Maxwell and the *Alceste* in the capture of a French frigate, said to him, "Your government must not blame you for the loss of the *Alceste*, for you have taken one of my frigates."

Maxwell was knighted the following year, but never got command of another ship.

Other ships' companies and captains were not always so lucky. In 1807 the *Blenheim*, 74 guns, with Admiral Thomas Troubridge and 590 men, and the *Java*, 32 guns, with 215 men, disappeared completely in the Indian Ocean, probably in a typhoon.

It was not until after World War II that anyone connected an actual wreck with the Admiralty files. The story begins in 1744:

I am extremely sorry this should be the messenger of such dis-
agreeable news as the loss of H.M.S. *Loo* . . . will you please
acquaint their lordships that . . . at a ¼ past one in the morning, the officer of the watch sent down to let me know he
was in the middle of breakers. . . . Just as we hauled the main
top sail the ship struck abaft . . . the Captain [sailing master]
came and told me the tiller was broke short off . . . . the ship,
continued striking . . . there came three or four seas and
bulged her immediately . . .

This was written by Captain Ashby Utting in a letter
from Port Royal on February 15, 1744, to the Admiralty,
reporting the loss of his late command on the reef now
called Loo's Key which lies off the southwestern tip of
Florida.

Almost exactly two hundred years later, a fisherman
named Bill Thompson found some cannon on the reef. In
October of 1950, Thompson showed the cannon to Dr.
and Mrs. George Crile and their children. Dr. Crile is a
surgeon from Cleveland who, aided by his wife Jane, built
his first diving helmet in 1934 and has been fascinated by
diving ever since. Their book, *Treasure-diving Holidays*,
is an amusing account of the enormous fun the Crile fam-
ily had with diving, and their progress in learning its dangers and pleasures in the days before it became a popular
sport.

What the Crile party saw through their facemasks was
typical of the coral reef wrecks that had been found in the
past and were to be found in the near future. Its interest is
that the Criles tried to make sense out of what they saw on
the bottom. Their description is worth quoting:

Below us the bottom was covered with oblong bars, heaps and
piles of them, tumbled and strewn as far as we could see. The
whole length of the deep narrow channel between the coral

banks was filled with wreckage. On one bank two thirds of a huge anchor was buried, like King Arthur's sword, in solid stone. The hawser ring was big enough to swim through. There were cannon deeply embedded in sand and rock; others leaned against the coral banks. Two were criss-crossed in the white sand. Above them, grey skeletons of sea fans hung like cobwebs from the deep coral of the walls. Scattered among the cannon were coral covered cannon balls, twisted shapes of metal rods, and those mysterious oblongs as big as building stones. All the oblongs were the same size. A dozen or more were stacked in each of the rough heaps. There were square ones too, some of them single, some in piles of twos and threes . . . Except for one little patch of sand, the bottom was like concrete; a hard white conglomeration of broken bits of coral reinforced with the iron remnants of the wreck . . .

They thought that the bars were silver, and were excited. They were only able to work one more day, however, before a hurricane drove them off the reef. They had salvaged cannonballs, musket barrels, a coin of 1720, silver buttons, and a pewter mug.

They returned to the wreck on May 30, 1951, accompanied by a large party which included Mr. and Mrs. E. A. Link, Commander Mendel Peterson, and Art Mackee. They were disappointed to find that the bars they had hoped were silver were really iron ballast blocks.

The party dug on the site with airlifts and water jets for five days. They recovered coral sand–encrusted cannonballs of six and twelve pounds each, marked with the broad arrow of the Royal Navy. Imbedded in the coral were hundreds of smaller objects such as fragments of English salt-glaze stoneware, bits of broken green glass bottles, Chinese porcelain, cow and sheep bones from the ship's salt-meat supplies, pot handles, a Queen Anne pewter teapot, and more coins. Covered with a thick layer

of coral sand, making it unrecognizable, was a large collection of ship's hardware, wrought iron rigging fittings and
hull bolts, an iron broadax, a rusty iron lock, bits of sheet
lead, a lead scupper pipe and brass barrel hoops marked
with the broad arrow.

One of the last objects recovered from the wreck was
one of the cannons, which Ed Link managed to raise and
sling alongside his yacht and bring to Marathon, Florida.
It proved to be a long six-pounder with its wooden
tampon still in the muzzle. It was marked with a Tudor
rose, which meant it had been cast before the death of
Queen Anne in 1714. When Peterson returned to Washington he looked up the losses of ships in the Royal Navy
from 1720 onwards, and found that H.M.S. *Loo*, 44 guns,
Captain Ashby Utting, had been lost in America in 1744.
Peterson found nearly all the documents relating to the
Loo in London, and published many of them in 1955 in a
fascinating paper, "The Last Cruise of H.M.S. *Loo*."
They tell the story of the ship, her loss, the subsequent
adventures of Captain Ashby Utting and his men off the
Indian-haunted coast of Florida, and Utting's court-
martial, at which he was absolved of all blame.

Mendel Peterson's work with the *Loo* was a landmark
in the history of marine archaeology in America, because
it was the first time that someone combined research in the
archives with actual exploration of an underwater site, and
published the results as a serious historical paper.

The last landfall made from the *Loo*, seven hours before
she sailed into the breakers, was the Pan of Matanzas, a flat-
topped mountain behind Matanzas Bay on the north coast
of Cuba. Matanzas Bay was probably where a ship called
Nuestra Señora de los Milagros, alias *El Matancero*, was
launched. *El Matancero* went onto the reef on what is
now known as Punta Matancero on the coast of Central

America about a hundred miles south of the northeast corner of Yucatán, on February 22, 1741, in much the same manner as the *Loo* went onto the Florida Keys.

The later history of the wreck of the *Matancero* begins with a dynamic character named Robert Marx, who went to Yucatán in 1957 after several years in the United States Marines, during which he became well known for his nearly successful search for the U.S.S. *Monitor*. Marx is the classic example of a diver with a bad case of shipwreck fever who began as a treasure hunter and who has now developed into a serious and competent marine archaeologist and naval historian.

In 1958 he was scraping a living teaching tourists to dive on Cozumel Island, off the Caribbean coast of Yucatán. He soon began locating shipwrecks off the coast of Yucatán and Cozumel. In November he was joined by Clay Blair, who was at that time at the *Saturday Evening Post* (which afterwards published several articles about their adventures in Yucatán), and by photographer Walter Bennett. They hired a local fishing boat and went off to the most interesting of the wrecks that Marx had located, off Point Matancero, where he had seen a large anchor and some coral-encrusted cannon twenty feet down.

Embedded in the reef were green glass bottles, remnants of wooden chests, pewter belt buckles, and a handful of cut stones which marked glass and which the Americans thought were diamonds. After one day, a storm came up and forced them to leave the site. By the time the weather cleared they had to return to their jobs.

Mendel Peterson examined one of the bottles and thought that it had been made in England between 1720 and 1740. They were disappointed to find that the "diamonds" were paste, but this didn't dampen their curiosity about the wreck.

Blair and Marx spent the winter of 1957–58 organizing an expedition. They planned to set up a campsite near the wreck, hire the small boat and fisherman they had employed the year before, then make a systematic survey of the site, working slowly and carefully. Although not trained archaeologists, they knew they could count on Mendel Peterson to help them with their finds, and they were equipped for preserving the objects they hoped to find. They consulted the American Embassy in Mexico and Mexican officials in the capital of Yucatán, in Mexico City, and in Cozumel. They were told they needed no special permit.

They arrived at Point Matancero in June. The weather was bad. When it improved, they dived with hammers and chisels and struggled to hack objects out of the reef. They were in continual danger from the surf that washed over the reef and took them for twenty-foot rides which ended with a bang on a coral bank. They were using hookah or nargileh equipment, which substitutes a hose going to a compressor in the boat for the steel tanks carried by ordinary Aqua-lung divers. Blair nearly drowned when his air hose kinked, and Marx had a dramatic free escape when his air hose unscrewed itself because the surge had made him turn so many somersaults.

The coral was full of objects. There were thousands of identical examples of two types of brass crucifixes, evidently trade goods for the Indians. One kind, an inch and a half high, was inscribed VITAM PRAESTA ("Give us life"). The other, smaller, had MARIA MATER etched on the almost perfect brass. The wooden chests they had seen the year before turned out to be full of silver-dipped brass spoons. There were thousands of beads, and a lump of coral full of pewter plates.

They were very excited. It seemed certain that they had

One of the crucifixes from the Matancero.

found a wreck which had not been salvaged. Even though they weren't finding treasure, they began to be obsessed with curiosity. "What was the ship?" they asked themselves. "Where was she bound, and where had she sailed from?" The spoons seemed to be English, like the bottle. By the third day they were convinced that they had found all that remained of the wreck of an English vessel trading to the Americas.

After several hours on the bottom Marx and Blair surfaced, exhausted, to find a large gray launch alongside their fishing boat. It was the police. They were under arrest.

Their little expedition had been sunk by rumors that they had found vast quantities of gold. From the moment they had left Cozumel, the island had bubbled with stories that would have been comical if their outcome had not been so unfortunate. A relation of someone who had once owned a treasure map that was now lost but had supposedly shown the location of a treasure near Point Matancero, filed an affidavit demanding half the gold. There was a rumor that the Americans planned to murder their boatmen and sail to Cuba with the treasure. So much pressure was put on the local officials that they were forced into action.

When they got back to Cozumel, Marx and Blair were told that they had not broken any law, but that the political situation required that they obtain permission from Mexico City before working further. The finds were confiscated. They spent ten days in hopeless politicking, until time ran out and Blair had to return to America and Marx to his diving lessons.

A short description of the Americans' attempts to obtain permission to dive on the wreck takes up eight pages of the book Blair later wrote about the adventure. He includes it as an object lesson to anyone attempting the same sort of thing in any Latin American country. Mexico had no laws which covered underwater exploration or underwater archaeology. A new law was immediately passed, requiring all finds to be turned over to the Mexican government, which also put sunken galleons under the authority of the antiquities service.

It became clear that permits for underwater research would be granted only to Mexican nationals. Now there appeared an organization called CEDAM — Club de Exploraciones y Deportes Aquáticos de México. The club had staged several expeditions, including one which involved placing a large bronze statue of Our Lady of Guadalupe, the patron saint of Mexico, underwater at Acapulco.

CEDAM got a permit to work on the wreck. Marx and

Blair were to be allowed to go along as guests of the CEDAM expedition. CEDAM's recruiting drive for the expedition included a series of advertisements in the Mexican newspapers inviting anyone who could dive and would pay eight dollars a day to join the expedition on the romantic coast of Yucatán.

Dozens of recruits turned up at CEDAM's headquarters in Mexico City. The "crew" included apprentice movie stars, airline pilots, and a man whose principal qualification was that he had been the first man in the world to water ski on one bare foot. The official party included an archaeologist from the ministry of national patrimony, more than a dozen reporters and photographers, a mysterious person in dark glasses who was said to be a secret policeman, and a man with "magic capsules" which he claimed would react if the proper formula were recited to them as they passed over gold.

Mercifully, the official party included Commander Argudín of the Mexican navy, who was to be camp commander. It took two DC-3's and a flying boxcar to transport this contingent and their equipment from Mexico City. The flying boxcar crashed in the jungle and was totally destroyed, along with most of CEDAM's diving equipment. The DC-3's arrived safely.

Marx was put in charge of diving operations, "because of his experience in diving on the wreck." The portable air compressor had been lost in the plane crash. On Monday, the first day of the expedition, the water over the wreck site boiled with nearly fifty badly disappointed skin divers, most of whom had expected to see a coral-encrusted galleon and were surprised to find that they would be expected to spend their diving time, when diving became possible, in pounding at the coral with chisels and hammers.

[51]

That night there was nothing to eat in camp. On Tuesday the weather was bad. It was impossible to land food or water. There was a gale on Wednesday, but a replacement air compressor was landed and the empty tanks were filled. The diviner discovered what he said was either "gold or the anchor of the *Santa María*," and a hapless group was set to digging a hole in the beach. At the bottom of the hole they found an unlimited supply of salt water.

On Thursday the first diving with Aqua-lungs was possible, and the CEDAM divers had their first experience with the surf. On Friday Marx raised several cannon and the big anchor. A week after the expedition had begun, only six of the CEDAM recruits were left. Most of the hangers-on had decided that Yucatanian underwater archaeology was not nearly as agreeable as it had seemed in Mexico City. The remaining divers, led by Marx and by Alec and Reggi Arnold, professional sport divers from Acapulco, continued to hack tons of object-filled coral from the bottom. This was processed by an efficient laboratory which CEDAM had set up in Cozumel.

During the second week the Arnold brothers found a folded bundle of about a hundred pieces of gold leaf, weighing altogether about a pound. Rumors spread that the divers at Matancero had found hundreds of pounds of gold.

A few days later they heard that a band of Fidel Castro's rebels were about to attack the camp. Commander Argudín distributed guns and ammunition. The Mexican navy dispatched two corvettes and a party of sailors. The army contributed a company of soldiers. The secretary of national defense flew in from Mexico City. The rumored attack never developed, to the relief of the divers, who had grown beards and were concerned about being mistaken for Castroites by the soldiery. The gold was shipped to Cozumel under guard, but the armed soldiers and one corvette remained for the rest of the expedition.

On the first day of the third week Marx found a hall-marked gold pocket watch marked *Wm. Webster Exchange Alley London.* Although its works were completely rusted out, the face and hands, stopped at 8:20, were in good condition. There were two scraps of an eighteenth-century English newspaper in the inner case. The print was still legible.

That night Marx had a violent headache, developed severe pains in his back, arms, and legs, and collapsed, delirious. The camp doctor had him flown to Cozumel by navy helicopter. There his illness was diagnosed as malaria, but the men left in camp thought he was suffering some strange malady caused by prolonged exposure underwater. A few days later the expedition broke up, its end hastened by bad weather which made it impossible to work on the reef.

Back in Cozumel, Blair and Marx saw for the first time the more than twelve thousand objects recovered from the wreck. There were hundreds of devotional medals, brass spoons, thousands of metal buttons, crucifixes, buckles, beads in metal settings, knife handles, and musket balls. There were fourteen bottles, of which four were still tightly corked and held their original contents. One of the most startling finds was a paper package marked IOHANES EER VON. ACH. It had contained needles which had turned to rust stains, but the paper of the package remained.

Blair and Marx found the documents relating to the ship in the Archives of the Indies in Seville, after Marx noticed the mention of a ship called *El Matancero* in a Mexican newspaper article of the 1740's. They found the manifest and a general description of the ship, a list of supplies and equipment on board when she sank, and documents relating to her loss and attempts at salvage. They established, among other things, that some of the material they had found was not on the manifest. The rest of the story belongs to Clay Blair, who tells it so well in his book that it would be redundant to repeat it here.

After the Public Records Office in London and the Archives of the Indies in Seville, the third great source for the age of European exploration is the Algemeen Rijksarcheif in the Hague, where the records of the Dutch East India Company are preserved. The great ships bound for the Indies rounded the Cape of Good Hope and sailed due east with the trade wind behind them until they made a landfall, after more than three thousand miles, on the barren western Australian coast. Then they tacked to the northwest, and the long chain of Indonesian islands a thousand miles away. Other great ships, bound for India and Ceylon, sailed up the African coast to Zanzibar, then across the Indian Ocean to Surat, where they bought Mogul silver rupees at a discount for gold, then to Calicut, around the island of Ceylon and southeast to Java and Sumatra. They were following a track which had first been laid down in the early centuries after Christ, when enterprising traders sailed from the mouth of the Red Sea to India and Ceylon to exchange Roman gold for silks and precious stones and spices. It is probably not a coincidence that Roman lead anchor stocks were made like Chinese ones in junks of the last century. The big junks came from China to Ceylon, where they traded with merchants from the Levant. There is evidence of this trade in the form of Roman pottery and coins that have turned up on the west coast of India and in Ceylon.

In the summer of 1962 I surveyed a Roman shipwreck in Greece with the aid of two young American engineers,

Bob Kendall and Roger Wallihan. They had just come from Ceylon, where they had been diving with Mike Wilson and Arthur C. Clarke. At their suggestion, I wrote Clarke and Wilson to ask if they knew anything about Roman ships in Ceylon. In reply I got a cable asking if I could come to Ceylon to help them and the Ceylon department of antiquities survey an interesting wreck.

I arrived in Colombo to find Arthur Clarke still limping from an accident that had left him partially paralyzed, but full of excitement over the marvelous wreck that Mike had found two years before, which they now intended to survey. Mike's finds were stored in a double-locked teak chest in Arthur's office. There were two small bronze guns, and some heavy white lumps of coral. Sacks of silver coins were held in their original shape by coral growth, although the fiber sacks had long since rotted away. They were rupees stamped with the name of the Mogul emperor Aurangzeb, and the date according to the Moslem calendar was AH 1114, or 1702–03 of our era. Except where they had been worn by objects in the sea, the coins were in mint condition. There was little question but that this was a shipment of new coins, direct from the imperial Mogul mint in Surat.

Once the box was opened, explanations came fast. In March of 1961 Mike Wilson was filming at the Great Basses reef, a line of rocks several miles long off the southern coast of Ceylon. One of the largest rocks protrudes a bit above the waterline, and is marked by a large lighthouse built by the British in the 1870's. Mike had observed a small bronze gun on top of the reef and, when he dived to raise it, saw that a nearby hollow of the reef contained overgrown iron cannon and that the reef itself was full of silver coins.

The place was ten miles offshore, and completely exposed all year round. It was only possible to dive there during the interval, early in the spring, when the northeast monsoon which had been blowing since November changed to the southwest monsoon, which would blow until September. This time could last, with luck, a month. The longest calm period on record, said Clarke, had been when the Basses' lighthouse had been built in 1873. It had lasted for 43 days.

Clarke and Wilson had gotten expert help in their efforts to identify the wreck. Major Raven Harte of Colombo, a specialist in Ceylon's colonial history, had searched the old Dutch archives and turned up several references to possible shipwrecks. One particularly interesting one concerned the *Overness*, a *fluyt* belonging to the East India Company, which had been lost on the Basses reef on her way from Batavia. This was fascinating, but did not explain the Surat rupees, which were normally bought at a discount by the Dutch in Surat, on the west coast of India, for gold, then carried to Batavia, where they were used as common currency by the company.

A more interesting hint was provided by a transcript of the meeting of the Governors' Council of February 11, 1704, when it was discussed: "Whether or not to hold up the Yachtlet *De Pool* any longer . . . Since, to the surprise of the Governor and Council, there had not been the least news from Surat since the previous November . . ."

The implication here was that perhaps the annual pay ship for the garrison of Ceylon, carrying silver from Surat, had been lost in 1703 or 1704.

This was not proof of anything much. The coins did not bear the VOC stamp which they should have had if they were company currency. Furthermore, the guns that Mike had raised came, according to Mendel Peterson, from somewhere in Southeast Asia.

If we could show that the ship that had left that heap of silver on the Basses reef was Dutch or English, then it might be possible to find her records, including a manifest of her cargo. Like all sensible treasure hunters, Clarke and Wilson wanted to risk their future investment against a known possible profit. They had the blessing of the government, which only demanded that the project be conducted as an archaeological rather than salvage operation. The question of who owned the finds was more vague, but it seemed certain that Clarke and Wilson owned at least half, although there was a question as to whether the wreck was legal salvage or an archaeological find.

We drove around the island to Tangalla, the nearest good harbor to the Basses reef, where Mike had left his launch. The country there cannot have changed much since Roman times, nor the people, who smiled back at us as we passed them on the road, the same kind of smile that forgotten sculptors had carved on the Buddhas looking out from their rock cut shrines along the way.

This sandy coast, with its beautiful beaches, is where the traders of two millennia ago made their landfall. They called Ceylon "Taprobane," possibly after the small island of Taprobane which still shelters fishing boats just off the beach in a sandy bay.

We stopped for the night in a government rest house made of upright palm trunks with matting walls. The smooth red cement floor was a delight to walk on barefoot. The rug-covered porch looked out at the Indian Ocean. An inscription on the doorstep read DOORMYN OP GEBOUWT 1774.

Arthur Clarke limped up with a bottle of cold beer and a glass which he filled and handed me. "There is nothing between us and Antarctica."

We sat with our legs stretched out on the long arms of

the polished hardwood chairs in the cool of the evening, wondering who Doormyn had been, the man who built this house and sat on the same stoop and looked out towards the southern continent in the same year that Captain James Cook had sighted the lands hinted at, but never found, by Tasman and Van Dieman.

The next day we fueled and loaded Mike's new boat, and sailed with two Christian boys named Lazarus and Martin for Hambantota, halfway between Tangalla, where the rest house was, and Kirinda, the lighthouse supply station on the mainland opposite the great reef where the wreck lay. A modern hotel had been built near the great house at Hambantota, where in the years before the First World War Leonard Wolf had written *Sowing, Growing,* and *The Village in the Jungle.* He had once been the colonial administrative officer of the district.

Mike and I arrived at Karinda covered with diesel oil and dead tired after an unfortunate struggle with the boat's new exhaust pipes, which had been made from the wrong kind of flex tubing and continually broke, filling the boat with smoke. There we found Rodney Jonklaas, the third partner in the Clarke–Wilson–Jonklaas diving team.

Rodney is a graduate biologist educated in England, a native of Ceylon from one of the aristocratic group of European Ceylonese called Burghers. He makes his living collecting tropical fish, and knows more about the reefs of Ceylon than any living person. He traveled with a van containing a coffin-sized icebox, usually full of beer, and had brought his cook Anthony, an unsmiling Tamil Catholic, black as night. Anthony had set up his cooking shed by the time we arrived. In all the time we were together, he never failed to feed us on time.

Rodney gave us a beer and regaled us with his latest diving adventure. He had just been sexually attacked by a large male sea turtle which weighed, Rodney swore, not less than seven hundred pounds.

The principal industry of the village of about a hundred thatched houses was the shrine, or rather the shrines, for there were two of them, one Muslim and one Buddhist. The Muslim shrine honored an Arab trader, one of those who had followed the monsoons from the mouth of the Red Sea. His name, I was told by an earnest young man who carefully wrote it out for me in swirling Tamil, Singalese, and English as well, was Assaiq, Said Mohammed Yoosuf Oliyullah. He had three brothers, all of them holy men too, who were buried in the district.

The Buddhist shrine honored Viramahadevi, a beautiful princess who jumped into the sea to appease the sea gods when the ocean was encroaching on Colombo. She was thrown up alive and well in Kirinda, where she married the local princeling and lived happily ever after. The *dagoba* which honored her was a stone's throw from the Said Oliyullah's tomb. The government had had to put a police station in Kirinda to prevent the rival religions' fighting over the shrines. The Buddhists were most militant.

The Moorish Muslims were now mixed with Malays — Muslims too, but of a different sect. Their ancestors had been soldiers of a Malay regiment which had been paid off and had settled there in colonial times. They still spoke their own language and looked down on the "Moors."

We set up camp inside the tin-roofed boat sheds of the Imperial Lighthouse Service, with our beds beside the clinker-built surf boats which ferried supplies to the lighthouse. The boatman was a Roman Catholic Tamil from

Jaffna, like Mike's boat boys, but the lighthouse crews that they supplied were Buddhists. Tuan Hamin, the foreman, was the only Muslim.

When Mike had worked on the Basses reef in 1961 he had camped in the lighthouse. This was not possible now, as there was not space for all of us and our equipment. We planned to live at the Lighthouse Service base camp at Tangalla and commute, so to speak, to the wreck with Mike's motorboat. We had two Avon rubber dinghies which we planned to use as diving boats. They were safe to take into the breakers on the reef. If overwhelmed in the surf, the only danger was to the boatman, who would have to dive deep and swim to seaward, under the breakers, to avoid getting rolled on the coral.

When we arrived at the reef, we saw that it would be dangerous to put *Ran Muṭu*, Mike's motorboat, over the wreck, which lay almost under the first break. We ran around to the inside of the reef. While we rigged our tanks, the great waves broke on the outer reef with a crash to send spray right over us, and the surge roared through the channels of the coral.

Mike explained that Rodney and I were to follow him, and that if either of us got into trouble we should swim to the rubber dinghy, from which Martin, the boat boy, would watch for heads to appear in the boiling surf. This was to be my first dive in the Indian Ocean, and while it was all very well for Jonklaas and Wilson to be indifferent to scorpion fish . . . what was it that Mike had told me . . . ah yes, if you hit one, head for the surface before the paralysis affects your breathing. And sharks. Rodney had been attacked by a small tiger the week before, near where we were. I remembered his laconic description in his clipped English. "I turned my head. If I hadn't he would have got me, but as it was all he got was a poke with the spear gun."

The Indian Ocean water was almost body temperature. We reached the bottom, a completely unspectacular plain of coral, and then, following Mike, swam towards the cloud line ahead of us which marked the surf. Mike found the gully he was looking for and led on through. The wash was shocking. When it hit us we clung to the bottom for terrifying seconds. When it stopped, we had a minute or so to swim before the next swell set up another surge. The coral grew ever more colorful as we struggled through that gully. It was inhabited by big reddish-brown groupers with mean-looking doggy teeth, who watched us curiously.

Halfway through, a big wave got me and I was swept into a nest of dogtooth barnacles growing on the rock. One chopped a groove in my thigh a half-inch deep which didn't hurt a bit then, but gave trouble later. By this time I was panicky and tired, but more afraid of being alone than of following Mike.

The water deepened; the waves roaring over the reef stopped grabbing with maniac force, and only pushed. We were in a valley in the coral which lay at right angles to the sweep of the waves. Mike headed for a ledge where the rock ended and the white coral sand began. I joined him there.

The rock was full of silver coins. It was as if a madman had mixed tons of cement with silver money for gravel, and dumped it onto the reef. A bronze gun was embedded on top of the mess. We swam up and down the gully, which was over a hundred feet long, finding coins and overgrown iron guns everywhere. Four huge anchors lay tumbled in a heap at one end.

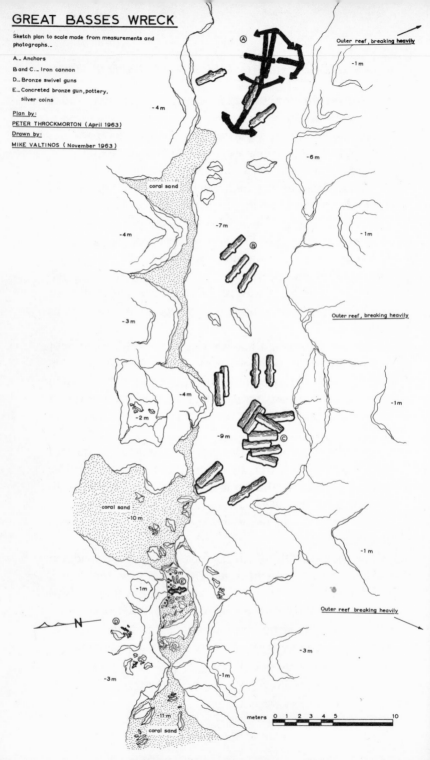

GREAT BASSES WRECK

Sketch plan to scale made from measurements and photographs.

A.. Anchors
B and C.. Iron cannon
D.. Bronze swivel guns
E.. Concreted bronze gun, pottery,
    silver coins

Plan by:
PETER THROCKMORTON (April 1963)
Drawn by:
MIKE VALTINOS (November 1963)

Outer reef, breaking heavily

-1 m

-4 m

coral sand

-4 m

-7 m

Ⓑ

-1 m

Outer reef, breaking heavily

-6 m

-1 m

-3 m

-4 m

-2 m

-9 m

Ⓒ

-1 m

coral sand
-10 m

-1 m

Ⓔ

Outer reef breaking heavily

Ⓓ

-3 m

Ⓓ

-3 m

-1 m

-3 m

N

meters 0 1 2 3 4 5   10

-11 m

coral sand

Ⓐ

Plan of the Great Basses wreck.

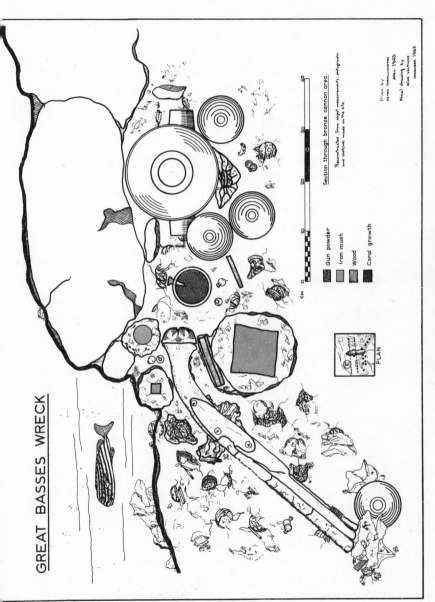

GREAT BASSES WRECK

Gun powder
Iron mush
Wood
Coral growth

Section through bronze cannon area.

Reconstructed from slight measurements, photographs and sketches made on the site.

PLAN

Plan by
PETER THROCKMORTON
APRIL 1963
Final drawing by
MIKE VAUGHAN
NOVEMBER 1963

CM 0   10   20   30   40

A cross-section of the Great Basses "silver gully."

Then we noticed that Rodney Jonklaas was not with us, decided we had better find him, and struggled back through the channel in the rock, not nearly as frightened by the surf this time. We found Rodney safe and sound. His regulator had quit while he was right in the surf, and he had been forced to surface. He had been lucky not to be caught by a big wave and smashed against the coral while helpless on top of the reef, or drowned in the cave we had passed through. He had put on a new regulator and swum back to us, but could not find his way.

Tired after our long swim through the surf, we decided to look at another wreck which Mike had found. He had seen a large anchor and a heap of ballast stones. Arthur thought it might be the wreck of the sloop *Aletta Adriana*, lost in late 1765 or 1766 on her way to Colombo from Trincomalee.

It was on the lee side of the reef in about twenty feet of calm water. Looking towards the reef, a hundred yards or so to seaward, you could see the groove that the unfortunate ship had bashed in the coral as she drove over it. The bottom between the reef and the heap of ballast stones was littered with bits of copper sheathing.

A good look showed that the ship was modern. The "ballast stones" were really nineteenth-century mortar shells, covered with coral. Mixed with them were corroded iron objects shaped like giant washboards. In the interstices were dozens of bottles with pointed bottoms marked LEMONADE CLARKE ROMER AND CO CEYLON and SUPERIOR SODA WATER CLARKE ROMER AND CO CEYLON. A bottle of soda and a bottle of whiskey, still full of brown liquid, were stuck side by side.

We found the bronze gudgeons, the great hinges that had held the ship's rudder, and the pintles on which the rudder had swung, lying on the bottom in the middle of the track the ship had plowed in the coral. There were lead fuse plugs marked with the broad arrow, and full bottles of red wine which smelled ghastly when we pulled the corks out. There were only a few bits of the teak planking left, protected by the leaching of green copper corrosion products into the wood.

Like the *Aletta Adriana*, this ship had probably been on her way to Trincomalee from Colombo. The cannonballs and mysterious "iron washboards" might have been destined for the British base at Trincomalee. They would have been transshipped in Colombo, where later research showed the soda bottles were manufactured. Later on, a friend of Arthur Clarke's searched the Ceylon papers but found no reference to a wreck in the middle 1800's off the Basses. It would be interesting to search the records of the officers' club at Trincomalee for the period. One might find that there had sometime been a period of great drought and hardship.

The most interesting and important thing about the wreck of this country-built ship was the remarkable state of consolidation of the wreck. Although the wood of the ship was gone, as if dissolved in acid, the rest of the ship seemed to have stayed in place. Waves had not had much effect on it, which was remarkable in view of the location.

That evening we decided on our plan of action. The "silver wreck" had been a large ship, and a lot of material from the ship was there. While the weather held, we should remove the silver that was on the surface, as well as the bronze gun, which was the only object that stood out conspicuously to mark the site. Mike Wilson would do the main job of hacking out coral, while I scouted around, trying to find objects to help identify the ship and making a rough plan of the site.

During the next few days a fairly accurate plan, made

by taking innumerable tape measurements from a series of fixed points, began to take shape in my notebook. The channel in which the wreck lay was formed by two ridges of coral rock running east and west, with an average of twenty to thirty feet between them. At the eastern end, all together, lay four great iron anchors, each thirteen feet long by about twelve feet across the flukes. The great spade-shaped flukes were typical of the seventeenth and eighteenth centuries.

The fact that they lay together suggested what might have happened to the ship. Four anchors were standard gear on a ship's forecastle in the 1700's. If she had been making a passage from Surat to Batavia or headed for Batavia after a stop in Colombo, the anchors on the fo'c'sle head would have been lashed securely. The ship could have been running at night, like the *Loo*, booming along at ten knots, the wind strong enough to build up whitecaps so that the lookout would not have seen the seas breaking on the Basses until it was too late. Whatever happened then happened fast, because there was no time to get even one of the four anchors on the forecastle over.

At least part of the story may have been very like that told by Captain Utting, recounting the loss of the *Loo:*

At 12:30 A.M. and again at 1:00 the deep sea lead line was cast . . . no bottom found at 300 feet. At about 1:15 Robert Bishop (the master) sent the lead line crew to clear the line for heaving and followed them to the gunwhale himself, to see to this. To his great surprise he found the ship in white water and saw breakers ahead. He instantly ordered "helm alee" and sent a message down to Captain Utting . . . As Utting rushed on deck . . . he found the ship coming into the wind and away from the reef . . . as the ship veered off the wind the headsails were caught across wind and the ship struck the reef aft . . .

Anyone who has sailed even a tiny dinghy will remember the heart-in-throat feeling one has as the boat, handled badly, hangs in stays a minute or so, while the current pushes you onto the dock and the inevitable derisive audience makes uncomplimentary remarks. Emotion increases in intensity in direct ratio to the size of the boat. I remember with awful clarity putting a ten-ton cutter on shore a few years ago. There was the shore, fifty feet away, with little waves breaking on the sandy beach. The wind was right on shore, and rising. We had no dinghy. The boat was supposed to be hauled.

I sailed past the shore, hailing the people in the yard. It was five o'clock and they were quitting. No one paid attention. On the last pass, a block caught, the jib got stuck on the wrong side, she hung in stays and drifted broadside. We dropped the anchor but it dragged. We went onto the shore. There was no damage, except to my ego, but the three minutes before she struck lasted a long, long time.

The same sort of thing happening at night in a place like the Basses would be horrible. Imagine the lookout's cry, all hands running to put the ship about, the sickening moment as she misses stays and fails to come about, then the last lift of the ship as she rides over the waves which rise higher as the first line of reef constricts them below. Then the shattering crash as three or four hundred tons of ship fall twenty feet down a wave onto the coral. Then chaos, with great seas sweeping her decks until she sinks into a channel large enough to hold her.

The *Loo* went onto the reef in calm water, and did not break up, although she was bilged. There was time to get boats launched and people and some gear off. The Basses ship must have been smashed to bits almost at once. The heavy iron guns, lashed securely, must have soon pounded through the deck, which probably broke amidships. The swivel guns that Wilson found in 1961 might have been on the bulwarks aft, which would explain how they got onto the top of the reef.

The anchors, weighing many tons, settled to the bottom with the smashed remnants of the forecastle under them. Over a hundred feet away the lazarette, the area under the great cabin where the silver was stored, sank too. The bronze gun, which had perhaps been on the poop, fell on top of the mess.

Fourteen iron guns, each eight feet long, lay together fifteen feet east of the bronze gun and the mass of concreted silver, so overgrown that they no longer resembled guns. It took many dives before we found all of them, though they lay within a few feet of each other. Nearby was a larger gun, over ten feet long, towards the stern. Halfway to the anchors three more guns were lying on hard coral rock. Four smaller ones lay beside the anchors in the place where the gully narrowed at the east end of the wreck.

The coral which almost covered the bronze cannon was packed with all the things which had washed into the bottom of the gully, to be overgrown by the cementlike coral. There were cannonballs, which had lost almost all their weight through oxidation, but which still retained their shape although they were as fragile as soft pottery. Grenades, hollow spheres of iron full of gunpowder, still had their wooden stoppers in place.

The bronze gun was the only object which would be readily visible to a casual skin diver swimming over the site. We decided to remove it. With hammers and chisels we set about hacking it out of the coral. In order to stay in place we had to lash ourselves down to pitons driven into the wreck, like mountaineers. I especially had trouble with the backwash of waves breaking on the reef, since I had to do a good deal of swimming in shallow water as I searched for objects and measured for the plan. There was nothing to catch hold of in the shallow water, where the wash was much stronger, and I learned to curl up in a ball when a wave got me, face the current, and wait for the ringing crash of my tanks bringing up against the coral.

The most frustrating thing about the wreck was the quantity of identical silver coins. It was, after all, my job to find the little bits of material that would identify the wreck, not to mine silver. I searched, and all I found was silver. When Mike and I, working in relays with our hammers, had gotten a trench dug beside the bronze gun, we began to find more useful material. The ship had been fastened with iron nails, which had corroded into mush leaving perfect molds of their dimensions in the sea growth. We pried up lumps, black with the stain of corroded iron and smelling strongly of gunpowder and pitch, until finally we could get an auto jack under the gun and break it loose. This was the system we had used at Cape Gelidonya on the Bronze Age ship. The gun was raised with a plastic balloon, and when cleaned, measured four feet seven inches. It was inscribed 23–23–8 on the breech.

The lumps contained what must have been a typical sample of material in the after end of the ship. There were the remains of a pair of matched flintlock pistols. The wooden stock of one was like new, but the barrel had been dissolved by corrosion. There were the forearm of a musket; a pewter decanter stopper; bits of broken blue-and-white china and other shards; a bronze pestle; a gold-washed brass earring with green glass pendants; bits of green glass bottles; fragments of bone; the brass buttplate of a musket; pistol and musket balls; and a silver-plated copper salver. Pieces of the coconut fiber bags which had held the coins, probably a thousand to the bag, were mixed in the solid mass like straw in bricks. Coins were everywhere, loose if the bag had rotted away before the coral had cemented them together, or in the shape of the original bags.

After two weeks the weather changed. Great monsoon clouds built up to the south. The wind grew a little stronger each day and the seas got bigger. When one of the engines of the boat quit, we were forced to stop work. We had several hundred pounds of silver, a sketch plan, lots of fragments of wood in plastic bags, and a collection of bits of bronze, pewter, glass and pottery.

Loaded with samples of material, I departed for Athens and began the correspondence which would, I hoped, lead to identifying the ship. It seemed likely that there was no record anywhere of the loss of the vessel, since there can have been few survivors of a ship that went on that reef in monsoon waves ten miles from a hostile coast.

As reports began to come in, it seemed less and less likely that the ship was the *Overness*, the East India Company *fluyt* which had seemed a likely possibility at the beginning. Mendel Peterson wrote that the cannon was probably English, and that the numbers on its breech indicated hundredweights, quarterweights, and pounds, corresponding to the cannon's weight, which proved to be 332 pounds.

Mr. C. G. Goins, firearms expert of the U.S. National Museum, said that the pistol stocks were characteristically English or German. Mr. B. Francis Kukachka of the USDA Forest Products Laboratory studied wood samples from the wreck, and identified the stopper from the brass cannon muzzle and stoppers of the iron grenades, fragments of broken chests, and the musket forearm as teak. What might have been a bit of the ship's planking was also teak, which suggests that the ship was at least fitted out and perhaps built in southeast Asia.

Dr. N. M. Japikse, archivist at the Algemeen Rijksarcheif in Holland, found records of three ships called *Overness* owned by the Dutch East India Company between 1697 and 1776, but none of them was listed as lost. The British East India Company lost fourteen ships between 1702 and 1719, but none was known to have sunk near the Basses reef and none with 22 guns. There were, however, two other possibilities: the *Gloucester Frigot*, 350 tons with 70 men and 30 guns, was lost somewhere between Plymouth and Bencoolen in 1702, and the *Albemarle*, 300 tons, 66 men, 30 guns, was lost in 1704 with a cargo worth twenty-thousand-odd pounds.

The ship might have been a Moorish vessel from Surat, suggests M.P.H. Roessingh, who searched the Dutch East India Company's records. This would explain the lack of the VOC mark on the coins, and the Oriental wood and guns, but raises the problem of the European pistols, pewter, bottles, and china. And why should a Moorish ship carry armament typical of an Indiaman?

Richard Russell, the chemist who examined several of the coin lumps and the black "cement" which held the larger lumps together, offered information of a different sort. He found that the sand in the lumps contained particles of quartz, rose quartz, garnet, and a few bits that looked like rubies. In some of the lumps were a few very small pieces of obsidian, with conchoidal fractures and razor-sharp edges, which Mr. Russell thought might have come from the explosion of Krakatoa in 1883.

A second proposal by Mr. Russell suggests that, since the black stains were from hydrated iron oxide and the silver had been blackened by a coat of silver sulfide, the iron in a wreck does not simply oxidize as it would on land. The wreck area was probably infected with sulfate-reducing bacteria, whose action produced the considerable quantity of iron sulfide found in the lumps. Russell concluded that a thorough study of material from the wreck required not only a chemist but a marine microbiologist.

The plan shows that the ship must have been well over a hundred feet long, assuming the bronze cannon and silver coins mark the stern of the ship. This would be close to the specifications made in 1697 by the central board of the Dutch East India Company for a third-rate Indiaman of 130' × 33' 6½" (Amsterdam feet), carrying 26 guns.

The identity of the Basses ship will probably not be known until we get more material from the wreck. Some of the problems are tantalizing. For instance, two of the anchors are over 13 feet long. An anchor this size should weigh about two and a half tons. Yet the guns, which were the right size to have been six- or nine-pounders except for the long gun, which cannot have been smaller than a twelve-pounder, seem right for a frigate or a third-rate Indiaman which would have carried anchors half that size. Does this mean that the ship was a very large merchantman of the period? As we could not raise any of the smaller guns, and only a few cannonballs, we cannot be sure. It seems possible that some of the guns could have been twelve-pounders. All we have to go by are the rough dimensions of the coral-encrusted lumps that were the guns, and these measurements were made while I was being flung around by the surge.

Was the project worthwhile? Certainly not in a commercial sense, though Clarke-Wilson will probably break even eventually. Arthur Clarke has produced a popular book on the wreck (*Treasure of the Great Reef*, New York and London, 1964) and Clarke-Wilson made a successful TV film. However, the 350 pounds of silver coins, equaling about 15,000 silver rupee pieces, which were salvaged in 1961 and 1963 are not worth much more than $15,000, judging from their value on the world numismatic market of about a dollar apiece. This is, in any case, a rather specious argument, since there cannot be fifteen thousand collectors interested in Surat rupees. The half-rupee pieces were worth a good deal of money before the wreck was found, since they were very rare, but the first few dozen flooded the market and the value dropped.

What else can we conclude from the Basses wreck? There, on the Basses reef, is what remains of a large ship that sank before 1705. Her guns, her anchors, and many of her fittings can be salvaged. Although smashed, a good sample of the small objects that were on board can be recovered and preserved. The project, especially the preservation, will cost more than any private individual can be expected to pay.

Luckily the wreck is in an inaccessible place, unapproachable for eleven months a year, and is guarded by the lighthouse keepers.

At the eastern end of the Dutch sea route to the Indies is the barren west coast of Australia. Forty miles off the coast is a group of small islands called Houtman Abrolhos. The islands are close to the path of Dutch ships which ran their easting down to a landfall on the Australian coast before tacking to the northwest for Indonesia. They are low, and their outlying reefs, like the Basses, are difficult to see at night.

On June 29, 1629, two hours before daybreak, the Dutch East India Company ship *Batavia* struck on what is now called Morning Reef. She had split open and flooded by ten that morning, but luckily remained in one piece on top of the reef.

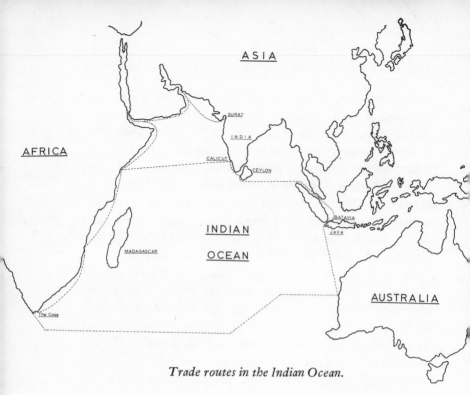

Trade routes in the Indian Ocean.

The commander, Francesco Pelsaert, sailed in a small boat for Batavia with the captain in order to get help for the survivors who were waiting on a nearby island. When Pelsaert returned he found that 125 of the survivors had been murdered by a gang of mutineers, who tried to capture the rescue ship, failed, and were caught in their turn. The story has been well told by Henriette Drake Brockman, Hugh Edwards, and others.

In 1960 a fisherman found a very old skeleton and a piece of a pewter pot with an inscription in Dutch, which he took to C. Halls of the Western Australian Museum in Perth. Halls identified it and realized that it could be a relic of the *Batavia*. Soon afterwards the wreck itself was found by divers.

An expedition was organized in 1963 under the joint leadership of Hugh Edwards and Mr. M. Creamer. They were joined by groups from the Australian army and navy. In the nine days the group worked on the site they found twenty-four cannon, five of them bronze, from 6 to 22 feet deep. Two of the bronze guns were raised. They were inscribed *Rotterdam* and dated 1603 and 1616. Besides the cannon there was a treasure-house of seventeenth-century finds: sounding leads, pewter plates, a coffeepot, bellarmine jugs, Rhenish stoneware flasks, and a bronze chemist's mortar inscribed *Amor Vincit Omnia*. There were seventy coins with dates from 1588 to 1626, and the bottom was scattered with limestone blocks, fluted column drums, pieces of carved stone architraves and heaps of bricks, all stowed as ballast but usable in Batavia, like the cargoes of bricks that English ships brought to America during the same period.

The interesting characteristic of the wreck is that it seems scattered in the same way as our wreck at the Basses. Although the ship herself is gone forever, the cannon and the cargo remain, in understandable context, in a channel in the reef.

There are literally thousands of wrecks like the ones described in this chapter, and more are being found every year. The most spectacular from the point of view of the general public are the wrecks of the 1715 Mexican plate fleet off Florida, and the recent discovery of the remains of Sir Cloudesley Shovell's fleet, lost off the Scillys in the early 1700's.

The usefulness of such sites to the would-be marine archaeologist wanting to study more ancient wrecks is that they illustrate the local dangers to navigation, and the problems that confronted the commanders. The study of shipwrecks in recent historical times is the key to understanding what happened in the more remote past.

III

∞∞∞∞∞

The Wreck of the *Nautilus*

Cape Malea, Cape Malea, help us, Christ and Holy Mary!
— Greek seamen's saying

THE most renowned danger area in the Mediterranean, both for modern and for ancient mariners, is probably the entrance to the Aegean Sea, past Cape Malea. Here nineteenth-century naval archives can be used directly as a means of understanding what happened in ancient times. Here sponge divers in the early 1900's found the first and most important Roman ship that has ever been found. A few miles away lies the tragic, well-documented wreck of H.M.S. *Nautilus*. Here we find even the ubiquitous shade of Lord Elgin, whose hired ship foundered on Kythera island, off Malea, with its cargo of Parthenon marbles.

Several summers ago we spent some days there with a friend's boat, curious to see the sites of several memorable shipwrecks, curious to understand the problems the sailing ships had faced. It was late afternoon by the time we got the schooner precariously anchored at the edge of Nautilus Reef, baptized by the H.M.S. *Nautilus* a century and a half before. We had come to see if there were something left of the *Nautilus*.

The water here in the middle of the channel was so

clear that we could see the anchor teetering on the rock
ledge forty feet below, the ledge then sloping away to in-
finity. Jon Smith cut the engine as the anchor took hold
and the little ship swung with the current to lie parallel to
Nautilus Rock.

It was the time of day when sea shadows bring out the
hunters, when sharks attack. There are not many sharks in
the Aegean, but there are sharks in that channel, which is
traversed by every ship passing to Piraeus or the Dardanelles from the west. Once the big blues and the fat tri-
angle-toothed white man-eaters were normal only in
tropic seas, but since the opening of the Suez Canal they
have followed big ships and their trail of rich refuse into
the Aegean. Rocks that rise from great depths tend to at-
tract them.

That evening the rock seemed ominous, perhaps because I knew a little of its history, and imagined more. I
always find a wreck or reef a bit frightening the first time
I dive on it, or swim near it; the ghosts of imagination can
only be exorcised by familiarity.

If any reef in the world is haunted, Nautilus Rock must
be. Among the men who died there were the English sailors of the *Nautilus* from the winter of 1807, following
whatever unrecorded Aegean adventurers who must have
run afoul of the same ugly rock before and after the men
of the *Nautilus:* Phoenicians and Greeks, Romans, Turks
and their Christian galley slaves, Venetian traders and
Rhodian sailors on pirate patrol.

These clear blue waters had seen the death of modern
ships as well. In the first week of May, 1941, Stukas sank
H.M.S. *Gloucester* within sight of the rock, and machine-
gunned the survivors in the water. Earlier that same morning, Ju–88's put two bombs into H.M.S. *Greyhound*, a destroyer. She sank in fifteen minutes. The week before, a

Nautilus Rock. Nautilus *struck on the far right.*

The fangs of Nautilus Rock on which Nautilus *struck.*

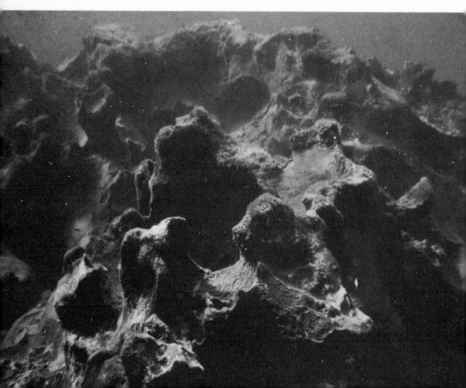

few miles away off Malea, the Germans had sunk a British troopship, the *Slamat*, packed with the last troops from the evacuation of the Greek mainland. The destroyers *Diamond* and *Wryneck* were sunk with her. Fifty men survived out of more than a thousand. A month earlier and fifty miles to the west, the battle of Matapan had cost the Italians the heavy cruisers *Pola*, *Zara*, and *Fiume*, the destroyers *Alfieri* and *Carducci*, and twenty-four hundred men.

So many battles have been fought here because this is the main gate into the Aegean Sea. A submarine ridge between Grabusa and Malea forms the sill to the door. It is not large, only sixty miles along the ridge, averaging three to five hundred feet in depth and nowhere more than a mile wide. Both sides of the ridge slope down to the deep central floor half a mile below. From this ridge rise the stumbling blocks in the door — the islands of Kythera and Antikythera, Pori, and several sunken reefs and islets, including Nautilus Rock.

The place can be a caldron of gales in winter. Captain Henry Denham (R.N. Ret.), who knows as much about the Aegean as anybody, remembers a day in January, 1917, when he was a very junior officer on board H.M.S. *Raccoon*, a destroyer patrolling the east side of the channel for German submarines. They were hit by a northeast gale that rose in half an hour from a hearty breeze to almost hurricane force. When seas began breaking over the ship, they hove to, going slow ahead on both engines. Even so, the guns could not be manned, and as they worked up to windward towards Milos, the galley and then one boiler room were flooded. By afternoon the following day the wind had begun to ease up and they reached a lee under Milos.

A much larger ship, the 9,000-ton passenger steamer

Heracleon, was caught in a southerly gale in December, 1966, while en route to Piraeus from Crete. She foundered between Malea and Falkonera in half an hour, and took over one hundred fifty people down with her.

Pirates thrived in the channels right through to the nineteenth century. An inscription in Rhodes, cut in the second century B.C., records the death of a Rhodian sailor killed fighting pirates "between Malea and Crete." Piracy persisted all through classical time, until the Romans, like the Rhodians before them, managed to suppress it. From the seventeenth century onwards, the straits were infested with mustachioed Maniots from the mainland, fierce men in small fast rowing boats which they concealed, when they took to the hills, by filling them with stones and sinking them in shallow bays. When cornered, the Maniots fought like wolves. It took the Royal Navy to stop the Maniot pirates, but not before the loss of H.M.S. *Cambrian*, a 48-gun frigate, off Grabusa. The big ship ran aground chasing pirates and was a total loss.

It was a happy coincidence that I had heard these stories, knew of the loss of the *Nautilus*, and had been lent the schooner for a trip to the channel while the weather held calm enough to allow us to anchor at Nautilus Rock. Still, the water looked too blue and the current ran too fast for comfort. It was late and the sharks could be there. I wished we could call it all off and dive there the next day.

The crew was scrambling for masks and fins. My daughter Paula, aged almost two months, slept happily in her basket slung from the boom, which gave me no excuse to suggest that my wife Joan stay on board. So I grabbed mask, fins, and my Nikonos from the cabin top and jumped into the clear water. When I got the mask on, the bottom loomed up through the water, its claws covered with a hard green growth that looked like someone had spilled a pot of paint. It was late August, but the water still felt cold at first, then tolerable. The current ran hard, but not so hard that we couldn't swim across it. I was halfway to the rock when I saw that I was alone, so I headed towards the point. The water shoaled fast. Soon I would be close enough to get out of the water if jumped by sharks.

From accounts of the wreck, I judged that the remains of H.M.S. *Nautilus* must be inside the eastern point of the island. Still alone, with the others following, I rounded the thin ridge of the point, spinning in the water, nervous, looking into the deep blue water to the north, away from the twenty-foot ledge of rock which surrounded the island. It was from the blue depths that sharks might come.

I sensed something behind me and shivered, thinking of the time, years before and a couple of hundred miles to the north, when five blue sharks over ten feet long had jumped me when I was swimming on the surface in just such a place. It was only Joan, with Jon Smith behind her. I hung in the water, peering down to the ledge twenty feet below and saw man-made debris forty feet ahead.

There was a heap of iron ballast blocks, each about three feet long by six inches square, scattered over the bottom. Then I saw a cannon, and knew we had found what was left of *Nautilus*. It was the first time in my twenty years as a diver that I'd ever found an old wreck just like that, from information given in her obituary paperwork.

As the sun fell, the sea seemed to light up. I shot thirty-five pictures with my Nikonos. Film finished, we swam back to the schooner. It was almost dark.

We climbed back on board shivering, for we had stayed naked in the sea too long. After a struggle with the anchor, which was jammed in the rocks, we started the engine and headed for the island of Antikythera, whose black westerly cliffs loomed five miles away across the channel. We were making for Potamos, on the north side of Antikythera. It was a deep inlet, surrounded by high cliffs, where survivors from the wreck of the *Nautilus* had been landed in January, 1807, after their ordeal on the rock.

As we came into it, Jon cut the engine and our little ship, barely under way, slipped through the still water, leaving hardly a ripple of wake. Although it was almost dark, we could see that the bottom was rocky, in most places with huge boulders big as houses rising from sixty-odd feet to within twenty feet of the surface. We picked a likely looking sand patch between boulders and anchored near a big fishing boat. Our friend Rick climbed down the side into the dinghy and took our stern line to the rocks. We were moored for the night.

It was dark by the time we put on shirts and blue jeans and headed for shore, a happy party of summer sailors and children. Although there was a crowd by the dock, no one greeted us. At the head of a long flight of stairs, two combination general store–coffeehouse–bars were lit by dim oil lamps. The general impression was of idleness, uselessness; shabby houses lacking that last pride of impoverished island villagers, whitewash; the mild hostility of people so familiar with desperation that they no longer trouble even to despair.

The children, Mark and Sarah, stayed near the dinghy while we climbed the steps towards the coffeehouses. Old men sat around outside them, talking in the semidarkness. Jon and I each ordered an ouzo and sat down a couple of tables away from them. No one said a word. Silence, like a smelly blanket, lay all around us. Chilled, we drank up and walked up the hill to the end of the road, trying to buy food, but no one had any to sell us. As we walked past a group of men, one remarked to another in an amiable voice, "Damn masturbators, after the treasure again."

We acted as if we had not understood this curious but common Greek epithet. It was a much chillier reception than that given the crew of the *Nautilus* in 1807, but then we were a bunch of frivolous tourists, not survivors of a disaster so terrible that it led, in the end, to cannibalism. A contemporary account describes how the rescued crew had been greeted:

Twelve or fourteen families of Greek fishermen dwelt . . . in a state of extreme poverty. Their houses, or rather huts, consisting of one or two rooms on the same floor, were in general built against the side of a rock; The walls composed of clay and straw, and the roof supported by a tree in the center of the dwelling. Their food was a coarse kind of bread, formed of boiled pease and flour, which was made into a kind of paste for the strangers with once or twice a bit of kid . . . they (the islanders) made a liquor from corn, which having an agreeable flavor, and being a strong spirit was drank with avidity by the sailors.

We continued to the second general shop at the top of the hill, where we fared a little better. There the owner and captain of the big fishing boat we had moored alongside, filled us with raki, probably the liquor that the English sailors "drank with avidity." First-class home-brew raki makes good lighter fluid as well, though sticky if used continually. By the time we started back to the boat, we had been filled with raki and with sea stories as well.

I'd tried to show only mild interest when an old man, who seemed to be a poor relation hanger-on in the store, had told about the seven fabulous golden turtles lost on the bottom of the sea at Cape Glyphada. Then some Frenchmen in a big ship, especially fitted with electronic devices for underwater research, had come to carry away the turtles. Although they had been watched, they had somehow stolen away in the night.

He must have been talking about the visit paid by Cousteau, in *Calypso*, to the site of the Antikythera wreck in 1953. James Dugan, Cousteau's literary collaborator, was there, and he told me that the water had been so clear that a snorkler on the surface could see the divers working 180 feet below. They had spent only a couple of days on the site and had had to leave because they were literally running out of food. Too many uniformed officials had found pressing business on board at mealtime.

We wanted to do a little modest exploration of the *Nautilus*, but would never have a chance if we were thought to be the same sort of alarming scavengers. Hoping for the best, we headed for the rock next day at dawn. Even on a calm day, the channel was choppy with swells running against the current. When the sun came over the horizon the wind dropped, and we knew we should be able to look forward to six hours of calm weather before the afternoon breeze began.

We moored the little ship very carefully, right over the ballast blocks, with her anchor hanging down the 300-foot slope ahead of us and with lines to the rocks on both sides so she could not swing. We were safe for the day, unless a squall from the north hit us, or the anchor dragged, or the engine failed to start. In the bright sunlight all the ghosts of the day before had disappeared. The only hint of the *Nautilus* drama was the ballast blocks and a photostat of a yellowing document from the Admiralty library.

ADM 5381 is entitled: *Minutes of the Proceedings of a Court Martial assembled and held on board His Majesty's Ship* Atlas *on Friday the 15th Day of May 1807.* The court-martial board was directed by "the Right Honor-able Cuthbert S. Collingwood, Vice Admiral of the Red and Commander in Chief of HM's Ships and vessels em-ployed and to be employed in the Mediterranean . . . to Investigate and enquire into the circumstances which led to this unfortunate Event. And to try Lieut. Alex^r Nesbitt and such of the surviving Officers and Ships Company of his Majesties late sloop *Nautilus* as are now in the Squad-ron for their conduct on that occasion. . . ."

Every officer and man in the Royal Navy knew that when a ship was lost, the survivors would stand trial for their lives. Nesbitt was only the second lieutenant of the *Nautilus*, the third-ranking officer. But it was his sword which lay on the table, separating him from the eleven captains who formed the board, and from the president of the court, Rear Admiral of the White John Child Purvis. It was a calm spring day off Cadiz, a long way from the freezing surf-swept rock where Lieutenant Nesbitt had made the decisions and given the orders, as senior surviv-ing officer of the *Nautilus*, which would determine his fu-ture naval career.

When the ceremony of swearing in the members of the court was finished, the president of the court asked the assembled petty officers and the rest of the crew if they thought that the "loss of the *Nautilus* was occasioned by any misconduct on the part of Lieutenant Nesbitt." The reply was a murmured "No," and the tension in the court relaxed. No accusations would be made. Nesbitt was now safe.

It is certain that the loss of the *Nautilus*, on an un-charted rock, must have been common gossip in the fleet, and that most captains and masters had by now made ap-propriate notations in their personal charts. In those days charts were not issued by the Admiralty, but were the pri-

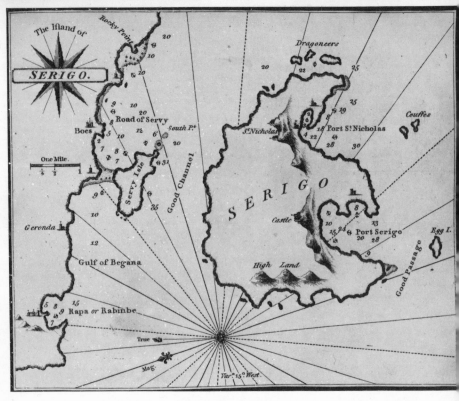

Heather's chart of the region around Kythera. (John R. Freeman)

vate property of the officers and sailing masters of the fleet. Heather's charts, which were being used by the late Captain Palmer, did not mention the rock on which *Nautilus* struck.

The others were ushered out of the great cabin, leaving Nesbitt to further examination by the court. Their intention was to find out what had happened as quickly as possible, and only in regard to the loss of the ship. Other issues were not brought up. The fleet knew that the survivors on the rock had eaten several men who had died of exposure. Perhaps Admiral Collingwood himself had even suggested that certain rumors had best be ignored.

The court questioned Lieutenant Nesbitt, Mr. Shillingsworth, and the gunner, Mr. Drummond. It was soon apparent that the dead captain of the *Nautilus*, Edward Palmer, had been entirely responsible for the wreck, and that he had been unlucky rather than incompetent. He had quashed, by enthusiastic persuasion, Nesbitt's doubts as to the advisability of running at night before a gale through an unknown passage at nine knots. Shillingsworth, the master, had advised Palmer to heave to shortly before the ship struck and had been told to go to bed. The nearest he comes to criticism of the captain is when, asked by the court if he attributes the loss of the *Nautilus* to anybody's misconduct, he replies, "Captain Palmer took the charge out of my hand at two o'clock."

Unhappy Shillingsworth! He had come on deck to relieve Lieutenant Nesbitt at 4 o'clock, and found that Captain Palmer had changed the course he had laid out two hours earlier. Nor had he been notified that they were between the islands of Pori and Antikythera. He had just taken over the watch from Lieutenant Nesbitt when the lookout man forward shouted "Breakers ahead!" and the ship struck.

The court then asked the master if he had "mentioned to any officer in the ship what might be the probable consequence of the captain's perseverance of carrying sail and going on." This one had teeth in it. As master, Shillingsworth was legally responsible for the navigation of the ship, under the command of the captain. He was required, according to the *Regulations and Instructions Relating to His Majesties Service at Sea*, to "represent to the Captain every possible danger in or near to the ship's course and the way to avoid it, and if it be immediate, to the Lieutenant of the Watch."

The master answered that he believed not. He had just as well have said of course not. He had only been master for two days.

The next question was along the same line. "Were there any soundings at any distance from the island of Cerigotto [Antikythera]?" This referred to another article in *Regulations and Instructions*, which required the master, when in "pilot water," to "see the lead carefully hove though the pilot should not require it . . ."

Everyone in the court knew that there were no soundings in the channel, and that the rock rose from very deep water. Who could blame a master only two days in the ship for being overruled by his captain? The responsibility was the captain's. He had taken it squarely, against the advice of the Greek pilot, the navigator, and Lieutenant Nesbitt, and had paid for his error with the King's ship and his own life.

The navigational problem, as Palmer must have seen it, was simple. When he left Anti Milo at dusk on Sunday, the fourth of January, he had seventy-odd miles to run to the high cliffs of Pori, or Antikythera, or Cape Grabusa in Crete. They should be visible a good way off, and easy to avoid. Then *Nautilus* would be clear of the archipelago, and might make another couple of hundred miles before she lost the gale. He was taking a chance to run on a dark night through a badly charted channel. But he carried urgent dispatches from the Dardanelles, and knew that the road to success in Nelson's crowded navy was only open to those who took intelligent risks.

Like Lieutenant Nesbitt, George Smith, the cox and second master, had been long in the ship. They are both down on *Nautilus*'s latest surviving muster roll of January, 1805. Smith was the hero of the whole affair. One can imagine the discomfort of Smith, an unpretentious man, pigtailed, sunburned from a lifetime at sea, as he stood to testify before the row of imposing captains.

The president asked him to tell his story, and he replied,

Bounty Paid	Nº	Entry.	Year	Appearance.	Whence and whether Prest or not	Place and County where Born.	Age at Time of Entry in this Ship.	Nº and Letter of Tickets.	MENS NAMES.	Qualities	D. D.D. or R.	Time of Discharge.
	1	Jany 1805	Jany 1						Widows Man	ab		
	6	"	"	"	"				Thos Needham	Cook		
	10								Ino Crothers	2 Gunner		
	13	"	"	"	"				Edwd Graham	abd		
	14	"	"	"	"				Ino Donaldson	Gunrs Mate		
	15	"	"	"	"				Ino Anderson	abd		
	16	"	"	"	"				Thos Jones	abd		
									to Mary Capt Afflen and			
	17	"	"	"	"				Ino Quayle	abd		
	10	"	"	"	"				Wm Wilkinson	ordd		
									2 August ob	ab		
	19	"	"	"	"				Wm Castaway	ord		
	20	"	"	"	"				Robt Murray	ordby		
	23	"	"	"	"				Wm Webber	2 Masr		
	25	"	"	"	"				Robt White	abd		
	29	"	"	"	"				Robt Wiggons	ord.		
	32	"	"	"	"				Ino Carthy	Idle		
	35	"	"	"	"				Ino Lewis	Idle		
	39	"	"	"	"				F anthy Reedr	Masr		
	40	"	"	"	"				Wm Row	Idle		
	45	"	"	"	"				Thos Coulson	Capt Forecastle		
	46	"	"	"	"				Robt Smith	Gunner room		
	47	"	"	"	"				Jas Douglas	2 Masr Mate		

The last muster of the Nautilus. *(© Public Record Office, London)*

"I took the conn [i.e., watch] at 2 o'clock. My orders were a SW course which continued till 3. The lookout man forward called out 'Land Ahead.' The captain immediately said to Lieutenant Nesbitt, 'Haul your wind on the starboard tack and make sail [that is, sail as close to the wind as possible].'" The wind was coming from north northeast, and the land seen was Antikythera, which Gilley says showed up in a flash of lightning.

Having seen the cliffs, Palmer knew he was passing to the north of Antikythera and wanted to get the ship to the northward as far as possible. On the course he was sailing he could, if the wind held, get right across the Adriatic and all the way to Cape Passero at the southern tip of Sicily without losing ground by having to tack, if he could keep to the north, away from the African coast.

Smith continued. "This continued till four. After asking me how high she laid, my reply to him was NW by N. At four the captain was on deck again. Lieutenant Nesbitt told me to 'keep her west by north and be very particular who you have at the helm. . . .' The captain called me down in his cabin and I found him and the pilot holding a chart in his left hand, the dividers in his right."

The impression this scene made must have been very strong: the big cabin, with its settee on the after bulkhead; lantern light on Palmer's and the pilot's faces; the ship bashing along in the roaring darkness. Palmer was worried. Smith knew he had not slept for the past twenty-four hours, and that he had not had his clothes off since the Dardanelles. (As cox of the captain's gig, Smith was also his valet and knew him well.) The detail of the chart and dividers must have stuck fast in Smith's mind as the last moment of normal ship life before the end of his world.

"He asked the pilot if he knew this land. The pilot said he did not, as he had never been through this way before.

The Captain then asked me if his bed was made. I told him yes. He said 'Go and tell the officer of the watch I want him.'

"When on deck I saw Mr. Shillingsworth taking the charge from Lt. Nesbitt. I told Mr. Shillingsworth the Captain wanted him. He went down, and I after him and just as I got to the foot of the ladder I heard someone forward cry 'Port, hard a lee, breakers ahead.'

"Lt. Nesbitt ran aft and ordered the helm to be put a lee, which we had scarcely done when she struck.

"The people ran on deck crying out, and Mr. Nesbitt ran fore and aft pacifying the men, saying, 'If you are Britons, behave like Britons' until he saw the sloop bilged [that is, her side knocked in], when he said 'It's of no use, get the yard tackles down.' [These were the tackles used for handling the boats, which were normally stowed on skids on the main deck.]

"The people ran to the captain's gig and I ran around the deck to find the captain to tell him of it. I found him in his cabin, putting some papers in the fire and the private signal box by him. . . . I shut the door, went on deck, saw that they had lowered the gig halfway down. Conceiving nothing but death before my eyes I jumped into the gig, pulled her clear of the quarter, laid on our oars and divided our clothes amongst many that were naked, all telling me to command the boat as I was so well used to her. We pulled up to the island of Pori, got there at 8 o'clock, all went on shore except myself and another. They soon came back saying they could see nothing of the ship nor any person on the rock, that no water was to be found, and that one part of the island was overrun with wild leeks. On the other part were hundreds of goats and pigs but no men to be seen on it.

"We rested in the boat all that day thinking the weather

would moderate, for to pull over to Cerigo, as we could see a fortification there."

As the gig, with Coxswain Smith at the tiller, shouting to the straining oarsmen to pull for their lives, had been bashing into the big seas towards Pori, Lieutenant Nesbitt led the crew in their struggles to get the cutter off skids and over the side. It was very difficult. The boat weighed nearly a ton.

Captain Palmer, alone in the great cabin, hung on grimly as the ship pounded against the rocks. Very carefully, he fed the dispatches and signal book into the small coal stove; the magazine was only ten feet forward, in the hold. A particularly heavy crash warned him that there was little time. He stood at the door wondering what to do about the fire in the stove, but there was little danger of fire. Already a wave had washed through the door leading from the officers' quarters into the tween decks. The magazine must now be under water.

Nautilus was his first command, and he had made himself as comfortable as he could manage with fine furnishings and personal comforts including his own silverware. He must have had a last, grief-stricken look around as there was a heavier crash and the angle of the deck began to shift. Men screamed in the tween decks. The ladders leading to the upper deck had collapsed as the ship opened up.

He sprang up the cabin companion to the poop, to find Nesbitt in the waist, still struggling to get the boat over the side. Every time a wave picked up the ship and flung her onto the rock, the men heaving at the tackles collapsed in heaps. Finally an extra-heavy sea swept the deck, picked up the boat, and smashed it against the lee bulwarks.

The ship was breaking up. Big timbers, probably part of the keel, keelson, and deadwood, were drifting off in the white foam to leeward, and every time a big sea hit them white water spouted out of the forehatch. With the weakening of the timbers holding the iron fittings, the guns began to move. Then the lashings chafed through and the guns, each with its carriage weighing a couple of tons, began to skid across the deck and smash through the bulwarks.

The deck became untenable. Survivors had to take to the rigging, unable to help men who were swept off the deck to drown in the frothing darkness to leeward. Half an hour before daylight the main mast gave way. The great pine stick, which weighed over ten tons with its sails, fittings, and yards, smashed bulwarks and then cracked as it hit the rock. Although several men were injured or killed in the fall of the mast, the spar now formed a shaky bridge by which the survivors could crawl to a rock, thirty feet long by ten wide, and almost level with the sea.

Palmer stayed to the last. When the survivors had gotten onto the rock they found that he was missing, and sent a party of volunteers back onto the wreck to search for him. They found him, badly injured and unable to move alone. They managed to half carry, half drag him back along the unsteady mast to the rock.

The Nautiluses had gotten out just in time. The ship formed a sort of breakwater just to windward of them, and by the first light of dawn they saw that less of her was visible with every great sea that struck. When she fell apart, the seas would be free to sweep their rock with full force.

As it got lighter they saw that the rock which lay next to theirs was larger, and that parts of it were visible even when the largest waves struck. A shallow channel, which sucked dry every time a wave receded, separated them from it. The channel was about thirty feet wide, and it might be possible to run across it in the interval between one wave and the next.

The first lieutenant led the way across the channel and scrambled up the side of the rock to a safe place above wave level. At intervals the rest of them followed. Many more were now injured, and all their feet were lacerated by the volcanic rock with fangs like animal claws.

When we tried to walk around the rock 159 years later, we found we could not do it in bare feet, and kept our swim fins on. But the channel itself had been smoothed somewhat by water and covered with weed, making it just possible to run that stretch. It is full of potholes, and then was cluttered with great chunks of jagged wreckage threatening the little groups of frightened men.

As day broke, the surviving officers took stock of the situation. Out of about 121 on board at evening quarters the night before, 90 men had reached the rock. Ten had gotten away with Coxswain Smith in the gig. The others were dead. Only two hours had passed since *Nautilus* had struck. Some sailors were half naked: they had literally been washed out of their hammocks. They made a division of clothing and began to fish useful things out of the surf that pounded on the rock. It was cold. There had been ice on the ship's decks the day before, and the gale was not yet blown out. They had no food and no water. Many were injured.

They were four miles from the nearest land, the uninhabited island of Pori where George Smith kept his men searching for water all through that day. By nightfall they had found several holes full of rainwater, and had captured a goat, whose blood they drank. They posted sentries and settled down in the boat for the night. Smith decided to wait until the weather made it possible to get over to Cerigo (now called Kythera), fourteen miles across the channel to the north, where they had sighted a fortress from the cliffs. Antikythera, to the southwest of them, seemed to Smith a less likely place.

After midnight the weather cleared slightly, and the sentry on the cliff shouted down that there was a light on the rock. Stiff and shivering, Smith clambered up the goat path to the sentry. Someone had indeed managed to light a fire.

Although it was rough next morning, twenty-four hours after the wreck, the weather had somewhat moderated. Smith asked for volunteers to come with him to the rock, to see how the survivors fared. By eight, the gig was dipping in the great seas, heading across the channel with four men at the oars. It was bitter cold.

The ship had disappeared, but the rock was swarming with men. A pole with a panel from a torn sail had been erected on the highest point of the rock, and a canvas lean-to gave some of the men some shelter from the spray. Smith's crew pulled up in the lee of the rock, welcomed by cheers all around. Neither party had believed that the other could have survived.

Smith was glad to see Captain Palmer still alive. There was a strange consultation between them, the boat hanging in the lee of the rock, Smith keeping a watchful eye that she never got too close, the captain standing just above the high wash of the seas. At times the boat was twenty feet away, at others so close that the men on the rock stood by to fend it off.

Smith said he could take ten men. Palmer told Nesbitt to choose ten, including the Greek pilot, who said that help could be gotten from Antikythera. The men, still disciplined, made their way into the boat one by one. The Greek was fifth. Apparently considering himself in charge, the pilot then ordered Smith not to take any more

men into the boat. Greek seamen seldom suffer from rash
heroism, nor in all probability had the pilot anything like
Smith's experience in handling a crowded boat in heavy
seas.

They took no one else aboard, and began the long pull
for Antikythera, into a rising sea. By the time they
rounded the cape and entered Potamos bay, the sky had
darkened and the gale had begun again. They had great
difficulty beaching the boat on the shingle under the
houses.

No sooner was the boat safe than they found themselves
surrounded by a crowd of black mustachioed Greeks in
baggy pants tucked into sheepskin gaiters at the knee,
wearing rawhide sandals. The Greeks leveled firelocks and
loosened long knives in their sashes. The pilot parlayed
with the leaders, who accepted his explanation, and together they pulled the gig higher on the beach beside some
local fishing boats, which Smith saw were big enough to
hold a couple of dozen men each.

The starving sailors were taken into the houses built
along the cliff, and given black bread, olives, and raki by
women in long black dresses with embroidered vests.

That afternoon they got a party of villagers to help
them get the boat off the beach so that they could make
the trip with another volunteer crew. But they failed. It
was impossible in such weather.

On Wednesday morning, forty-eight hours after the
wreck, the Greeks flatly refused him their large fishing
boats, but promised they would definitely man a boat
themselves "in the morning." By ten that night, the wind
had dropped, although the sea was still up. Smith and his
crew, apparently without help, launched the gig and
pulled to the rock with the news and with amphoras of
water. But the surf was still so high that it was impossible

even to land the water jars, and so they rowed back to Potamos again in the frozen night.

On Thursday it seemed to Smith that the weather had moderated completely, but he was put off with more promises by the islanders. All that day he pleaded, through the pilot-interpreter, for the use of one of the big fishing boats. The villagers pointed to the sea and shrugged their shoulders. It was too rough for them.

Besides the weather and a lot of peasants he must have considered none-too-docile savages, Smith was battling an enemy whose existence he did not even suspect. The Greek calendar varied from the European one (it was not altered till 1923, and the *Nautilus* survivors had arrived on Antikythera at the beginning of the twelve days of the Byzantine Christmas, when local belief is that boats must stay in port. It is unsafe to sail until Epiphany, when the sea is hallowed by a priest who throws a cross into the sea. During those twelve days, demons called *kallikantzari*, who some say are like men, but dark, ugly, and tall, with iron shoes or cleft hooves or monkeys' arms, and who appear to piss on hearthfires, turn new wine sour, and generally make trouble. A sailor abroad on so horrible an unholy sea had a doubtful future, if any.

It was not till Friday, six days after the wreck, that the villagers let them launch the boat. They skidded it into the water at noon and pulled for the rock, with the news that the villagers had promised to come the next day.

On the rock, the situation had steadily worsened. After Smith's first visit, the gale increased until the waves swept away the tents and put out the fire. The survivors huddled on the highest part of the rock, with green seas sweeping over them every little while. They were saved from being carried away only by ropes lashed to the rock.

By dawn Wednesday, half a dozen were dead and the

remainder exhausted and apathetic. Captain Palmer had refused to leave the island the day before, feeling that his duty lay with the men on the rock. He was now too weak to stand.

At dawn Wednesday the wind dropped again and the seas moderated. Someone, standing swaying against the wind, shouted with joy. He had seen a sail. In a minute the half-frozen, demoralized men were filled with hope, and the rock was alive with activity. Ragged sailors waved their shirts and bits of torn canvas, and struggled to set up a spar for flying a signal. In a little while they saw that it was a large ship, thrashing along with all sail set before the wind. As they watched, she changed course for the rock. Soon they could see that she was manned by Europeans.

She hove to a hundred yards away and hoisted out a boat, which pulled close to the rock where men swarmed, cheering. The boat's crew hung on their oars twenty feet from the nearest naked English sailor. The men in her gazed at the castaways in silence for a few minutes, and then rowed back to the ship.

The survivors watched, raging, while the ship stayed hove to, occasionally tacking back and forth, all during that day. Her boat salvaged spars, canvas, rope, and float-ing barrels from the tangle of wreckage that still washed around the island. In the afternoon, with no word ex-changed with the castaways of the *Nautilus*, she hoisted in the boat, hauled her yards around, and set sail for the westward.

The eighty-odd men still on the rock had now been four days without food or water. Now some disobeyed their officers and their own certain knowledge, sated their thirst with great gulps of sea water, and died in convul-sions not many hours later.

That night was bitter cold, but there was no wind and

Rick Hawes in the hollow of the rock that sheltered the shipwrecked men of the Nautilus.

Jon Smith on Nautilus Rock.

SHIPWRECKS AND ARCHAEOLOGY

not so many men died. Thursday was a bright, sunny January day, quite calm. The gale was over, but no one arrived from Antikythera. Captain Palmer was dying, as was the first lieutenant. The men had now been five days without food or water. That evening they cut up and ate the youngest of the fresh corpses. That evening Captain Palmer died. He was twenty-six. The first lieutenant died at about the same time.

Still more men died on Thursday night. By Friday morning most of the survivors were too apathetic to do more than shelter themselves behind the ridges, twisting and turning against the painful rock in the bright sunlight. One group found the strength to improvise a raft and launch it on the lee side of the island, but it broke up in the surf before they could man it. Five men built another tiny raft and managed to get aboard. They drifted away with the current, and were not seen again.

On Friday night Smith returned with the gig. He managed to pick up two men, and watched another drown trying to swim to the boat.

Saturday morning was calm and sunny, and at last the boats from Antikythera came to the rescue. Little more than half the original survivors of the wreck reached Antikythera that morning; thirty-four had starved or died of exposure. Smith judged that perhaps ten of the fifty-odd who were rescued would have survived another night on the rock.

After Smith made his way back to Antikythera with those who had lived through the ordeal of the rock, they were weatherbound for eleven days there and then again in Kythera for three weeks. They were hospitably received in Kythera by the English vice-consul, Emmanuel Caluci, and the local notables. Caluci had played a part in the salvage of the Elgin marbles which had been lost off nearby San Nikolo bay five years before.

There was to be still another shipwreck before the survivors got off Kythera. The master, Shillingsworth, took a local boat to the Peloponnesus to search for a Russian frigate which was said to be patrolling there. He was wrecked on the way, and nearly lost his life. He finally found the Russian, which put into San Nikolo bay to pick them up on the fifth of February. They reached Corfu in March, two months after the wreck.

The *Nautilus* incident passed almost unnoticed. The news did not get to England until April. It rated only a paragraph in the papers.

The court-martial's verdict was that no blame attached to Lieutenant Nesbitt or the other survivors, and that they had used "every exertion that circumstances could admit." The court's final words were heartwarming, despite the official prose "And it appearing to the court that the conduct of George Smith [the coxswain] who was ultimately the means of saving so many men, was such as induced the court to recommend him to the Commander in Chief, and the said George Smith was hereby recommended accordingly."

There were several George Smiths in the Royal Navy then, and I do not know what happened to Smith of the *Nautilus*. But I like to think that he is the Geo Smith (A) who was commissioned as a lieutenant on September 20, 1811. This is unlikely, as he was "lower deck" and probably illiterate. But it is possible, if Admiral Collingwood had taken him under his wing.

The young Lieutenant Nesbitt applied that June for leave "for the reestablishment of my health, which in consequence of our late sufferings, is not a little impaired."

The first lieutenant's request for leave.
(© Public Record Office, London)

We next hear of him being promoted to commander in 1809, then married in 1811. Marshall's *Naval Biography* says that "he married, in 1811, Maria, youngest daughter of William Fisher, Receiver-General for the county of Norfolk; and died, we believe, in the year 1824." Norfolk being a green and pleasing county, we can hope Nesbitt had a prospering life, and certainly an easier death than that of others he had seen on Nautilus Rock.

The last irony of the *Nautilus* is that the messages she carried with such unfortunate haste were redundant. Rear Admiral Louis had been sent to the Dardanelles with a considerable fleet (*Canopus* 80, *Thunderer* 74, *Standard* 64, *Active* 38, and *Nautilus* 18.) These had been detached from the fleet off Cadiz to strengthen the hand of the British representative in Constantinople, who was trying to prevent Britain's old allies, the Turks, from making an alliance with Napoleon and going to war with Russia.

But the sultan declared war on Russia on the thirtieth of December, 1806. Louis got to the fleet in the Dardanelles on the second of January, and the *Nautilus* sailed with her dispatches at dawn on January 3.

But it had been apparent a month earlier to the foreign office that Turkey's declaration of war was inevitable. Orders to Collingwood to reinforce Admiral Louis had already been sent from the Admiralty on December 22, and arrived on January 12. Admiral Duckworth and a fleet of eleven ships sailed on January 15, though they did not go into action until late February.

Now, in 1966, we did not expect to find much left of the *Nautilus*, but were curious to see how much of her story we could read from what we found. Assuming the weather stayed fine, we had a full day to try.

She had been a good-sized ship, probably about the same size as the Antikythera ship described in Chapter 4.

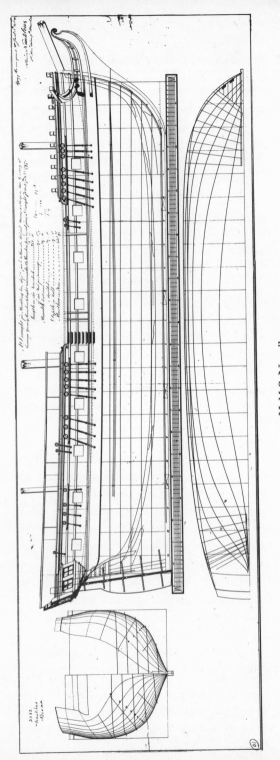

H.M.S. Nautilus.

Her total weight when equipped for foreign service was 456 tons. (Her measurement tonnage was 382.) We could expect that the hull had disappeared completely, smashed by waves and eaten by marine organisms. We might find some of the 40-odd tons of iron ballast, 24 guns, 4 or 5 tons of coal (unless she had been burning wood in her galley stove), 22 tons of shot, 4 anchors, and a lot of miscellaneous things such as the brass hoops of powder barrels. Royal Navy specifications for a sloop of this type called for more than five tons of copper fastenings. (These ships were fastened with copper below the waterline, as iron fastenings and copper sheathing caused electrolytic action which destroyed the iron.) She had had three tons of copper sheets, and over fifteen tons of iron bolts. Such a sloop also carried over four tons of lead of all sorts.

We got the little compressor rigged on the deck aft, which was right over the wreck, and Rick helped me rig up for the first dive. He spun the flywheel, and the little engine sputtered alive. I waited until it was running well and then, at a nod from Rick, dropped over the side.

The water was very transparent and, as I hung for a while waiting for my ears to clear, I got a good idea of the wreck. To my left, in a little valley in the rock, was a single iron gun, heavily overgrown. No other guns were visible. The bottom was almost clean, with very little sea-growth, in contrast to the slope which began thirty feet away and was covered with weed. Just below me was the heap of junk we had seen the day before — a mass of iron bars 90 centimeters long by 15 square. As my ears made strange squeaking sounds and I swam up and down waiting for the pressure to equalize, I realized that these must be *Nautilus*'s iron ballast.

There was a pop as my ears cleared, and I swam down to the patch of ballast twenty feet below. The bars were

One of Nautilus's *cannons resting on Nautilus Rock*

Ballast bars and cannonballs from H.M.S. Nautilus.

cemented to the bottom by limestone growth. Mixed with the ballast bars were cannonballs of varying sizes. That was all. I spent the next hour, until I was cold, searching the mass of iron bars for something that would prove that this was what remained of the *Nautilus*. I found the bronze cheekpiece of a block and two bronze pins, one of them satisfyingly stamped with the Royal Navy's broad arrow. At the very last I spotted something gleaming white, wedged under a stone. It was a silver spoon concreted to an overgrown lump of iron. When cleaned, much later, it was possible to distinguish Palmer's crest, a greyhound sejant. Hallmarks showed that the spoon was made in 1805.

I surfaced with a bagful of odds and ends, to find that Jon Smith and my wife Joan had seen other cannon on the other side of the ridge of reef. The others, including the older children, Mark and Sarah, swam off to search for more cannon. Joan and Roger Stafford set about measuring the reef, the relation of the remains of the ship to the reef, and the locations of the cannon we found.

Jon Smith and I got out the chart and the record of *Nautilus*'s course at 4 A.M. Monday, January 7, 1807. When we combined this with the rough plan that Joan and Roger had made, and had learned that the only mass of ballast bars was the one we had anchored over, it was easy to see what had happened to the *Nautilus*.

Jon shook his head. "Poor Palmer," he said. Jon had been the skipper of a yawl which had sailed from Australia to the Mediterranean the year before, and had made lots of decisions like the one that Palmer had made.

The plan showed that if the man on watch had spotted the breakers a half-minute earlier, or if the breakers had not appeared when the watches were changing and there was some slight confusion as to who was in charge of the ship, there would probably have been no wreck. The ship would have escaped if she had passed only a hundred feet to the westwards.

The positions of the guns in relation to the ballast showed that the gun deck, with some guns still attached, had washed right over the reef when the ship broke up. A few bits of crumpled copper sheathing in the rock showed where she had plowed into it. We swam right round the island, searching the shallows, and found nothing more. It was understandable that we did not find small objects, for a heavy sea breaking in the exposed rock could be expected to scour it clean of any light objects which did not catch in the interstices of the rock. We found only seven cannon out of twenty-four which we know must have been in the ship. The total weight of iron ballast on the reef, though difficult to estimate exactly, did not exceed ten tons, less than a quarter of the total probably on board.

Joan and Jon Smith dived to draw the heap of ballast bars and to search the bottom for more small finds. Then we got the little compressor into the dinghy and, with Rick at the oars, I headed for deep water. At about forty or fifty feet the character of the bottom changed from a hard, desert expanse of rock with only black, wild sponges on it, to seaweed so dense that the bottom was invisible. Here, in deeper water, it was colder. I zigzagged across the area into which debris from the ship might have swept, found nothing, then searched the bottom between the beginning of the weed and the rocks where the ship struck. There was nothing. It was hard to believe that cannon could have been swept for two hundred yards by wave action in fairly deep water.

Then I went around the reef where *Nautilus* struck and searched the area below the ballast bars, down to over one hundred feet. There was nothing except a piece of corroded iron about a yard long and as thick as my wrist, and a pall of cloudy stuff which streaked the thermocline at eighty feet.

Nautilus had disappeared except for the cannon on the reef, ballast bars, and the documents in the Public Records Office. It seems likely that the wreck was picked over by sponge divers soon after the ship sank. Cannon were valuable, as were her copper tanks. It is even possible that the Royal Navy had sent a salvage party. The ballast bars are only twenty-odd feet deep. Perhaps they just removed the missing guns from the northern side of the reef where the ship struck, and never found the ones that had washed over it to be found by us over a century and a half later.

The evening wind had begun to rise. It was time to go. Little waves were beginning to slap the schooner's sides and she tugged at her mooring, a hawser bowlined around a snag in the reef where *Nautilus* had struck. The children, Mark and Tim, both eleven, and small Sarah, nine years old, were worn out from a day of helping hunt for cannon, and hold measuring tapes. They had nearly caught a big octopus which had swarmed right up on the rock trying to catch someone's rubber swim fin, which it apparently thought was edible.

Jon started the engine, and while he and Roger heaved in the stern line, Rick and I hove the anchor up and lashed it to the cathead. Hearts a bit in our mouths, we watched as Jon, bluff, Australian, and very unconcerned, jockeyed us out of the basin in the reefs in which we lay, and out into the channel. As we started over the channel between the rock and Antikythera, the route that George Smith had traversed so often, and moved steadily at six knots under power, the shadows lengthened and threw the barren fangs of Nautilus Rock into high relief.

PART II

IV

~~~~~~~

The Antikythera Wreck:
The Beginning of Marine Archaeology

W<small>E</small> anchored again in Potamos, in the same place that we had been the night before. Jon and I spread the chart again and ticked off distances and courses for square-rigged sailing ships out of the Aegean. Palmer of the *Nautilus* would have needed only a slight southerly set to the current to have piled up on Antikythera, and as we know from the surviving records, that was the danger he was watching for. The skipper of the big Roman ship that struck on Cape Glyphada, on the northeast side of Antikythera, could have been set south by the same current.

If he were coming late in the year from Rhodes or from the Asia Minor mainland to the north, he too might well have been struck by a northerly gale and decided to make the best of it, keep the island of Crete well to leewards, and make for the Kythera channel. If, like Captain Palmer, he were under orders to "proceed with the utmost dispatch" and decided to chance running at night, he can well have piled up where he did.

It seems unlikely that he would have been trying to make Potamos harbor. It was a dangerous place into which to take a square-rigged ship in a northerly gale. Only a smaller ship could lie there safely, as did the boat commanded by Dimitrios Kondos, the Greek captain who found the Antikythera wreck. He and his men had been returning home to the island of Syme, in the Dodecanese, after a season of sponge diving on the banks off North Africa. A southerly gale had caught them in the Antikythera channel, and they had come here to shelter from it.

That evening, after we had moored the dinghy safely so that she wouldn't smash on the tiny concrete dock, Jon and I sat again with the owner of the fishing boat. He said that Potamos was impossible in a northerly winter gale, but safe at other times. Sponge boats coming back from Africa in the fall still use it. Like Kondos's group, today's diving boats travel in pairs. A fairly large schooner serves as the depot ship. Most of the men live in it, and it is large enough to carry all the supplies necessary for thirty-odd men who work for months off the barren coast. The diving boats depend on the depot ship. In the old days they were rigged with hand-cranked compressors, oars, and sails. Today the boats are similar, but have engines.

These divers and their boats had fascinated me for years. We talked late that night, as I explained the wonders of the sponge business to Jon and Rick and Roger, wanting them to share my excitement about seeing Cape Glyphada in the morning. Antikythera had been something of an obsession with me ever since I had written a paper on the fragments of planking in the National Museum in Athens. I had bothered the librarian at the American School of Classical Studies until, in desperation, she had translated the scanty Greek archaeological reports for me. Eventually I chased down all the printed material on the wreck. I learned, finally, enough Greek to read the yellowing newspaper reports in the Greek National Library, and at last found the relatives and friends of the men who had actually done the work there so long ago.

My chief source was John Lyndiakos, whose uncles had owned the ships commanded by Kondos. Lyndiakos had spent a year on Antikythera as a boy, when his father was working there. He was the last surviving participant of the expedition, but said apologetically that he had been only eight years old at the time, and could remember only the things a boy would remember. I laughed, thinking of my stepson Mark, who had helped survey an ancient wreck in Italy when he was nine years old, then given a talk at school that fall explaining marine archaeology.

Many of the old Syme houses had been bombed and burned in the war, with the loss of whatever old receipts, diaries, and logs might have added to the old man's remembered story. Who was Kondos? What kind of a man was he? The story of the discovery of the wreck was so dramatic that it was not hard to reconstruct. Kondos was, after all, a man like me, a diver, and captain of his ship.

On the fall day that he found the wreck, he would have wakened in his bunk and felt that day was breaking soon. From the change in the rhythm of gusts rattling the rigging, he knew yesterday's gale was dropping. Like several hundred other sponge captains in the Aegean and off Africa on that same day, he crawled out of his bunk and climbed the ladder out of the stuffy little aftercabin. On deck he shivered. The only sound was the wind and the rattle of the big rudder, which gibbered on its worn pintles even though the tiller was lashed firmly to the starboard bitts.

Kondos made his decision while the others still slept. Although it was still blowing, they would be able to work on the protected north side of the island, under the cliffs. It was a difficult place to dive in, because the cliffs fell steep to great depths, but the slopes of the island would surely yield a day's wages. Anyway, the activity would settle the crew, who were getting bored and restless after three gale-bound days in Potamos bay.

He stamped hard on the deck, to waken Stadiatis, the diver who shared his cabin, then picked his way through the barrels and boxes that littered the schooner's deck to the cook shack, lashed to the bulwark behind the port foremast shrouds. In the crowded hold below, where the divers slept, bare feet slapped the deck and the hatch cover slid back to release the fug of nearly twenty men's sleep into the clear morning air.

The diving boat was moored alongside the schooner. She was what the sailors from Syme call an *aktarma*, a double-ended rowing and sailing boat, about thirty feet long with flaring bows that threw spray outwards so the decks stayed dry. Mercurio, the divers' tender and the second man in the crew after Kondos, was already up, shouting to the sailors as they pulled in the stern mooring, hove up the anchor, and with three of them heaving on the sweeps, rowed her alongside the schooner to load her crew of rowers and divers.

In the forty years that divers from the Dodecanese islands of Syme and Kalymnos had been working with helmet diving gear, they had evolved their own system of diving and of dealing with the problems of long voyages far from their home port. As divers, these men were unique. They probably had more experience of deep water at the time than any other group, anywhere.

The key of the system was the *aktarma*, the small, easily maneuverable diving boat that, driven by sweeps, could follow the diver on the bottom. The captain and the tender were responsible for maneuvering. The tender, sitting in the bow of the boat, followed every movement of the diver on the bottom with a very strong, pencil-thin, braided cotton or hemp line which the Greeks call a guide, or *kulaouzo*. The tender, therefore, is called a *kulaozeros*, "he who guides." Mercurio, the *kulaozeros*, was the man who took care of the diving gear as well.

It took a big crew to work the hand-pumped compressor and to row the boat. Divers can stay for limited times under water over thirty feet deep, and so a diving boat had to carry at least four divers, more commonly six or eight, as well as men to row and crank the compressor. Since so many men could not live comfortably on a boat small enough to be a maneuverable divers' tender, they had devised the system of the two ships working in tandem. On the big boat, the *deposito*, meals were cooked, and sponges cleaned.

It was still dark when the rowers went over the side of the schooner into the *aktarma*. The divers were already huddled together in their privileged territory on the foredeck, smoking cigarettes for breakfast. They never ate before diving, as they believed it brought on the bends. Mercurio took the tiller, Kondos the captain's place in the tiny round forehatch, and the rowers, without an order, bent to the big sweeps, which they worked facing forward, standing in the cluttered hold of the boat.

A gray dawn broke as they pulled around the big cape south of the harbor. Although the wind screamed at them from the tops of the cliffs, the water near the island was calm. Kondos knew that a slight easterly current ran along the north side of Antikythera when the south wind blew, so he decided to head for the nearest promontory, Cape Glyphada three miles away, and work back to Potamos with the current.

It was Stadiatis's turn to dive. He flipped his cigarette

into the water, dipped some soft soap out of the can that always hung on the mast, and sloshed his wrists with it. Then he picked his way through the lounging divers to the dressing bench, where the ship's boy waited with the diving dress. While the boy held the neck of the rubberized canvas suit, he stepped into it, sat down on the bench to get his legs into the legs of the suit, then stood up as the boy pulled the dress up over his shoulders and held each sleeve in turn so that Stadiatis could slip his soapy wrists through the tight red rubber cuffs.

The sun came over the horizon as the boy swarmed around Stadiatis under Mercurio's watchful gaze. He fitted the rubber neck of the suit over the copper studs of the heavy breastplate, slipped the iron clamps over the rubber, and spun the copper wingnuts down onto the clamps. They squeaked as they got a final tightening with a hand-sized hardwood dowel cut to fit over the lugs. The boy then knelt in front of the diver and whipped the lashings around the diver's shoes, which were steel-soled and very light, unlike the heavy boots worn by conventional divers. Then the boy dipped the helmet over the side and scrubbed it with a bit of what divers call soap sponge, to prevent fogging inside the helmet. Stadiatis and Kondos each took one of the heavy diving weights, which were tied together with the lanyards that served as shoulder straps. It was good lead. Like most of the lead used by sponge divers, it probably came from a Roman anchor stock.

Stadiatis was ready. Sitting on the diver's dressing bench in the bows, facing aft, his left leg resting on top of the bulwark, he cannot have seen the shore, the cliffs, or the red streak in the rock. It was a place the Antikythera people called "Pinakakia," but it is not likely that anyone on board knew that then. For the sweating oarsmen, for the divers, Kondos, Mercurio, it was just another cape past which the current ran carrying food for sponges.

Captain Kondos, right up in the bows, legs curled crab-like in the little round hatch fitted into the tiny foredeck, strained his eyes to see a ledge or bottom through the glass-bottomed bucket. He must have been thinking as he did so that this was a godawful ugly deep place, with the pure blue of deep water to his left and the cliff on his right falling sheer without a ledge or even an easy slope where a diver could get the buoyancy of his diving dress under control after leaving the shot line. It takes no mean skill for a helmet diver to float along a sheer wall, adjusting his weight with perfect delicacy by little taps of his head on the valve in the helmet. Hands are a final control, but the weeds of the cliff offered only an insecure grip. A diver rigged too light can rocket upwards, out of control. Too heavy, and he can sink, to die of squeeze caused by the difference of pressure, unless the boy on the hose and the tender are very careful of their jobs.

All these things, and others, will have been in the captain's mind as he peered through the water glass into the abyss. A ledge heaped with boulders swam into sight sixty feet below. Kondos lifted his head and glanced at the cliff, thinking that the red streak would make the place easy to find again if they did hit virgin sponges here, thinking any-way that it was probably not much use, since too many other divers worked these waters.

He nodded to Mercurio, who picked up the helmet, spilled the last of the water out of it, and handed it to the boy. The boy slipped it over Stadiatis's ears and locked it. Two sailors stepped out of their places port and starboard, and stood to the cranks. Air rushed into the helmet from the pump, which turned smoothly at the sailors' hands. Old Mercurio banged Stadiatis's battered copper helmet

The cliffs of Pinakakia on Antikythera.

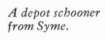

A depot schooner
from Syme.

twice. The diver swung his right leg over the side, and pushing himself outward, splashed into the water facing forward, his left hand holding the descending line. The boy, midships in the boat, began calling the depth in fathoms from the gauge on the pump:

"Five, seven, seven . . ."

This was the time when the diver reached the end of the descending line and balanced his weight, releasing himself then to float under control to the bottom.

"Eight, nine, ten . . . eleven, twelve, twelve, fourteen, fourteen, fifteen, fifteen . . ."

Kondos nodded. The boy turned to a little shelf on the mast and inverted the minute glass.

"Sixteen, seventeen, eighteen, nineteen . . ."

The diver was well under control now, with old Mercurio holding the hard twist lifeline. The slight negative weight of the diver was balanced by the old man's hand on the line above. The sand ran out. The boy turned the glass again. The pressure gauge turned smoothly to 30 fathoms, 180 feet. Kondos made sure that he was conscious of the time, since too much time at that depth was very dangerous. The gauge settled at thirty. A steady chant came from the boy on the depth gauge: "Thirty, thirty . . ."

"Five minutes," Kondos thought. "I'll let him stay five minutes."

Then the boy, his squeaky voice rising, shouted, "Twenty-eight, twenty-seven, twenty-six, twenty-five, twenty-four, twenty-three . . ."

Was Stadiatis blowing up? It shouldn't happen with an experienced diver. The gleaming copper helmet broke surface in a ring of foam near the boat. Kondos slipped the loop that held the diving ladder out of the water, and lent the tender a hand on the lifeline. When they had pulled the diver to the ladder, he clambered up it far enough so that the helmet protruded over the bulwark. The boy bearhugged it, twisted to unlock it, and straightened up with it in his arms. Kondos leaned the diver over, so that the water that had leaked into the fold of rubber under the breastplate could splash onto the bulwark. The boy set the helmet down in the middle of its coil of hose, then ran back to pull the slipknots that held the kidney-shaped weights.

Stadiatis's eyes were rolling, and he was sickly pale. He was babbling, half screaming, something about women. Kondos shook him.

"What was it, man?"

The diver made no coherent reply, but mumbled "Holy Virgin" over and over again, as they worked him over the bulwarks to the bench in the bow. He was trembling. They sat him down and Kondos asked again what the trouble was. Elias kept mumbling. Heads turned in the boat. Everyone's attention had been caught by the hysteria in Stadiatis's voice.

"Never mind virgins," said Kondos, very steadily. "What's wrong?"

"Horses, women, naked women, beautiful women with syphilis . . ."

"Somebody give him a cigarette." Mercurio reached into the pocket of his dirty shirt, fumbled out a mashed cigarette, lit it, and put it into Elias's mouth. He took a deep drag. Kondos felt past the copper breastplate for his shoulder, and shook him.

"Come on, Elias. Calm down, man. What happened. What did you see?"

"People . . ."

"What people?" Someone sniggered and remarked that Elias had gone off his rocker at last. With a dozen faces staring at him, Stadiatis tried desperately to explain that he had seen dead naked women, their obscene flesh half eaten by disease or the fish, and horses.

"Like a city, with men and horses . . ." His voice trailed off.

Kondos waved the men back to their places, and when Stadiatis had gotten out of the diving dress, put on his own socks and crawled into the damp canvas dress. In five minutes he was on his way to the bottom, ignoring the oarsman who asked him to bring back the best of the girls. Stadiatis sat crouched beside Mercurio in the bows, mumbling about the city and horses upside down while the tender, his hands very delicate on the lifeline this time, waved directions to the oarsman. At just under thirty fathoms the chant steadied; Kondos was working on whatever it was. The lifeline jerked. Mercurio let it go slack. The boat rocked, silent except for the slap of the compressor, the panting of the men turning it, and the squeak of the oars against the wooden tholepins.

It seemed longer, but after less than five turns of the minute glass, the man tending the hose felt three jerks, the signal that Kondos was on his way up. When Mercurio began to heave in the lifeline it didn't come. It was stuck fast, a sign that Kondos had taken it off and tied it onto something. He was coming up on the hose.

He surfaced near the side, was dragged over to the ladder and climbed up to the bulwark with the help of a heave from the boy. The men babbled, crowding forward so that Mercurio had to yell at them to get back. When Kondos was on deck with his helmet off, he gestured towards the line.

"Heave it in, boys."

Half a dozen men gathered around the fo'c'sle and gave the lifeline a great heave. It stuck for a moment and then came free, easily hauled by two men. They got it to the bulwark, and with a final heave, Kondos's find came over the side to land with a thump on the foredeck. The men stared.

It was a man's right hand, life-size, of green metal filled with sand. The first two fingers were extended as if to hold an object which had long since disappeared. Kondos laughed.

"Statues, you cuckold idiots, statues. A whole shipload of statues."

There are several versions of what happened next. The official story, published in the Greek archaeological journal *Ephemeris Archaeologiki* soon after the wreck was salvaged, says that Kondos found the wreck in the spring, took only the bronze arm, and went to the Greek government in the fall from motives of pure patriotism.

This version is hard to swallow for several reasons. It is extremely unlikely that any sponge boat would return from Africa in the spring of the year. Sponge expeditions from the Dodecanese traditionally sail just after Easter to the banks off Africa. It is reasonable and normal, however, that a boat should return in October or November, which is also the right time of year for the kind of southerly gale which drove Kondos into shelter in Potamos. Such gales are rare in the spring. Furthermore, it seems equally improbable that a crew of sponge divers would abstain from looting a wreck for patriotism or sentiment of any kind. Even if Kondos had wanted to, he could not have kept from robbing the wreck, since most of the crew were shareholders in the expedition and would have forced him to make whatever profit could be made from this or any other wreck.

In Syme they say that Kondos and his men salvaged what they could before the weather changed, and that the small bronzes they got were sold in Alexandria between

1902 and 1910. The proceeds are supposed to have been invested in a schooner which had a lurid and highly profitable career smuggling surplus French army rifles to the natives of Cyrenaica.

Neither version can be proved definitely after so many years, unless someone locates the lost bronzes. After sixty years, this seems unlikely.

There is another indication that Kondos and his men "mined" the wreck. Like all Aegean sponge divers, they were familiar with ancient wrecks. These were not and are not generally recognized by the divers as wrecks of ships, but are seen as heaps of clay jars or bits of calcined wood or piles of copper ingots. Generally sponge divers pick the sponges off the clay jars, search the area for lead or copper, and move on. It is generally known that a diver who finds a heap of clay jars on the bottom is likely to find large "bars of lead" nearby. These bars of lead are ancient anchor stocks. The anchors' flukes were made of hardwood, as were the shafts. A wooden anchor would obviously not sink to the bottom, so ancient Mediterranean seafarers cast the stock — that is, the crossbar of the anchor — in lead in order to sink the wood and cause the anchor to lie on the bottom at an angle to let the flukes dig in. It is interesting that there has never been a recorded find of a lead anchor stock in the Aegean, although every sponge diver has seen them. Hundreds of stocks, however, have been found in the western Mediterranean, which has not been combed by Greek divers.

The Antikythera wreck was a ship of the right size and period to have carried at least five large lead-stocked anchors, the stocks weighing from 500 to 1000 pounds apiece, like the ones we found in Taranto. Although tons of material were eventually salvaged from the Antikythera wreck, the only anchor found was a rusted iron fisherman's anchor, undoubtedly modern. If Kondos and his men had salvaged what they could from the wreck when they first found it, they would certainly have removed the anchor stocks to sell for scrap. If other divers before Kondos had found the wreck, they would certainly have taken the lead anchor stocks and probably the portable bronzes as well, leaving none for Kondos. It follows, then, that Kondos was probably the first to find the wreck, and decided to get out of it whatever he could.

They stayed on the place for a fairly long time, making three five-minute dives per diver per day. The wreck, they found, lay parallel with the face of the rock on a sandy ledge which jutted out at the thirty-fathom level and ended at thirty-five fathoms in a steep slope leading to very deep water. It was fantastic good luck that the wreck had fallen in that particular place. If the ship had sunk fifty feet further out, it would have hit the slope and slid down it, to be lost forever.

The shape of the ship was outlined by the great oblong heap of statues which had frightened Stadiatis. This heap was cemented solidly together by a thick layer of sea-growth nearly as hard as concrete and several feet thick in places. The divers found several smaller statues and other things in the interstices of the heap, and pried them out.

Then the weather changed. In the fall of the year, in the straits, a southerly gale is most often followed by several days of calm, which can then be followed by a cold north wind. When it turned cold and big waves began to break on the cliffs, it was time for Kondos and his men to sail for home.

At that time Syme, like the rest of the Dodecanese, was officially a part of the Ottoman Empire, although its population was entirely Greek. It was to be forty-five years before the Dodecanese were united with Greece. Like other Greeks under Ottoman rule, the people of Syme had a fierce feeling of loyalty and patriotism towards the mother country where Greeks, governing themselves for the first time since the fall of Constantinople in the spring of 1453, were struggling to create a nation.

It was a time of archaeological discovery. Schliemann had dug at Mycenae and Troy, the French had begun to dig at Delphi, Germans were excavating at Olympia and Americans at Corinth. For the first time in history, Greek education, at least on the mainland, was out of the hands of the Orthodox church, which had indeed kept Hellenism alive through the dark time of the Turkish occupation but had certainly not emphasized Greek classical history. Now the government ran the schools, and Greeks were being taught to take pride in their pagan ancestors.

When the two boats moored in the harbor of Syme and the men swarmed ashore after more than half a year away from home, the news of Kondos's discovery must have spread like wildfire. Even had they wanted to keep the news to themselves, there is no such thing as a secret on a Greek island, certainly not a secret of this magnitude. Kondos must have realized that the shipload of statues he had found was valuable. It was impossible to say how valuable, and whether it would be worthwhile to undertake a difficult salvage job without a certainty of selling the statues for a good price. Furthermore, something had to be done very quickly, or another boat would get back to the site before him.

It seems very likely that rumors of a load of statues in the sea came to the ears of A. Economou, who was from Syme, and who was a professor at the University of Athens. Perhaps the owners of the boats, the Lyndiakos brothers, and Kondos approached Economou when they were trying to decide what to do about their find, and he persuaded them to offer it to the Greek government.

In any case, Professor Economou, accompanied by Captain Kondos and Elias Stadiatis, journeyed to Athens where they called upon the then minister of education, Professor Spiridon Stais, on the sixth of November, 1900. As evidence of their find they brought the bronze arm. When the arm had been examined, Kondos offered to raise the remaining statues if he and the Lyndiakos brothers were paid their full value, and if the Greek navy would provide a ship that could winch the heavy objects off the bottom. Stais, an imaginative and large-minded man and one of the best ministers of education that Greece has ever had, was fascinated.

He and Economou both believed that Stadiatis might have stumbled on a ship carrying Greek art back to Rome. Stais was, like all educated Greeks, familiar with the story of the Elgin marbles, how some of them had been lost on the way to England and salvaged by Greek divers. Elgin had been only an English millionaire with a passion for antiquity, who had done his looting at the end of fifteen hundred years of removal of Greek antiquities by men from the West. Imagination boggled at what kind of material a Roman emperor, someone like Hadrian or Nero, might have been able to collect in a big ship. It took Stais only two weeks to get the Kondos-Lyndiakos offer officially accepted, and to arrange a formal guarantee of funds and a navy ship.

Kondos, his divers, and the government that employed them, were not aware that they were undertaking the deepest salvage job in the history of diving up to that time. There had been only one comparable job, the recovery in 1885 of 90,000 gold pounds from the strong room of the wreck of the steamer *Alphonse XII*, which lay at 160 feet in the English channel. Alexander Lambert, the diver who did the job, was struck by bends and paralyzed for life as a consequence.

But if some busybody had told Kondos he was attempting the impossible, he would have laughed. Divers from Syme and Kalymnos had been going to the 300-foot theoretical limit for compressed air diving for years. Kondos and his divers wore watch fobs and used cigarette holders made from the black coral that grows in great depths off Africa, where few men have been even today.

Most of the twenty-two men in the boats with which Kondos returned to Antikythera seem to have come from Syme. The six divers were from several islands. One was a Turk from Crete, nicknamed George the Turk, or New George, or the Cretan. The "New George" nickname came from his conversion to the Greek church so that he could marry an Orthodox girl from Syme. Another diver was nicknamed "Rhodian." His proper name was John Piliou. (It is difficult to tell just who was aboard because of the nickname habit, which is still so strong that it is possible to know a diver for years without ever learning his real name. Even his shipmates won't know it, unless they have happened to look at the crew list or his identity card.

The Mundiades brothers, Kyriakos and George, were aboard for part of the time at least. There was a diver from Hydra named Vasilios Katsaras. Finally there was the wreck's discoverer, Elias Stadiatis, a neighbor and possibly a relative of Kondos. He was nicknamed "Sycophant." Old Mercurio, the *kulaozeros* or tender, was from Syme too. He had once been a naked diver.

The government expedition arrived off Cape Glyphada early in the morning of the twenty-fourth of November.

Big swells from the north were breaking on the cliffs. A gale, like the one that had sunk both the *Nautilus* and the Antikythera ship, was brewing. The captain of the navy transport *Michaeli* took one look at the place, with its sheer cliffs and steep shoreline that made anchoring almost impossible, and took *Michaeli* around the cape to Potamos harbor, where the northerly swell still made cooking difficult and kept a part of the crew hanging over the rail.

Kondos squinted at the clouds and decided to risk a dive. With the rowers straining at the sweeps to keep the boat headed into the waves, the divers made one dive each to attach lines to small objects. At noon they ran back to Potamos with the boat's spritsail pulling hard in the rising wind.

The haul was as impressive as Kondos had perhaps meant it to be. Professor Economou and the crew of the *Michaeli* gasped with excitement at the finds that were heaved over the transport's bulwarks. There was a life-size bronze head of a bearded man. He was probably meant to be a philosopher, but his face was so overgrown with sea-growth that he looked like a boxer. Even through the sea-growth, Economou could see that the head had been done by a great sculptor of classical or Hellenistic times. There was the bronze arm of a boxer, broken off at the shoulder but in very good condition; a corroded bronze sword, evidently part of a statue; two badly corroded marble statues of men, one life-size, the other slightly smaller, both lacking heads; and a couple of boxes full of bits of other bronze and marble statues, bronze bowls, clay dishes, and a sack full of broken pottery.

By the time they had transferred the finds, the wind had increased to a gale and it was obviously not wise to remain longer in Potamos harbor. *Michaeli* got under way to

Piraeus, and the diving boat headed for the nearest good harbor, San Nikolo bay in Kythera.

While the divers smoked and slept out the storm, the *Michaeli* thrashed across the channel, past Falkonera and Cape Malea, to Piraeus. When she arrived, pandemonium broke loose at the ministry. Stais had been right. Kondos had stumbled onto what was going to be the biggest hoard of ancient Greek bronzes found to that date. The first haul had included parts of at least ten statues, picked from what Kondos said was a huge heap on the bottom. The marble was badly pitted by marine worms, and some of the bronze was so fragile that it broke like bad pottery.

Red headlines broke in the Athenian papers next day: TREASURE AT KYTHERA . . . ARCHAEOLOGICAL TREASURE. Professor Economou and the officer commanding *Michaeli* reported that the transport was too large for the job, and that a smaller, more maneuverable ship able to work close to the cliffs was needed. The navy ministry assigned the steam schooner *Syros*, which was on the point of going into drydock, with most of her crew on leave. The missing officers and men were replaced from the naval depot, and rushed to prepare the little ship for work in the evil channels off Kythera.

She arrived in San Nikolo, where the divers were still sheltered, on the third of December. That day the storm subsided. Now the man in charge was the director of antiquities, Professor George Byzantinos. Economou apparently stayed back in Athens. It is possible that he even asked to be relieved; he was not a young man. Byzantinos said that:

The finds, and the divers' assurances that there were many more things on the bottom, convinced Mr. Stais and he instructed me to go to Antikythera to supervise. In spite of bad weather, we left Piraeus at midnight on the 2nd of December and ran down to Kythera where the diving boats were waiting. The divers gave us an enthusiastic welcome. We sailed for Antikythera the next morning and after four hours arrived where the ancient wreck lies. Ominous steep cliffs overhung the wreck, and the sharp blue reefs were cruel even in the sunshine. I looked at the cliffs, wondering where we would moor the ship, and was fascinated and frightened by the place, which seemed ready to destroy not only one trireme [sic], but a whole fleet. I imagined the awful night when the ship struck, the crash, the confusion of bronze heads and marble statues and live men. It seemed to me that the victims' screams still rang from the cliffs. Where did the ship come from, and where was it going?

Byzantinos was neither the first nor the last to ask that question, which has occupied three generations of students since his time. There is a passage in ancient Greek literature which it is tempting to regard as a clue. It was taken up at the time, but immediately abandoned for various reasons, the principal one being that the wreck could not, in 1900, be accurately dated. The passage occurs in a discourse by Lucian, a second century A.D. Athenian writer, discussing the works of the painter Zeuxis. No works of Zeuxis remain. He stood in about the same relationship to Athenians of Lucian's time as do Van Dyke and Vermeer to a contemporary Dutchman. Lucian says that:

Among the bold innovations of Zeuxis was the painting of a female hippocentaur, one, moreover, that was feeding two hippocentaur children no more than babies. There is a copy of this picture now at Athens, made with strict accuracy from the original. Sulla, the Roman commander, was said to have sent off the original with his other trophies to Italy, but I suppose the ship then sank off Malea with the loss of all its cargo, including the painting.

Sulla captured Athens in the fall of 86 B.C. and left for Rome in the spring of 83. All that could be said in December of 1900, as the several navy and diving boats rolled in the winter swell off Kythera with Byzantinos choking back his rising gorge and attempting to laugh at sailors' jokes about greasy pork, was that the wreck was carrying statues and other art works, and was probably Roman. The reference in Lucian seemed too pat, and in any case Lucian wrote "off Malea," not "off Aegelia" (the ancient name for Antikythera).

The ship ran to within a short stone's throw of the cliffs. The diving boat came alongside, and with help from the crew, Byzantinos clambered on board and worked his way to the tiny foredeck where Fotis Lyndiakos and Kondos were waiting. He watched with interest as the first diver was dressed, made the sign of the cross, and with a pick in his hand jumped over the side.

"After three minutes the lifeline jerked. Captain Fotis [Lyndiakos] shouted 'Brabmata.'" (Dialect spoken by the men of Syme altered the Greek *pragmata*, "things," sufficiently for Byzantinos to trouble to quote directly. He was much struck by this dialect, and quotes it frequently.

The diver had found an antiquity. When he came into the boat several minutes passed before he could answer our questions. He then said that 'there is a mound [of statues] stuck together with cement with a bronze foot sticking out of it.' . . . This he detached. A second diver then descended to tie the foot so that it could be raised . . . a second signal then told us that the foot could be safely pulled to the surface. It was quickly hauled to the boat, where everyone crowded around to admire it. This leg must be one of the best things found to date. The gilding on the sandal is still there, as if applied yesterday . . . It is hard to imagine what valuable, wonderful things must be down there . . .

Sometimes in January the Aegean falls calm. The sun shines and the clear sea invites swimming, although the water is cold. The divers worked without interruption for five days before the weather broke. They made two or three dives per man each day, each lasting four or five turns of the minute glass. The weather was calm enough so that the *Syros* could steam close to the cliff and pass a line to the diving boat. The line could then be attached on the bottom to heavy objects which were raised by the ship's winches.

It took several days to free the marble statue of a boy from the mud. The first diver who saw it thought that it was a "little dog." It took three dives just to lash the lifting cable. When it was on deck the divers and rowers crowded around. The last diver, says Byzantinos, cried "Little devil, you didn't want to be tied, you wanted to stay down there and eat crabs . . ." The navy crew cheered. A wit among them is said to have suggested that the statue be issued a uniform so he could stand watches.

When the weather broke at the end of the week they had stripped a colossal marble bull from the diminishing heap of stuff on the bottom, along with bronze parts of other statues and bronze fittings, probably parts of furniture. Byzantinos describes the end of the trip:

Then I must admit that along with the crew and all the loose objects in the ship, I did a bad dance . . . our ship nearly smashed on the rocks. If she had we should have gone to the bottom, to keep company with the ancient ship. We had a hard time getting ourselves and the diving boat into Saint Nicholas, where we were stuck for five days.

When *Syros* got to Piraeus, the statues were carried to the ministry of education, where they were put on public view. Long files of admirers passed through the hall. The emotions aroused by the discovery of the wreck were very strong, because this was the first major archaeological discovery made in Greece by Greeks. The wonderful wreck at Antikythera was full of Greek statues stolen by a foreign conqueror. Now it was being excavated by Greeks without foreign help. It became a symbol of unity which the struggling young nation badly needed. Seventy-three years had passed since Greek independence had become inevitable when a combined British, French, and Russian fleet sank the Turkish-Egyptian fleet in Navarino bay, but nearly half the Greek-speaking population of the Mediterranean was still under Turkish rule. The island of Crete, within sight of Antikythera, was autonomous, much like Cyprus in the 1960's, because the great powers would not allow union with Greece, out of consideration for Turkey.

While Athens admired the seagrown statues and politicians made speeches about the unity of Greece, the divers at Antikythera began to suffer from exhaustion. Tempers frayed as enthusiasm waned and the work got harder on the bottom. Mr. Byzantinos soon wearied of expedition life and appointed a Mr. Kritikos, an accountant in the department, as his replacement.

Kritikos was the first of a long series of junior officials who were in charge at Antikythera, and his appointment set a disastrous pattern which was characteristic of the archaeology of the day. In 1900 most archaeological excavations tended to be salvage jobs, with gangs of hired workmen more or less unsupervised as they dug for objects of value, which the archaeologist then classified and catalogued and commented on. Archaeology in the Aegean and Middle East had begun, half a century before Antikythera, as a treasure hunt. By 1900 archaeologists were just beginning to accept concepts like stratigraphy and pottery classification.

The idea of a sunken ship as a slice of a day in the far past, preserved under the mud like an insect in amber, was a long intellectual step from the state of mind of archaeologists of the time. They saw the Antikythera wreck as a marvelous treasure trove, unconnected with anything that they understood. The series of officials representing the department of antiquities seem to have been sent only to make sure that nobody stole anything. None of them seems really to have talked with the divers. If they had done so, they might have learned that the lead weights on the divers' suit had been cast from chopped-up Roman anchor stocks, and that the copper they used for repairing their compressors had been mined in Cyprus 3,500 years before, and that the Aegean was full of ancient pottery.

If one man had stayed through the whole excavation, he might well have made friends with the divers. Economou might have done it if he had been left in charge. Stais almost certainly would have, if he had had the time. As things turned out, the divers lived in a world apart. They were hired for a difficult salvage job, and they carried it out in the best way they knew how.

Their worst problem was exhaustion. Work day after day in deep water has effects which have not yet been adequately studied. In order to get an idea of what it felt like to be a diver at Antikythera, I hope that at this point the reader will excuse an excursion into personal experience.

In the late fall of 1959, I was working on an experimen-

Antikythera.

Aktarma working at dawn.

tal sponge diving project in Turkey with Tosun Sezen, a bright young ex-navy diver who was trying to combine modern diving technique with the Turkish divers' traditional methods. It was Tosun's idea that we would work with our modern equipment and decompression tables alongside traditional boats, hoping to prove to the captains that the system worked.

It was late in November, and the weather off Bodrum, where we were working, was probably about like that at Antikythera in January. We were working at an average depth similar to that at Antikythera, with equipment much better than that used by Kondos and his divers. Life on a sponge boat in cold weather was miserable. We were never really comfortable. Continued work at depth was exhausting. If we stayed only a few minutes beyond the correct time on the bottom according to the decompression tables, we found that we began to get mild bend symptoms — exhaustion, strange rashes and itches, aches in finger joints that had been strained a little while prying off sponges. We were irritable and often irrational. We only felt good under pressure. Following the sponge diver's rule of not eating during the day, we lost weight, which must have contributed to the fatigue. On deck we sat like lumps, full of a deadly calm. Our blood was bad. Small cuts expanded into sizable sores which refused to heal.

The old divers among us knew that we were ready to be hit by the bends, and although no one talked about it, the rest of us knew too. In the end, late in the year, diving deep, even with the aid of the decompression tables, our boat stank of fear.

Kondos had six divers. He worked them in five-minute shifts two or three times a day, taking the time from when the diver hit the bottom. This would be equivalent to a seven- or eight-minute dive on today's tables, which are calculated from the time the diver enters the water until he arrives at the decompression stop at the end of his dive.

A fifteen-minute dive to 180 feet requires twelve minutes of decompression, according to the USN diving tables. A twenty-minute dive to the same depth requires twenty-six minutes on the 30- and 10-foot decompression stops, before the diver can surface safely. It is easy to see that Kondos was working his men at the extreme edge of safe diving, in terms of our knowledge today. He was following primitive diving practice which had been developing for several generations, on a diving job which would have been rejected as impossible by any of the navies of the world.

In 1900 the physiological problems of diving were only beginning to be understood. Everybody knew that divers, and sometimes caisson workers, were occasionally stricken by a nasty paralytic disease which could cripple or kill them. Divers nicknamed it the bends, because its pains could twist divers into unusual shapes.

Greek sponge divers had known the bends ever since helmet diving gear had been introduced into the Dodecanese islands in the 1860's. The sponge capitals of the Mediterranean then were Syme and Kalymnos. Their seamen had roamed the Mediterranean since ancient times, diving naked from small boats. After the Royal Navy suppressed piracy in the 1830's, and the channels around Antikythera became accordingly safe, fleets of hundreds of boats from Syme and Kalymnos set off for the rich and comparatively untouched African banks every year.

The helmet diving gear was taken up with understandable enthusiasm by men who had spent their working lives feeling their way around the bottom of the sea without masks, while holding their breath. No one, including the manufacturers, had any idea of the lethal possibilities of helmet gear. Cases of bends were often diagnosed as chills or rheumatism.

For example, on December 4, 1867, Heinke Brothers of London published an advertisement in the *Levant Herald* which said:

HEINKE BROS.
SUBMARINE ENGINEERS
78–79 Great Portland St.

Beg to call the attention of shipowners, Merchants, Captains, etc. to the important improvements made by them in the submarine HELMET DRESS and APPARATUS which ENABLE A DIVER TO REMAIN AT ANY LENGTH OF TIME UNDER WATER, for the recovery of property from wrecks, working and repairing foundations of harbors and bridges and also for PEARL and SPONGE DIVING.

First class medal in the English exhibition 1851, FIRST class medal in the French Exhibition 1855, Submarine engineers to the English, French, Russian, Spanish, Portuguese, Sardinian, Canadian, Peruvian, Brazilian and Indian Governments.

That same year a sponge dealer in Kalymnos bought one of the new gadgets. Twenty-four divers learned to use it and ten died of the bends. The merchant was mobbed by the women of the island, led by the widows. The village priest threatened to excommunicate him, and the wise women of the town made charms against him. An Austrian biologist who happened to visit Kalymnos and Syme was so horrified at what he saw that he spent the rest of his life campaigning against the equipment. He did in fact persuade his government to get the Turks to forbid use of the helmet gear. But they used it all the same. The divers who survived made more money than they had ever dreamed of. The owners and merchants of Kalymnos and Syme grew rich.

The bends were explained in 1878 by a French physiologist called Paul Bert, in a book called *La Pression Barométrique*. Bert showed how nitrogen gas is absorbed into living tissue under pressure and then foams into the bloodstream as the pressure decreases. Millions of tiny bubbles, which stopped the flow of blood to the brain or the heart or through joints, were the cause of the bends.

Bert's research was however of no use to the Greek divers, thousands of miles away in space, centuries away in time. A Kalymniot captain was about as likely to know of French physiological research as he was of the Laplanders' recipe for reindeer stew. But meanwhile sponge captains had learned, through a game of trial and error in which there were no chips but the lives of men, that there was a manageable relationship between time spent on the bottom and the bends. A trail of divers' graves stretched from the Bosporus to Tunisia, and the rate of bends in the sponge fleets was reduced to something like five percent a year. Statistically, a diver had twenty years before being killed or crippled.

Decompression tables, which told divers how long they could stay on the bottom before the tissues absorbed a dangerous amount of nitrogen, were not published until 1906, after a series of experimental dives that took divers to a "record" depth of 210 feet. When, in 1904, divers had gone to 190 feet to inspect the sunken destroyer *Chamois* off Patras, their feat had been hailed as a diving record. Like so many similar "records," neither the Patras nor the Admiralty dives came near to the depths that had been familiar to Aegean sponge divers for a generation. It is all reminiscent of the delightful stories of the first foreign mountaineering expedition to scale Mount Olympus. They were said to have forgotten some bit of equipment, which was fetched down from the summit by one of the local villagers who explained that he didn't want thanks, it was no trouble since he and his neighbors, like their fathers and grandfathers, were up there all the time anyway, grazing their sheep and goats.

However, there was a catch. Captains like Kondos were used to working divers over vast reaches of sea bottom. General practice on deep diving boats was to send the diver to depth and then let him work his way to a lesser depth. Even when sponge boats became specialized in deep diving and some boats spent most of their time diving on reefs a couple of hundred feet below the surface, they did not generally find themselves involved in working divers for the maximum "no decompression" times at maximum depths, which is in effect what Kondos was doing at Antikythera. As I have said above, even when working on the navy tables as we did during Tosun Sezen's experimental project in Turkey, we were exhausted, probably because our bodies were still retaining some nitrogen. The problem of nitrogen retention is still not clearly understood even by specialists. But people involved with this sort of work generally agree that continual repetitive dives to depth, even on the tables, increase susceptibility to bends.

And so, while congratulations poured into Stais's office, trouble was brewing off Antikythera. At the end of January the divers struck for more money, and demanded that the government hire more divers. At the same time there was a well-publicized accusation that the divers were smashing antiquities on the bottom, and that the bronzes came up in pieces because the divers handled them carelessly.

This was denied by the ministry of education. Stais immediately formed a commission to study the finds. The commission concluded that most of the breaks were made in antiquity. The officials who had been at Antikythera all made statements praising the divers' gentle treatment of the material. The legend was so firmly planted that archaeologists were still praising the divers sixty years later.

Here the government seems to have erred on the side of excessive kindliness. Everyone admired the divers, and Byzantinos, the director of antiquities, was struck with the care they took of the material. They were gentler with the delicate objects than were some of the archaeologists present. Work on the bottom was a different question, which no one seems to have considered. The divers were being paid by the piece. Therefore they had to use their time on the bottom in salvaging material, not in thinking about how to salvage it.

The airlift, the giant underwater vacuum-cleaning device which moves tons of material in modern marine excavations, was not used in an underwater excavation for another fifty years. The Antikythera divers had no means of digging into the muddy sand which overlay most of the wreck. John Lyndiakos remembers the ramrods they used to probe the bottom, "to find objects to attach ropes to," so that the object could be pulled out of the mud by a winch from above. He says that many broke in the process.

In any case, whether or not their methods could have been improved on in those days of primitive salvage techniques, the divers' efficiency was lowered for other reasons. Recent studies carried out by a British physiologist, A. D. Baddely, show that with Aqua-lung divers, mere immersion in the water causes efficiency to drop 28 percent, while at 100 feet a diver is 50 percent less efficient than on the surface. Tests carried out by the United States Navy's Experimental Diving Unit showed that a diver's reasoning

F

ability under pressure was more affected than his manual ability.

Scientists are not yet agreed on the exact cause of this. It was once thought to be brought about by the effects of nitrogen under pressure. A more recent explanation is that it comes from a buildup of excess carbon dioxide not washed out by the "thicker" air under pressure, which does not flow the way air does on the surface.

Divers begin to be affected soon after 100 feet, and as they descend towards the limit of compressed-air diving at 300 feet, where they inevitably pass out, they get progressively "drunker." If the nitrogen gas that forms four-fifths of the air the diver is breathing is replaced by helium, divers can go deeper without ill effects.

The Antikythera divers, at over 180 feet, were at what we could consider today to be the limit of practical compressed-air diving. Down there, the effect of narcosis is rather like a couple of stiff whiskies on an empty stomach. One feels fine, gets into a car, drives with great skill, and then complains of injustice when had up for drunken driving. Like drunks, divers are loathe to admit that they were boiled out of their minds. Some cities in America convince day-after drivers by keeping a tape recorder or cine camera handy, so that he can see himself as he was. Salvage masters sometimes do the same thing, with a tape recorder hooked to the diver's telephone. There were no telephones at Antikythera, and the divers would have denied that they were drunk as hoot owls on the bottom, if anyone had thought to accuse them. There is no question but that they were, on purely physiological grounds.

To repeat, divers' ability to manipulate things and to do familiar jobs is not affected so much as is their reasoning ability. Diving deep, a diver is strong and active, and can work fast and well at a familiar job. It's the unknown and the unexpected that he can't deal with.

Helmet diving gear is much worse than the free diver's Aqua-lung system, which takes the exhaled air immediately away. The helmet, on the contrary, acts as a sort of trap for the diver's carbon dioxide–filled exhalations, especially if the compressor which is furnishing the air is designed for shallower depths. It seems certain that the Lyndiakos brothers had fitted their diving boat with the same kind of hand-cranked compressor that other boats used. These were the naval type advertised by Heinke. Experiments carried out by Haldane with this type of compressor in 1906 showed that they gave insufficient air in deep water, and Haldane recommended that the navy design a new type for work past 120 feet.

The effects of narcosis were further increased by the sand on the bottom, which floated up in clouds when the sponge divers tried to dig into it. It was, in fact, as if the tomb of Tutankhamen had been excavated in five-minute shifts by drunken stevedores who had never seen an Egyptian tomb, working in semidarkness, dressed in American football pads with coal scuttles over their heads.

At the beginning of February Stais decided to go to Antikythera himself. A group of dignitaries came with him in the *Michaeli*, which had been called back from her annual overhaul a week before. Among the group were Mr. Kavvadias, the new director of antiquities, and Mr. Emmanuel Likoudis, the ministry's lawyer, who was expected to straighten out the disagreements between the divers and the ministry concerning their salaries and advance payments. There was some confusion on the *Michaeli* because all her officers had gone off on leave; and her captain, Dimitrios Theoharis, and first lieutenant had to replace them with junior officers from another ship. They arrived, accompanied by the steam schooner *Syros* and a decked barge with a winch and sheerlegs (two spars rigged to form a triangle) rigged on its deck, to find the divers tired to the point of mutiny.

Stais and Economou pleaded with them. The next day was flat calm, and they finally agreed to go back to work after Economou personally guaranteed that they would be paid for the first statues as soon as they could be evaluated.

A heap of statues still remained on the bottom. They had been made into an almost solid lump by white coralline limestone growth. While the panjandrums argued about what to direct the divers to do, the divers themselves explored the central heap. New George found a group of amphoras, mostly upright, three quarters buried in the sand. The upper parts of the amphoras were covered by seagrowth. They got cables round some of them and heaved them up, and found the parts of the unbroken ones that had been covered "clean as eggshells," in the words of one of the young petty officers who worked there that winter. The amphoras were filled with sand, and the sand in some of them was full of olive pits. They raised twenty-seven jars.

One of the sailors, scraping idly with his knife, knocked a patch of concretion off one and found Greek letters and Roman numerals. One was marked XK, which inspired Mr. Likoudis, the lawyer, to make a long and complicated explanation which seemed to the sailors to be made chiefly so that he could demonstrate that he had read Homer. The first lieutenant made a feeble joke that pleased the ship's crew when he said it stood for "Xaridinos Konstantino-poulos . . . and whoever commanded that ship when her men were robbing statues from the forums and marketplaces of Greece had not neglected the harbor grocery stores. . . ."

Stais, who seems to have been a nice man as well as a good archaeologist, pleased the sailors with a crack about his cousin Xaridinos's olive business, referring to the tiny, dried up, salty, dark brown olives that appeared in the mess as the XK brand #1 quality. At that time the Greek navy fed its men on less than five cents per man per day.

The divers could not move the great stones which crushed the wreck. The solution was to tie them on the bottom with five-inch manila cables so that the knots would hold temporarily while *Michaeli*'s sailors maneuvered close alongside the cliff and Commander Theoharis squinted at the rock. His sweating men then winched up the great weight until the cable began to stretch and the ship listed ominously. Then a tight-lipped order from Theoharis would send *Michaeli* full astern so that the jerk would tumble the boulder down the slope to the abyss, which began only a few feet from the wreck site on the sandy ledge.

The operation demanded judgment and skillful seamanship. The stones were so big and heavy that they would have capsized *Michaeli* as they skidded down the slope if the loops which had been put around them by the sponge divers had been so tight that they could not slip loose as the ship jerked back. The whole operation of getting the big stones off the heap of statues was done with a party of sailors standing by with axes to chop the cables if *Michaeli* heeled too far.

When half a dozen boulders had been pulled off the wreck into the abyss, it was possible to raise the statues which had lain under them. In a few days *Michaeli*'s deck was cluttered with a collection of more than a dozen marble statues, all of them deformed by seagrowth and partly destroyed by borers. Sometimes ropes broke, and knots tied at thirty fathoms failed to hold. Once the statue of a horse slipped from its sling just as it was coming out of the water and fell, irretrievably, into the abyss.

The ephor of antiquities, Mr. Kavvadias, nearly joined the horse that same week when he fell overboard while getting into the diving boat from *Michaeli*'s gangway. A newspaper said, "It could have been serious, because the water was thirty-five fathoms deep and the Ephor could not swim a stroke." With his enthusiasm for underwater research somewhat dampened, he left a day or two later with *Michaeli* and the latest batch of statues, taking most of the archaeological tourists with him.

Stais moved over to the *Aegelia*. Of all the archaeologists who visited the Antikythera salvage while it went on, Stais and Economou seem to have been the most imaginative. If Stais had not been the minister, with heavy official obligations, and if Economou had not been outranked by practically everybody, the work might have been better done. If either of them had been younger, one wonders whether the world would have had to wait sixty years for the first classical archaeologist who was also a diver.

Left alone with the divers while *Michaeli* thrashed her way to Athens with her cargo of seasick panjandrums, Stais had time to think. There were still several great boulders preventing statues being raised. At the risk of sinking the ship, Stais ordered the next one brought to the surface. It was not a boulder after all. Through the clear water everyone saw that it was a huge statue of Hercules, with club and lionskin.

It was much too heavy to raise with *Aegelia*, so they slung it under the ship and proceeded precariously at two knots to San Nikolo bay, for *Michaeli* to lift onto her deck with her powerful winch. The "great boulders" had been statues all along, so improbably big, so corroded and over-grown, that ignorant men with depth-fuddled brains did not recognize them.

After a few dozen more marbles and pieces of marbles were raised, the divers began finding other things as they explored in the mud covering the lower part of the hull. Despite rough handling, dozens of delicate objects came up intact. There were flat roof tiles and rough kitchen pottery; beautiful glass bowls, blue and brown, some made of glass mosaic and mostly unbroken. There was a hand-some gold brooch decorated by Eros holding a lyre and set with seed pearls. By the time the weather changed again, *Michaeli*'s deck was so full that the sailors had trouble moving around.

On the recoveries, the mollusks which had destroyed the polished surfaces of the marbles rotted and stank in the winter sun. The divers were completely worn out. Before Stais had to go back to Piraeus, he and Economou per-suaded them to work for one more week. When that time was up, not even Economou could persuade them to work any more, for any amount of money, until after Easter.

There was talk in Athens of hiring another crew. Kondos and the Lyndiakos brothers protested to Stais, who allowed them to keep the job and reinforced the crew with four new divers, paid by the ministry.

Easter fell in the beginning of April that year. It was the ninth of the month before the divers got back to the cliffs off Pinakakia. Every crack in the rock bloomed with wild-flowers, and at last the weather allowed them to work in calm seas with no danger of going on the cliffs. Some days were cold and overcast. Then it was a hardship to pull on the wet diving dress and jump into the cold water, and a few ouzos in the evening in the bar in Potamos were a comfort.

Like all divers, Kondos and his men tended to drink too much when they had the chance, in order to make up for long dry months on the banks. It is only in recent years that research by the U.S. Navy's Experimental Diving Unit has shown what some sponge captains had thought all along, that susceptibility to bends is increased by alcohol. Working where they were, the divers naturally went ashore in the evenings, and just as naturally they often drank more than they should.

The week after the work had recommenced, the inevitable accident happened. After a heavy evening in Potamos, New George and some others got to bed very late. He slept badly. After the first dive the next day he remarked that he felt terrible and that his head was full of water. He didn't tell Kondos or Mercurio, who had made some pointed remarks that morning, and so was allowed a second dive. He surfaced gasping for breath and unable to speak. They broke off diving and ran into Potamos. The doctor there could do nothing for him. Kondos treated him in the traditional way, a cold water bath followed by splitting a live chicken in half and applying it to the diver's heaving chest. The treatment failed. New George died that evening, without speaking again.

The Greek government heard that Italian divers with special equipment could work longer and deeper than Greeks, and several well-publicized inquiries were made. Kondos, the Lyndiakos brothers, and a delegation of divers went to Athens on the *Michaeli* to protest and beg that they be allowed to finish the job. Stais again pleaded their cause, and the inquiries were dropped.

As spring wore into summer they were bothered by the *melteme,* the northern wind that cools the Aegean in summer. It became harder to work on the exposed side of

Antikythera. Kondos's crew snatched a few dives every morning before the wind began, then ran for Potamos harbor. Finds diminished, although every week there was at least one exciting discovery. One week they were fascinated by the discovery of parts of a human skeleton.

By the beginning of June all visible loose objects had been removed from the wreck. All they could see now on the bottom were thousands of bits of broken pottery and smashed marble that covered the area, 100 feet long by 40 wide, where the deck cargo once protruded above the fine sand. It was like a scar on the bottom. When the divers dug into the sand they continued to find objects, but little of value. They had no tools to dig with except their hands. Shovels and hoes had been tried, but did not work in the sand, which floated up in clouds and then settled back again after the befuddled diver had surfaced. The divers reported seeing other statues almost hidden under layers of seagrowth, but they could not be sure. In any case, the authorities had lost interest in the wreck, after spectacular finds ceased, and so, at the end of the summer of 1901, the work was temporarily suspended.

Kondos and his divers were paid off and went home for the winter. The men received 500 gold drachmas apiece, the equivalent of about a thousand dollars in today's drachmas, as a bonus, plus a share from the Lyndiakos brothers, who received a total of either 150,000 or 190,000 gold drachmas (depending on the source consulted), half of which they shared with Kondos and the divers. This would equal between $80,000 and $85,000 in drachmas of today, and roughly five times that in terms of purchasing power in 1901.

Kondos invested his share in a sponge boat of his own, but lost the boat when he used it as security in a shaky business venture that failed. He went back to diving, and after a few years got bent himself. He was a cripple for the rest of his life, almost completely paralyzed from the waist down. He was eventually reduced to keeping a tobacco kiosk on the waterfront in Syme, but that failed as well. He died in his daughter's house at Terplane, in Suez, about 1926.

In the early years of the century, several offers were made by foreign, mostly Italian, companies to finish the salvage of the wreck. They all demanded a share in the finds, which was not permissible under Greek law.

The wreck was forgotten for fifty-two years, until Captain Cousteau and his crew visited the site in the spring of 1953.

In the years that followed, there was much controversy over the date and provenance of the ship. Most of the material was never systematically studied, although many archaeologists were involved in the excavation. No one was assigned by the department of antiquities to study and publish the material as a group, from the beginning. The material was stored in the National Museum in Athens, where it was examined piecemeal by dozens of experts.

The bronzes were identified as belonging to the fourth century B.C. The corroded marble statues turned out to be later copies of classical originals. There was a heated scholarly controversy between J. N. Svoronos, who was convinced that the ship had been loaded at Argos and was on the way to Constantinople in the fourth century A.D., and K. Kourouniotes, who turned to the domestic pottery found on the wreck and maintained that it showed that the ship had gone down in the first century before Christ. He was correct, but it took more than sixty years before his thesis was proved.

Several heaps of unidentifiable material, roughly classi-

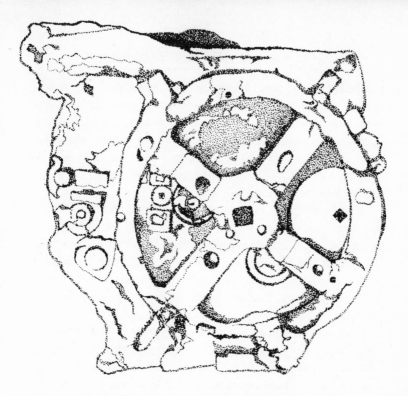

The famous "computer" from Antikythera.

fied into groups, had been piled up in the storerooms of the National Museum. Nearly a year after work had ceased, Valerio Stais, a young archaeologist who was the nephew of Spiridon Stais, was going through a pile of metal which had been put aside as possibly belonging to the statues. He noticed that a calcified lump of corroded bronze had split open as it dried out, revealing fragments of what looked like clockwork. Closer inspection showed a mechanism which he decided was either a clock or a navigational instrument. Parts of the machine were inscribed with astronomical inscriptions in ancient Greek.

Some experts decided that it was an astrolabe. Others maintained it was a medieval instrument which had found its way by chance onto the wreck site. Along with the rest of the material from the wreck, the "astrolabe" was gradually forgotten. In 1907, a much more spectacular shipwreck was found, again by sponge divers, off Mahdia in Tunisia. In later years, statues more important than the ones from Antikythera were found both on land and in the sea, and the wreck became less and less important from the art historian's point of view.

The "astrolabe" cum "clock" remained unique. Nothing like it was ever found again. In 1958 Dr. Derek de Solla Price, an English physicist and mathematician and student of the history of science who had been fascinated by the instrument for years, got a grant from the American Philosophical Society which let him visit the National Museum in Athens to study the instrument.

Four major pieces and several fragments had survived fifty-odd years of what Dr. Price refers to as "the delicate cleaning operations being carried out by the museum's technicians." From these he was able to reconstruct the instrument on paper. When new, it had looked like the working part of a small grandfather's clock, with brass gear wheels inside a wooden case which had dials on the outside, one in front and two on the back. The front dial had two scales: one fixed, which showed signs of the zodiac; the other on an adjustable slip ring, showing months of the year. Both scales were marked off in degrees.

The hand, which was connected to the inside mechanism, indicated key letters corresponding to other letters on an inscribed plate attached to one of the doors. These letters predicted the risings and settings of the major stars and constellations. Price suggests that the back dials indicated lunar phases and the setting stations and retrogradations of Mercury, Venus, Mars, Jupiter, Saturn, and possibly other planets.

The instrument was, in short, a computer. The complicated gearing inside the wooden box, when operated by a drive shaft that Price thought might have been made to run off a waterwheel, turned the hands of the dials so as to predict movements of the stars. His very interesting discussion of the interior mechanism is too technical to repeat here, and in any case is available to the interested reader.

He argues convincingly that the computer was made in Rhodes, because the most complete inscription on the machine is like part of a surviving astronomical calendar written by an astronomer named Geminos who lived in Rhodes at the beginning of the first century B.C. Price deduces that the machine was made about 82 B.C. and that it was repaired in 80 B.C., according to the position of the slip ring indicating the positions of the stars. It was probably set for the last time shortly before the ship sank. The gears were cut from a sheet of bronze two millimeters thick, and the gear teeth were cut by hand at the same angle, so that any one would mesh with any other. It was a working machine. Price found that it had been repaired twice.

When he visited the museum to study the "clock," he noticed that considerable material was still in the storerooms of the museum. Although most of it was uncatalogued, it obviously came from the sea. Some of the material mentioned in the early publications had been lost or mislaid because of the vicissitudes of the Second World War and administrative changes in the museum, but enough remained to show that it came from Antikythera. Mrs. Gladys Weinberg of the University of Missouri, for many years editor of *Archaeology* magazine, collected a group of specialists who undertook to study remaining material which had not been studied in the early 1900's.

There were bits of glass, amphoras, clay pots and bits of fragile, dessicated ship's planking which had shrunk with the years to a fraction of their original size.

The answers that Mrs. Weinberg's group came up with are a good demonstration of the progress made in archaeology in less than sixty years. The "junk pile" of material that had been put aside in 1901, since it could not be compared with similar material from other dated sites, had at last become meaningful and could be used to tell a good part of the story of the wreck.

Miss Virginia Grace, of the American School of Classical Studies in Athens, who is well known by Mediterranean divers and archaeologists for her interest in amphoras and willingness to help amateurs and professionals identify their finds, undertook to study the amphoras. She found that five of the clay wine jars came from Rhodes, where they had probably been made between 70 and 80 B.C. Another group came from the island of Kos, and belonged to the same period. There were two from Taranto in southern Italy, suggesting that the Antikythera ship might have been engaged in the Rome-Aegean trade, since Taranto was sometimes a stopping place in that passage.

Professor G. Roger Edwards of the University of Pennsylvania examined the clay lamps, the drinking cups, and the remaining jugs and pitchers. Most of these had been studied by Kourouniotes, as mentioned above earlier, leading him to conclude that they dated the wreck to the first century B.C. When he had worked on the material, there was insufficient dated material elsewhere to prove his ideas about dating the wreck, nor could he pinpoint the place of origin of the material. Professor Edwards was able to draw on later evidence to show that the pottery from the wreck comes from the central part of the Aegean coast of Turkey. The lamp is a type found in great quantities at

Ephesus. Professor Edwards does not believe that any of the material he saw came from mainland Greece.

Professor Henry Robinson, one of the world's leading experts on Roman pottery, examined the nine pottery plates identified as being from the wreck. He concluded that the plates came from Asia Minor, and belonged to the first century B.C.

The eleven glass bowls were studied by Mrs. Weinberg, who specializes in glass. She found them remarkable for their high quality. Several are molded. One of them is of blue glass with a pattern of rose petals. Others are made of strip and multicolored glass. All the bowls probably came from Alexandria, which was a center for the manufacture of luxury glass for the Roman market. Like the amphoras and all the rest of the material, the glass can be comfortably dated to the first century B.C.

The archaeologists of 1900 were amazed that wood planking was preserved, and one of the archeologists who worked on the material at the turn of the century was interested by the unusual nature of the technique which had apparently been used in the construction of the ship. The planks, which divers said came from the sides of the ship, were fastened one on top of the other by tenons neatly

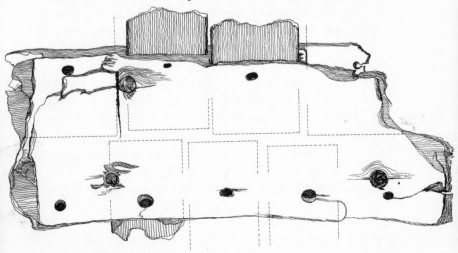

A plank from Antikythera: (A) tenons; (B) bronze nails; (C) treenails.

mortised into the planks. Before 1901 only one other Roman ship had been excavated. This was part of a small Roman cargo ship of about the same period as the Anti-kythera wreck. It had been found in Marseilles in 1864. It too was of tenon construction.

When, after some months of negotiations, I was finally able to get into the National Museum's storerooms to study the wood that remained, I found a box of powdery dried-out fragments that were fantastically light and broke with any pressure. The best preserved piece was only two feet long by about six inches wide. This piece and the several others stored with it tell a great deal, when they are compared with the wooden planking from other wrecks excavated in the 1950's.

A pattern of copper nails shows that the Antikythera ship was covered below the waterline with a layer of lead sheets, like the Mahdia ship and the big wine ship which Captain Cousteau excavated off Marseilles. The United States Department of Agriculture analyzed a bit of the planking and concluded that it was elmwood, which is only used for planking below the waterline today because it tends to rot if it is continually soaked, then dried, but lasts well if kept either wet or dry.

Like the other big ships of the period that have been found, the Antikythera ship was copper-fastened and was built shell first, that is the frames or ribs were put into the ship after the shell was built up, held solidly together by its tenons. Although the planks do not prove that the ship was big, they suggest that she was. I estimated roughly three hundred tons, about the size of the *Nautilus*. She was probably decked, because I found lead scupper pipes in the bottom of the box that contained the planking.

The wood from the wreck yielded another bit of evi-dence which would have been inconceivable to the researchers of 1900: a radiocarbon date. While a tree or an animal is alive, it absorbs Carbon 14 from the atmosphere. When it dies it stops absorbing C-14, which, being mildly radioactive, then begins to give off its radioactivity. If one reduces a bit of ancient wood to pure carbon and then measures its radioactive intensity, this can be compared with the known intensity of C-14 radiation.

A tiny piece of wood was subjected to this process at the radiocarbon laboratory of the University of Pennsylvania Museum by Dr. Elizabeth Ralph, who concluded that the tree that formed the plank had absorbed its C-14 between 260 and 180 B.C. Miss Ralph remarked that "If large logs were used, the particular sample which was dated may have come from the center of a log and would therefore have been earlier than the cutting of the tree by an amount equal to the age of the tree."

Elm trees live a long time. It is possible that the plank was cut from the heartwood of the tree. We cannot know if Roman owners, when making contracts with shipwrights, specified heartwood for planking. But in the eighteenth and nineteenth centuries, specifications for good quality ships like *Nautilus* commonly required the builder to use well-seasoned heartwood planking.

We can perhaps extract another hypothesis from the fact that the Antikythera ship was planked with elm below the waterline. Modern Greek ships of the approximate size of the *Nautilus* or the Antikythera ship are often constructed from Samos pine. Ancient Greek ships seem to have used either Samos or Aleppo pine. Elm is commoner in central Italy.

If the Antikythera ship had been built in Italy, she could have traded between the Aegean and Pozzouli, near Naples, along the standard ancient sea road down the west coast of Italy to the Strait of Messina between Italy and

Sicily, or around Sicily if the weather were favorable; then a passage reaching with the northwesterly behind them until she made a landfall at the mouth of the Aegean. The way back, in the fall, was not so easy, because the weather was erratic. Many Roman ships sailed from the Antikythera channel to near Methone, in the southwesternmost corner of the Peloponnesus, to wait for a favorable wind that would take them either up the coast to Corfu or Zakynthos, then a run across the mouth of the Adriatic to Brindisi, around Cape Santa Maria di Leuca to Taranto, then down to Messina or around Sicily. The Antikythera ship's Tarantine jars could well have been picked up when the ship stopped at Taranto or Brindisi sometime before she was lost.

According to Plutarch, Sulla was at Ephesus in the spring of 83 B.C. Ephesus is about a hundred miles from Rhodes, as the crow flies. The astronomer Geminos who, says Dr. Price, probably made the "computer," is known to have been in Rhodes in 77 B.C. The scholars who studied the pottery from the wreck are all convinced that the cups and bowls and dishes came, if not definitely from Ephesus, at least from that region. The island of Kos, where some of the commercial amphoras came from, is about midway between Ephesus and Rhodes. The fact that Koan and Rhodian jars were found on the wreck does not necessarily prove that the ship stopped at those islands. Both were big wine exporters, and one would suppose that any considerable merchant in the Aegean at that time had a stock of Rhodian and Koan jars. Still, it is agreeable to speculate.

We can go still further. Sulla landed in Italy in the summer of 83 B.C., after leaving his legate Terentius Varro in charge of a scratch fleet of warships in the Aegean. Sulla stormed the colline gates and entered Rome in the fall of

83 B.C. Dr. Price is certain that the computer was made in 82 B.C., used just long enough for repairs to be necessary, and last set in 80 B.C.

How then can the ship, if she is indeed Sulla's, have been delayed for two years? (There is of course the freak possibility that the computer did not really stop in 80 B.C., but was set inadvertently a couple of years ahead by some curious cabin boy.) And why did she sail in the late fall?

We can only guess. The Romans, when they suppressed Rhodes, unleashed a terrific wave of piracy in the Aegean, since the Rhodian fleet was no longer able to keep piracy down as they had previously done. The pirates joined Mithridates, a bloodthirsty Asiatic warlord who was forced to sign a shaky peace treaty with Rome in 84 B.C. Varro's fleet was enough to keep down Mithridates, but not sufficient to protect Aegean shipping effectively from pirates, especially the pirates of Cilicia, who waxed fat on the trade coming out of the Antikythera straits, like the Maniots eighteen hundred years later. The Cilicians, like the Maniots, used small, fast rowing vessels.

In 69 B.C., eleven years after the assumed date of the loss of the Antikythera ship, the Cilicians sacked Delos, the principal Aegean center for transshipment of cargo to the west. Finally, in 67 B.C., the Roman senate finally gave Pompey carte blanche to suppress the pirates of Cilicia, which he did with resounding success.

It is foolish to propose that the skipper of the Antikythera ship was being chased by pirates when she smashed into the rocks under Pinakakia, but reasonable to say that during that period the straits were as dangerous as they had ever been. With a big, seaworthy ship, one sure way of avoiding the Cilicians in the first century B.C., or the Maniots in the eighteenth century A.D., would have been to wait in the garrisoned and therefore safe port of Milos for a moderate northerly gale, and then run the straits at night.

We could go on and on, but the answers to the many questions remaining about the wreck lie in the elmwood hull, 180 feet below the surface, beside a great rock with poseidonia weed growing on it, beneath about three feet of muddy sand. The obstacles to work on the site are formidable. It is exposed to the prevailing north winds of summer, and to the winter's dangerous northerly gales. Ships can lie there safely for only two or three months each year. The depth allows bounce dives, but not the steady detailed work required for serious investigation rather than salvage. It can only be challenged by using advanced methods of diving which are still, in 1968, both too experimental and too expensive to be adapted to archaeological expedition work.

The most formidable obstacle is the Greek government's attitude toward marine antiquities. The official policy is that the necessary work will someday be done by the Greek department of antiquities, when money and personnel become available. This is liable to be a long time from now, considering that the cost estimate for an excavation of the Antikythera wreck comes to half a million dollars, five times the Greek government's expenditure for all archaeological research in 1965.

I had been curious for years to see the place where the wreck had happened, but it had taken till the summer of 1966 for this to be possible. From the schooner's deck Cape Glyphada looked as evil to us as it had seemed to Mr. Byzantinos a lifetime before us. The cliffs loomed gray-blue over the red streak in the rock, and the shore was fanged.

"Poor blokes," said Jon, and spat into the clear blue water.

Jon and I peered at the shore, imagining how we might one day moor alongside and, with a boom rigged on the cliff, get the generators and compressors and banks of helium bottles and building materials and iceboxes and stoves and goodness knows what else up those rocks. Someday. We paused in the dark blue water three hundred yards offshore, hoping it would seem to eyes elsewhere that we were having a spot of engine trouble. It would not do to dive, nor even to swim with mask and fins above the site. After a last look we opened up the engine and turned towards Kythera.

We were near the sites of two other shipwrecks as well, both part of the story of foreigners removing antiquities from Greece. Both ships had carried part of Lord Elgin's purchases back to England. One was the 42-gun frigate called H.M.S. *Cambrian*. She had missed stays, hit the rocks, and sunk while bombarding some Greek pirate schooners in Grabusa bay at the north end of Crete in February of 1828. She had on board a case of watercolor paintings made by Lusieri for Lord Elgin. They showed various classical monuments of Athens, many of which were destroyed soon after the watercolors were made.

The other was the wreck of the *Mentor*. In September, 1802, seventeen cases of antiquities acquired by Lord Elgin in Athens were loaded on board the British brig. *Mentor* got caught in a northwest gale after clearing Cape Malea, and began leaking dangerously. The pilot advised her captain to head for San Nikolo bay. She reached the bay safely, and anchored, but the anchors dragged. They cut their cables and got the ship under sail, but she missed stays and drifted onto the rocks at one side of the harbor, to sink immediately in sixty feet of water.

It would have been interesting to locate the *Cambrian*, but undoubtedly a waste of time. There was no chance that Lusieri's watercolors had survived over a hundred years of immersion, and I had no desire to salvage Captain Hamilton's dinner plates. They belonged, in any case, to the Greek government, along with the cannon, ballast blocks, and whatever else remained of H.M.S. *Cambrian*.

When we sighted Kythera, we headed for San Nikolo bay. It would be instructive, I thought, to see the site of the *Mentor*'s sinking, and the place where the Antikythera salvagers had ridden out so many gales.

We anchored in San Nikolo in the dark, off the ruins of a stone fort on the north point of the harbor. When we went to bed the wind was getting up, and the schooner danced on her anchor chain. Several hours later I woke up with the feeling that something was wrong. It was. We were drifting at sea. Our anchor had dragged, and so we hove it up and headed back into the harbor in the dark, thankful that we had not joined the bones of the *Mentor*.

The next day before the others woke up, I took mask and fins for a swim in the clear harbor. Our anchor had plowed a furrow in the bottom as it dragged the night before. Curious, I followed it. It was easy to see why both we and the *Mentor* had dragged. The bottom of the outer bay slopes gradually to seawards. Swimming along the anchor path, twenty feet below, I saw a heap of stones some twenty feet to the left of the path. They were the ballast of a fairly large ship. Between the ballast heap and the low cliffs of the eastern side of the bay, the rocky bottom was covered with fragments of identical amphoras. They were Rhodian hook-handled jars, a common kind which can be identified at a glance even through twenty feet of water. They belong to the end of the first century A.D. Thousands of them have been found, especially in Pompeii. The night before, our schooner had missed the rock which sunk that unknown Roman wreck by less than fifty feet.

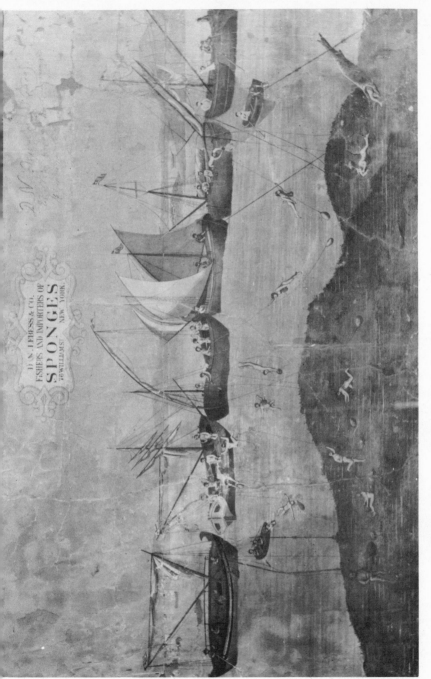

A nineteenth-century advertisement showing some of the dangers of sponge diving.

It was an interesting lesson in the cause of shipwrecks. San Nikolo, if you don't know the place well, is deceptive at night. Anchoring there, you should go further in than seems at first wise, or the anchor will drag on the sloping bottom. Jon Smith and I, Captain Elgin of the *Mentor*, and that forgotten Roman skipper had all made the same mistake. We were luckier than they were, but not by much.

I swam round the little cape to the place where I thought the *Mentor* might have gone down. There was a shelf, at about sixty feet under the cliff, which was big enough to hold her. But like *Nautilus*, *Mentor* had disappeared. The only parts remaining would be ballast and heavily overgrown and corroded ironwork scattered on the bottom. I had no Aqua-lung, and in any case it would have been unwise to have tried to dive on the wreck. There were undoubtedly local rumors about the fabulous treasures of the *Mentor*, even though Elgin's cargo was completely recovered by the naked sponge divers who salvaged the wreck within two years of the time it had sunk.

The job had been done by the great-grandfathers of the men who salvaged the Antikythera ship, divers from Syme and Kalymnos. A generation before the invention of the first practical diving dress (by Augustus Siebe in 1837), sponge divers worked naked. They had no masks or swim fins, but were guided from the surface by the captain or tender, who spotted sponges on the bottom through a glass-bottomed bucket from his station in the bows of the little boat.

There were various ways of dealing with the two major problems of the naked diver. Anoxia, caused by excessive breath holding, could knock a diver out without warning. He would drown if not pulled immediately to the surface. The islanders coped with this danger by attaching the diver's left wrist to the same line that held the flat stone he used to plane down to the bottom. This was done with a clever knot that allowed the diver to slide up the rope on his own, or be pulled up along with the flat stone if he passed out. As he was watched all the time through the glass-bottomed bucket from above, another diver could be sent to pull him up if he were to slip out of his lifeline.

Sir Francis Beaufort, who was on anti-piracy and chart-making patrol in the Aegean in command of H.M.S. *Fredericksteen* in the early 1800's, wrote about Kalymnos divers being hauled up *unconscious* and laid out on the boat's deck to recover. These naked divers were remarkable. One called Stotto Georgios (or George Stotti) dove to over two hundred feet in 1913 to recover a warship's anchor. This was hailed by the officers of the warship as a remarkable feat. It was probably more remarkable to them than to sponge diving Greeks, who claim that the old-time naked divers worked those depths regularly.

Sponge divers could not see well underwater in the days before the invention of masks. Apparently they were able to get some visibility by carrying olive oil in their mouths and releasing it at appropriate intervals.

A few naked divers still make a living around the Greek islands. Diving with the stone has pretty well died out. Today the naked divers use masks and fins like the ones used by spearfishing foreigners.

Hanging that day suspended in the clear water over the site of the *Mentor* shipwreck, it was easy to imagine those tough wild men from Syme as they made dive after dive into the tangled mess of rigging to clear it away, and as they struggled with *Mentor's* small hatches which Lord Elgin's representative had unsuccessfully urged the *Mentor's* captain to enlarge, and with the largest boxes containing part of the Parthenon frieze jammed in the hatchway.

The English vice-consul, Emmanuel Caluci, had difficulties with the divers on the island of Kythera. He found them a bunch of barbarians who were drunk all the time and a continual cause of trouble. Hamilton, the Englishman who supervised the salvage job, wrote to Lord Elgin that "Never did an unfortunate prisoner look with more anxiety for the happy moment of his release, than I for that day on which I may escape from this wretched island . . ."

Nobody has recorded the sponge divers' opinions of either Hamilton or Caluci.

The salvage of the marbles cost Lord Elgin more than he had paid for them. They lay on the beach for a winter, covered with seaweed, until a transport sent by Lord Nelson came to take them to England.

Five years later, Caluci took care of the *Nautilus* survivors. And it seems probable that one reason we found so few of the *Nautilus*'s cannon was that the same divers who salvaged the *Mentor* worked on the *Nautilus* as well.

The wonderful job done by the naked divers on the *Mentor*, like the Antikythera salvage nearly a hundred years later, was forgotten. Archaeologists remembered only the vast expense of Antikythera and Mahdia, and the myriad difficulties of dealing with the strange wild men of the sponge diving islands.

Nearly half a century passed before diving technology developed to the point of allowing nonspecialists to explore the sea bottom. Then archaeologists could begin to explore ancient wrecks. The first to do so was an archaeologist familiar with discoveries of the sponge divers and fishermen of the Mediterranean, with ancient sources, and with the new discoveries made by Aqua-lung divers on the French Riviera. He was an Italian; his name was Nino Lamboglia.

V

~~~~~

Trial and Error:

The Development of Marine Archaeology

> . . . To condemn Layard for not using the technique of
> today is as ridiculous as to make light of Alexander the
> Great's generalship on the grounds that he did not employ
> the atom bomb. If Rawlinson and Layard had not demon-
> strated the value of what could be recovered from the city
> mounds of Iraq there might have been no story of Meso-
> potamian excavations to write.
>
> — Sir Leonard Woolley, Preface to Seaton-
> Lloyd's *Foundations in the Dust*

THE great steel grab hung for a minute over the mass of
broken pottery, barely visible on the muddy bottom.
The diver in the steel observation shell peered through the
gloom to make sure that it hung over the place where the
concentration of pottery began, and spoke into the telephone.

"Aria tutto . . ." Lower everything.

A hundred and fifty feet above, on the deck of the salvage vessel *Artiglio*, the salvage officer swept both hands
palms down towards the deck. The winches spun free,
shaking the ship as the heavy grab slammed into the bottom. A great cloud of mud suddenly darkened the interior
of the observation chamber which rested upright on the
muddy bottom.

"Haul away."

The big winch coughed as the sailor handling it turned the steam valve. It spun for a minute, then came almost to a stop. The ship heeled a bit, and swung to port as something broke free on the bottom and the grab came up easily. The white marks on the cables flashed past the blocks on the winch drum.

"Slowly."

The grab broke water and swung higher than the men watching from the deck. The salvage officer waved at the winchmen and the grab, dripping with water, swung inboard and down to the deck where eighteen years before the first gold ingots from the sunken liner *Egypt* had tumbled.

This time the grab's haul had no intrinsic value. But it excited Nino Lamboglia, the government archaeologist in charge of the Italian Riviera, just as much as the *Egypt*'s gold had excited the veterans of the *Egypt*'s salvage who watched with him now, for there on the muddy deck were chunks of timber from a large ship concealed in the mud under the mass of broken pottery that littered the bottom.

The discovery was the culmination of a long search. The wreck had been first reported to the authorities by three fishermen, the brothers Bignone. In November, 1933, they had hung their nets on an obstruction 120-odd feet deep, nearly a mile off the place where the ancient mouth of the Centa River had left a gully in the beach near the modern town of Albenga. They heaved and the line broke. They then dragged the area with a small grapnel anchor and caught the net. It took the three of them over an hour to pull the net free and get it into the boat. Caught in its folds were three identical Roman amphoras.

They were intact. Full of mud, they weighed over a hundred pounds apiece.

Antonio Bignone reported the find to the local authorities, and said he was certain that there was a shipwreck on the bottom. Nothing could be done about it then, but the declaration was filed in the records of the antiquities service.

In 1946 the trawler *Aurora*, working off Albenga, found amphoras in her nets on two separate hauls. There must have been hundreds of other finds not reported, since Lamboglia, when he began making inquiries, found that local fishermen referred habitually to "The Amphoras" as a good place to fish. The mound of Roman wine jars formed a kind of artificial reef where small fish could breed and octopi found nesting places inside the ancient jars.

Lamboglia was fascinated, and transmitted his enthusiasm to the city fathers of Albenga. They in their turn interested Commandatore Quaglia, owner of the Sorima Company and famed salvager of the "impossible" *Egypt*'s cargo of gold ingots, sunk 396 feet down in the Bay of Biscay, in the late 1920's.

When he stood on the deck of the *Artiglio* on February 11, 1950, Lamboglia himself had no idea of what would be the result of this preliminary exploration. The week before, Antonio Bignone, now gray-haired, had guided the *Artiglio* to "The Amphoras." One of *Artiglio*'s divers had crawled into the deep sea observation chamber and strapped on his oxygen purifier. They had slapped the hatch shut and dropped him to the bottom, where he saw a great heap of amphoras, some broken, some complete. The mass was roughly in the shape of a ship, ninety feet long by thirty wide.

A helmet diver sent dozens of complete amphoras to the surface. There was no way for him to know what lay under them. The grab was the only available instrument which could dig down into the soft mud. Lamboglia needed to be certain that the heap of amphoras was not a cargo jettisoned when an ancient ship had been in danger of foundering, or even an ancient dump of some kind which no one understood. Thence the grab.

By the eighteenth of February, enough material had been recovered so that Lamboglia could state that here, under the mud, lay the wreck of a large Roman ship of the first century B.C., of which a large part of the cargo was intact and, where protected by mud, in as perfect condition as if it were made yesterday. He realized that the steel grab was not the right tool for excavating an ancient shipwreck. Still curious, but restrained by his archaeological conscience, he called off work the next day.

The *Artiglio* steamed back to Genoa and conventional salvage work, having demonstrated that a ship lay beneath the pottery and that, as at Antikythera and Mahdia, commercial salvage divers with conventional equipment could not do a satisfactory undersea archaeological excavation.

Lamboglia was left with several tons of broken pottery and a series of technical problems that neither he nor any other archaeologist had any idea how to deal with. The most obvious problem was that of excavation. How were divers to dig under the mud which overlay the wreck? The *Artiglio*'s helmet divers had worked in darkness from the time they began prying the first amphora loose from the bottom. The grab stirred up the mud so badly that the divers who controlled it from the observation shell could see nothing for hours after one bite. In any case it was too crude. Out of 728 amphoras recovered only 110 were intact.

Other things that had come up in the grab hinted tantalizingly at what lay in the soft alluvial mud under twenty-odd fathoms of sea. There were bits of three bronze helmets; a strange circular disc cast from lead; lead plates that had been fastened, perhaps to the outside of the hull, by copper nails; and pieces of planking and ribs from the ship. Some amphoras probably contained resinated wine; these had been stopped with pine cones. One held walnuts. There were plates and cooking pots which might have come from the ship's galley; a lead horn which Lamboglia thought might have been part of the ship's figurehead; and fragments of lead piping and clay roof tiles.

Concluding his report on the work at Albenga, Lamboglia wrote that the road was now open for development of new techniques of underwater excavation, and that good work in the future could only be done by well-organized professional groups. Here lay the root of the problem that still plagues the development of underwater archaeology. In 1950, "divers," to most people, were salvage divers. A little band of enthusiasts was learning to use the Cousteau-Gagnan Aqua-lung, and these were, in the process, piling up more time underwater than all the salvage divers in history. But they were still classed as amateurs. Like boat-builders faced with the invention of fiber glass, which in a sense makes their woodworking skill obsolete, helmet divers defended their professionalism as well as they could to anyone who asked them. The last attempt to excavate an ancient wreck using sponge divers was made in Greece in 1952. Even in 1958, that archaeologist was still convinced that good work could only be done by "professional" salvage divers in helmet suits.

Like so many of the other sciences and techniques that began to grow in the time of the Victorians, archaeology itself had not been long out of its own Dark Ages. Part dreamer, part necromancer, part pirate businessman, Schliemann had dug Troy with more enthusiasm than painstaking technique. General Pitt Rivers had excavated at Cranborne Chase between 1880 and 1900, had laid down principles and methods of stratigraphy, written all this down and been for the most part ignored. At the time of the First World War the teaching of archaeology still meant art history. Directors of digs dropped in now and then to see what valuable objects had been recovered, and otherwise generally let the treasure hunt go on by itself.

Archaeology under water remained, in fact, impossible until the 1940's, when a limited freedom of the seas was given ordinary men through the work of a Frenchman, Jacques-Yves Cousteau. Before Cousteau, men explored the undersea world like timid savages living at the edge of a hostile jungle which they visited with trepidation and explored at risk of their lives. Cousteau changed all that. As a young naval officer before World War II, he dived with the Le Prieur autonomous diving apparatus, and became fascinated by diving and the world under water. He then got Émile Gagnan to adapt to underwater use an air-regulating device originally built to meter gas in wartime woodburning automobile engines. The result was the Aqua-lung, which has done more than any other device to open up the shallow depths of the ocean to man.

In 1944, after two creative years of thinking and experimenting while immobilized under the German occupation of France, Cousteau founded the Undersea Research Group of the French navy and then, by a superlative stroke of diplomacy, created his own brilliant group out of it, with the support of the French navy, the National Geographic Society, and other institutions. They gathered recruits for their wonderful gadget, the Aqualung. They collected biologists, geologists, and oceanographers, taught them to dive, and took them on a series of expeditions which have changed the whole pattern of man's study of the sea.

Cousteau and his group had always been interested in ancient shipwrecks, and the possibilities of excavating them. In 1948 he and Commander Taillez had relocated the Mahdia wreck off Tunis, but were able to work for less than eleven diving hours on the site. By 1952 Cousteau was independent and determined to make an experimental undersea excavation.

The ideal wreck was found by Gaston Christiannini, an independent diver who scraped a living scrounging scrap and lobsters from the waters around Marseilles. Crippled by bends, he was treated by Cousteau's Underwater Research Group in Toulon, where he told Frederic Dumas about a heap of "pots" off a rocky islet near Marseilles called the Grand Congloué. They explored the site, and found the biggest heap of amphoras that any of them had ever seen. It was spread out for over a hundred feet along a slope that went from 125 to 245 feet in depth.

Cousteau moored *Calypso*, the group's research ship, under the sheer cliffs of the Congloué rock. Like the men who had worked at Antikythera, the crew of the *Calypso* looked up at the cliffs and wondered if their ship would end on top of the ancient ship far below, driven onto those forbidding rocks by a mistral, one of the bad seasonal winds of the region.

Teams of divers, working to strict decompression schedules, removed tons of broken and complete amphoras and black glazed dishes. The wreck was the oldest yet explored, belonging to the first half of the second century B.C. Soon the old problem of mud stopped work. Cousteau's group then built the first archaeological airlift, or mammoth pump, for removing the mud. The device

G

had been invented long before, at the turn of the century, and had been used for pumping water from mines and for mud-pumping in harbors. In principle it was simple: a noncollapsible, flexible pipe led from the surface to the bottom 150 feet below. Air injected into the bottom of the pipe rose to the surface, creating a strong suction at the bottom. It functioned as a giant underwater vacuum cleaner. With it, divers were able to clear off the surface cover and get to the timbers of the ship.

The airlift technique was still crude. None of the divers had any training in archaeology. The archaeologist in charge, Fernand Benoit, was an old man and had to remain on deck with only occasional glimpses of the bottom through a closed-circuit television system developed for the job.

The mistral made it difficult and dangerous to moor *Calypso* over the site, so Cousteau built a platform on the rock above the wreck. It held air compressors and a crew of divers who could work the year round regardless of the weather, descending to the wreck from the boom that held the airlift pipe.

Teams of divers worked on the wreck for five years. They recovered over two hundred tons of material, including thousands of amphoras of two main types and hundreds of black varnished Campana-ware cups. Like the Albenga and Antikythera ships, the Grand Congloué ship was sheathed in lead, and the planks were held together by tenons. In addition to the cargo, there were lead ship fittings, domestic pottery from the galley, the ship's anchors, lamps, and even parts of the ship's keel, frames, and bottom planking.

Cousteau demonstrated that it was physically possible for free divers, working under a discipline that strictly controlled the time they spent underwater, to work for

The working end of an airlift.

thousands of hours with little or no danger. This was re-markable in terms of the past records of archaeological diving expeditions. Antikythera, where Kondos and his men had spent a total of less than a hundred hours under-water, had cost one life. Mahdia, where the sponge divers had spent under four hundred working hours on the bottom, had made three cripples. At Artemision, where in 1926 Greek sponge divers had worked for less than a week at about the same depth as the Congloué, work had been called off after a diver died of bends. The Congloué did take one life. Jean Pierre Servienti suffered a heart attack at 240 feet while recovering a mooring anchor lost a long way from the wreck. This, unlike the disasters at Anti-kythera, Artemision and Mahdia, was a pure accident which could not have been prevented.

The Congloué was the developing ground for all the tools that are today a necessary part of the underwater archaeologist's equipment, such as the airlift, underwater pressure jets, underwater photography, and by default, underwater surveying. Cousteau demonstrated both that it was possible to excavate an ancient shipwreck and that such a project was worth carrying out. The Congloué was the largest and most important closed group of Roman trade material of the second century B.C. that had ever been found. The cargo of the ship was not as valuable as the cargo of the Antikythera and Mahdia ships. Its worth lay in the fact that here in this ship had been an assorted cargo of thousands of ancient objects all loaded into the ship at more or less the same time, and all sunk on the same day. "Common things are of more importance than partic-ular things, because they are more prevalent" (General Pitt-Rivers).

The great problem of the wreck, however, remains unsolved. In 1961, ten years after Frederic Dumas learned the location of the wreck from Christiannini, Professor Benoit published the final archaeological report on the wreck. Called *L'Épave du Grand Congloué*, it was the most detailed treatise published to date on the excavation of a shipwreck. Benoit concluded that the ship must have sunk between 150 and 130 B.C., that it had been fitted out in Delos and taken on further cargo in Sicily and the Bay of Naples, and that it had been a very large ship.

There are discrepancies, however, which make Benoit's conclusions arguable. Some of the amphoras can be securely dated to between 220 and 180 B.C., while others are much later. The *Calypso* divers say they found lead sheathing on the *underside* of the ship's deck, which might be taken to mean that there were two ships at the Grand Congloué instead of only one. M. Benoit is sure that there was only one wreck. Some of the divers who worked at the site thought there were two, but Frederic Dumas, who directed the work for part of the time and has more underwater experience with shipwrecks than anyone in the world, feels that there was only one.

The only thing that could prove or disprove the two-wreck theory would be a plan of the site, but such a plan was never made. At the time of the excavation it did not seem necessary, and by the time questions arose which could only have been answered by archaeological sections dug to land standards, Port Calypso was dismantled.

Today small groups of amateur divers go out to the Congloué on weekends to mine the huge remaining heap of pottery for souvenir amphoras and Campanian cups. Sometimes, digging with small airlifts, they uncover bits of wood, still in place. There is hope that someday someone with adequate funds will be able to follow after Cousteau's excavation of the Congloué, like Blegen followed after Schliemann at Troy, and finally solve the one- or two-wreck question.

To say that the question still exists is surely no criticism of Professor Benoit, one of the first professional archaeologists to tackle a problem of this kind, nor of Cousteau, the first man since Dimitrios Kondos with the technical ability to attempt a wreck excavation and the courage to carry it out.

French archaeologists took little notice of the Congloué excavation, not from any particular opposition or hostility but simply because it did not occur to them to do so. No one capable of studying a Roman cargo and publishing his findings was inspired to learn to dive. The same was true in Italy, where Professor Lamboglia felt so strongly about separation of the two departments that he forbade his archaeological assistants to swim or learn to wear masks.

It was more natural for oceanographers and marine biologists to learn from Cousteau. Indeed, as long ago as 1844 Professor H. Milne Edwards had dived in Sicily to observe sea animals in their natural surroundings. But on land, archaeologists were still sending out workmen to fill their baskets with whatever they managed to sift from sites. If they did not visit their own trenches, it was unlikely that they would be seized with the professional desire to plunge to the bottom of the alien sea.

Still today most "classical" archaeologists are by training Latin or Greek scholars or historians or epigraphers or numismatists or philologists. Photography, surveying, and sufficient chemistry to ensure conservation of finds are just now beginning to be obligatory tools of the student of the buried past.

Whatever they were, archaeologists were very rarely sportsmen, and it was the sportsmen — skiers, sports car drivers, light-plane fliers, bobsled racers — who rushed like lemmings to explore the world at the bottom of the sea. Archaeologists and divers would have had trouble talking to each other at dinner; it was all the more improbable that they would consider their occupations involved with one another.

In short, no one meant the marine archaeological situation in France to go sour, but it did. Other groups of divers were formed, and found more amphoras on the bottom of the sea. Wrecks began to shrink. Aside from being an exotic souvenir of an afternoon's outing, an ancient amphora can be a wonderful thing, and this wonder is shared by tomb robbers, antiquarians, archaeologists, artists, historians, and everyone else with a little imagination. It is splendid to hold in one's hand an object which has been used by other men, other women, perhaps thousands of years ago, and even better to have it at home holding geraniums or being a doorstop.

Some groups like the Club Alpin Sous-Marine urged their divers to report and turn in finds to the local authorities. All through the 1950's Professor Benoit at the Musée Borely struggled to cope with floods of reported wrecks. The law forbade removal of objects from ancient sites, but the notion of enforcing the law at the bottom of the sea was absurd. And what difference could it make, thought one souvenir hunter after the other, as amphoras vanished like flies in Flit, if there were one amphora more or less among hundreds of identical ones on so many sites? In any case the law was unclear, being confounded with salvage laws fixed in the time of Colbert, in the mid-seventeenth century.

Honor Frost's account in *Under the Mediterranean* of what happened to the Chrétienne A wreck is in its way a classic:

1948

M. Henri Broussard, president of the Club Alpin Sous-Marine de Cannes, discovered a wreck which became known as the Chrétienne A. . . . Fishermen had for some time been finding pottery in their nets at that place. Broussard reported the wreck to the appropriate authorities, and received permission for his club to dive on the site.

In its virgin state the wreck was covered with concretions and overgrown with poseidon grass. Samples of the surface cargo had to be extracted from the stony crust that soldered them together, while, to gauge the size of the wreck, it was necessary to clear the weed . . .

1949–50

During the two following summers the Groupe de Recherches Sous-Marine of the French Navy also made several visits to the site. Frederic Dumas dived on the wreck five times in 1949 and four times in 1959 and was able to make a sketch of the site while it was virtually undisturbed.

Dumas made a sounding of the site, and found three layers of amphoras. The inner sheathing of the hull and ribs were found in good condition on the bottom of the excavation.

1953–54

Members of the C.A.S.M. made frequent visits to the site during the winter of 1953 and the summer of 1954. They discovered the large lead anchor stock and cleared it of weeds and concretions . . .

1961

In June of 1961, seven years after the anchor was raised, I received a letter saying that all the amphoras had been removed . . . but that, in the middle of a desert of sand and sherds, the cut end of a sizable timber, like a Roman keelson, was emerging from the bottom . . . Two months later I returned to have a look at it. By then the tourist season was over and even the wood had disappeared . . . holiday-makers from a nearby camp had taken the wood because of the copper nails which it contained, and which they prized as souvenirs . . .

Honor Frost and Frederic Dumas dived on the site together and found that "the site had become a bare and empty desert. It is apparent that the ship had been preserved in the sand." Miss Frost concludes that: "There is very little doubt that had the Chrétienne A wreck been subjected to methodical research, sufficient structural parts would have been found for this ship to have been at least partially reconstructed." The Chrétienne A wreck dated from the last century B.C.

Frederic Dumas, working almost alone and with almost no funds, has recently made a plan of the remaining timbers and excavated parts of the wreck. He has found the mast step of the ship, and in it a coin, already a hundred years old when some ancient seaman put it in its place. His book, *Épaves Antiques*, is full of pictures of the remaining timbers and plans of the remains of the ship's structure as they lie on the bottom. One wonders what might have been had Dumas excavated the wreck from the beginning.

The summer that saw the end of systematic work at the Grand Congloué saw also the beginning of a project which had been agitating Commander (now Capt. Ret.) Philippe Taillez, Cousteau's old partner and diving companion, for several years. Taillez's excavation of a wreck on the Titan Reef grew into a demonstration of what could be done, given responsible discoverers of a wreck, sufficient funds and equipment, and an excavation director with a clear idea of how to go about the job.

The wreck had been found several years before by Dr. Piroux of the Club de la Mer at Antibes. Although considerable pressure was put on him to do otherwise, he realized its value and refused to reveal the location, even after the publicity given it by photographs, taken by a friend supposedly sworn to silence, which appeared in the popular press. The situation rapidly grew complicated. There was considerable emotion among the various "discoverers" who were soon squabbling over the wreck.

Eventually a friend of Piroux, who knew the wreck's location, was bent. Like Christiannini, discoverer of the Grand Congloué wreck, he was treated at the GERS station. There he met Taillez. With the approval of Benoit, who was afraid that the well-publicized although still "secret" wreck would simply disappear as had Chrétienne A, the recovered diver took Taillez to the site.

Like the others who had seen the wreck, Taillez was amazed. A 90- by 35-foot heap of amphoras lay undisturbed, still stacked as they had been in the hold of the ship. The upper works had disappeared, but wood existed just below the sand. Four amphoras were salvaged. Fernand Benoit said they belonged to the first century B.C., and came from Italy.

Taillez determined to excavate the wreck before it was discovered a third time by less benevolent divers, and so he began a tedious journey through the administrative jungle. First he needed permission from the navy, then from the Administration des Beaux-Arts. Then he needed funds. By the spring of 1955 he was arranging for a museum to receive the great quantity of expected finds, when he was transferred to Germany as commander of the French navy's Rhine flotilla.

It was three years before he got back to the site of the Titan wreck. During that time it had, as feared, been found again and the process of dissolution by divers, so much more efficient than nature at destruction, was well begun. The whole top layer of amphoras had disappeared.

But Taillez returned in a perfect position to do a good job. He was commander of the French navy's diving school, and the wreck, which lay at a hundred feet, was an ideal training ground for divers. The French navy, kindly disposed to research projects of this sort, loaned him the necessary equipment and seconded to him the nucleus of officers and men needed for a skeleton crew.

His plan was simple and effective, but as always when someone tries to do something new, the experts were delighted to point out errors. His first requirement was a floating base, one which could be easily towed to the site and remain there for the duration of the work. On it would be mounted the high-pressure compressors for filling Aqua-lung tanks, and the big low-pressure compressor needed for running the airlift. A shack on the barge would serve for storage of finds, office, and sleeping quarters for the men who stood watch at night.

He managed to borrow a barge, and was fitting it out when a high-ranking officer decided it was too small. When Taillez got around this problem and got the barge moored over the wreck, it was hit by a storm which proved his doubters wrong but made such a mess of the equipment that ten days were needed for repairs.

For two weeks they cleared hundreds of tons of sand and concretion with the airlift, then photographed the exposed amphoras. Raising of the material began on July 31. First they removed the amphoras, which, loaded into steel wire baskets by divers on the bottom, came up by the hundreds. They were brutally heavy, weighing over a hundred pounds apiece. Sand had filtered even into those which still had their stoppers. In these, mixed with sand, were hundreds of fish bones. The ship had been carrying tons of fish preserved in olive oil, which Professor Benoit thinks may have been rations for Caesar's legions which were invading France at the time the ship sank.

Beside the amphoras of the main cargo, divers found bowls, cups, cooking pots, roof tiles which might be from the cabin of the ship, and various other objects. There were coins, and even a weighted fishing line preserved by concretions.

Early in August ship timbers began to appear. Two finely worked wooden plates, caught between two ribs, disintegrated when the divers touched them. By the end of August the keel and ribs of the whole ship were uncovered. They lay on the bottom like the articulated skeleton of a great fish. The frames were about two feet apart. The planks, like those of other Roman wrecks, were tenoned and uncaulked.

Taillez decided to bring the remains of the ship up in two sections. The keel was sawn in two, a special frame built, and the wood slipped onto it. The ancient fastening did not for the most part hold, and only a small part of the wood reached the museum in Toulon intact. There the shocking changes characteristic of ancient wood from the sea began to take place. As it dried out, the wood began inexorably to shrink.

A year later at the 1958 Conference of Undersea Archaeology, which had been promoted at the new naval museum at Albenga by Lamboglia, Taillez concluded his report on the Titan wreck by saying:

For the present, it must be said, underwater archaeology is still in the early stages. It must find its feet through the experience gained on the first sites. Titan is one of them. . . . We have tried sincerely, to the best of our ability, but I know how many mistakes were made. . . . If we had been assisted in the beginning by an archaeologist, he would surely have noted with much greater accuracy the position of each object; by personal inspection he would have drawn more information from the slightest indications.

But I can at least show that beginning and conducting an underwater [excavation] is definitely a difficult task which demands . . . faith, persistence, and courage. It cannot be undertaken by casual methods, but, on the contrary, necessitates over a long period the preparation of appropriate marine appliances and of specialized equipment.

Underwater excavation is a problem for sailors and divers rather than the archaeologist. How difficult it is, particularly in this century of specialization, to be all three at once! The archaeologist in particular must realize that he cannot accomplish this task without the help of the other two.

It is for the leader of the excavation to coordinate these three tasks. Sailors, divers, and archaeologists will ease his position if they work as a team and neither permit any activity on a wreck nor bring up any object for which the information obtained from its position on the site has not been recorded.

Unfortunately for students of ancient ships, Philippe Taillez's conclusions were ignored in France. The wooden parts of the ship, so carefully salvaged and transported by Taillez and his men, were wrapped in newspapers and old gunnysacks, and stored in the Tour Royale in Toulon. They were never drawn, except for one section which appears in Taillez's short report. Now, shrunk to half their former size, green with rot, they are crumbling to dust.

The only published information consists of the 23-page report in the *Atti* of 1958, and a mention in Taillez's popular book.

The Titan wreck was the last surviving known ancient wreck in reasonably shallow water in the south of France. In the short space of ten years the others had been destroyed without a trace, except for a few amphoras and other objects which found their way to the Musée Borely and were duly studied and published by Benoit. There was, for example, the Dramont wreck, a Roman ship of the first century B.C. Found as a heap of amphoras 21 meters long by 8 wide, impacted in a protective covering of seagrowth, it was dynamited by skin divers in 1957. We will probably never know anything more about the wine growers whose names were inscribed on the lips of the jars, wine growers of Campagna who exported to the new colony of Narbonne in Caesar's time. Who were they? Benoit gives their names, painstakingly constructed from the broken jars looters gave him: Bacchus, Dama, Evtactus, Onellus, Heraclius, Phillipus, Hermes and Mocconus. What was the ship like? Were the jars loaded together? How many were there? Did Phillipus load his jars with Dama, and could Hermes and Mocconus have been partners? A whole chapter in the history of navigation was blown to rubble by some mindless diver, perhaps hunting nonexistent gold, destroying not from malice but stupidity, like a bored child spilling the sugar on a rainy afternoon.

Other wrecks at the Planier islands, Maire island, La Ciotat, Cap Roux, Antibes, Fos, the Hyères islands, the Straits of Bonafaccio in Corsica, Saint-Tropez, Fréjus, Porguerelles, Nice, and Cagnes-sur-Mer did little better. One of the wrecks found in Nice was Etruscan, of the sixth century B.C. Such a wreck would justify, in any terms, the most enormous effort. It was completely robbed before Benoit even knew of its existence. His articles contain dozens of maddening photographs showing heaps of amphoras on the bottom, captioned again and again "Wreck so and so before its pillage." They contain no drawings of objects in situ or of the site itself. Though Professor Benoit has thoroughly studied each object he publishes, much of what he says as to locations of these objects must be taken with a grain of salt, since an angry diver, just arrested by the coast guard, can hardly be depended upon to furnish his captors with accurate information.

The south of France saw, in these years, a display of remarkably efficient destruction by witless "lovers of antiquity" which can perhaps be equaled only by the archaeological exploits of another Frenchman, Lucien Bonaparte. He retired to Italy after the downfall of his brother Napoleon, choosing for his seclusion the site of the Etruscan cemetery at Vulci. When the cemetery was accidentally discovered in 1828, Bonaparte put an overseer to mining the tombs, with instructions to smash the unpainted vases and save only the painted ones. The vase miners dug up a fortune in vases in a single summer.

The glory of the world must indeed pass away, but it seems wrong to speed its passage with dynamite and sledgehammers.

VI

$\infty\infty\infty$

A^2 Plus B^2

An engineer is a man who can do for five bob what any bloody fool can do for a quid.

— Nevil Shute, epigraph for
Trustee from the Tool Room

A BEGINNING had been made. Taillez, Cousteau, Lamboglia and others had made a valiant attempt to do something about the situation and had shown that systematic ship excavations were technically feasible.

But the material from these wrecks inevitably arrived at the surface as a jumble of junk. Out of context, rotten timbers of an ancient ship were of little value. A plan of an ancient ship would be something else again. The objects found in an ancient wreck were seldom worth much alone. But the pots, roof tiles, wine jars and such increased in value to the archaeologist as their context was understood.

For instance, a handsome Greek geometric pot, taken from a tomb by villagers and transported by whatever means to a Swiss dealer, has a more or less fixed commercial value as an art object. The same pot found in a Villanovan (i.e., pre-Etruscan, in central Italy) tomb along with a group of Villanovan objects would be of incalculable value. Geometric pots can be accurately dated, and Greek trade with central Italy at the beginning of the Iron Age is still a lively archaeological question. An archaeologist who could convince his sponsors that such finds were possible in central Italy would find almost unlimited support for excavation.

By 1958 many scholars, especially Benoit and Lamboglia, had seen the wonderful possibilities of the prosaic cargoes that were turning up on the Riviera, and they had seen their hopes turn to ashes in the hands of divers. Aside from telling the story of the ship's journey and construction, a shipwreck is valuable to the archaeologist because it provides a closed group of material. Before underwater archaeology, the best such closed group that archaeologists could hope for was an ancient city destroyed in antiquity by some catastrophe and never occupied again. But few ancient cities were truly abandoned, unscavenged by the looters who follow any disaster. Even if they were, the destruction date only gives what archaeologists call the *terminus post quem*, the latest possible date.

Furthermore, a city is by definition permanent, a place of storage as well as creation and daily use of objects. The room in which I write now contains, to pick a random list, a contemporary amphora from Korone, a fifth century A.D. Chinese sculpture, a sword from the American Civil War, a Turkish rug from Lesbos, and a World War I cannon shell with a dragon hammered into it — a muddle to make a field archaeologist run for a safe desk job. Tombs are better than houses, but they tell us of the ritual surrounding death, not life.

But a ship has little or no spare space for the nonutilitarian flotsam of life ashore. The St. Georges and Buddhas will have been left at home. Only very occasionally does something "old" appear in ancient wrecks, like the Greek vase found at the Grand Congloué, possibly an antique picked up in Greece by the captain or one of his officers.

The uninformed talk about raising entire ancient ships intact from the sea bottom, but this is obviously impossible. The wood uncovered by divers at Titan and the Grand Congloué fell apart as soon as it was moved. The only way anyone can reconstruct an ancient ship is to number, measure, and plot all the bits of wood that are uncovered on the bottom, then to remove the wood to the surface, where it has to be chemically preserved. This is an expensive and elaborate technique still in the development stage.

Even handling the wood is a problem. Big waterlogged timbers are light underwater, but incredibly heavy on land, having absorbed the weight of an equivalent volume of water. In addition, they are often the texture of cheese and have about as much strength. ("What kind of cheese?" asked a gourmet Belgian student. "Camembert pas trop fait," answered my wife, deadpan.)

By 1958 a lot of timber had been raised from ancient wrecks, and some of it had survived intact for Professor Benoit to study, but this was only a small percentage of what had been lost. The ship's fittings and its equipment are no less relevant when found in place. The lead pipes from Antikythera, the Grand Congloué and other Roman wrecks would tell their own story in situ, but are not much more than antiquarian scrap after divers raise them without plotting their position.

Part of the trouble was that divers are extremely limited in their time underwater. A survey done on land is a tedious, lengthy task, and few divers, in any case, are surveyors. There were some good suggestions. Dimitri Rebikoff, one of the pioneer French divers and a well-known inventor of underwater equipment, suggested photogrammetry in the early 1950's. Taillez had attempted to make a photo mosaic which would show the position of all the objects on the wreck. The trouble was that ordinary photographs are not suitable for mapmaking unless taken in a special way with special lenses, and the attempted photo mosaics were hopelessly distorted and therefore useless for measurements. Trying to survey with cameras turned out to be even more complicated and expensive, in terms of time, than conventional surface methods.

In land excavations the usual method is triangulation. The architect picks three or more control points, drives stakes into them, and measures the distance between them and their height in relation to a given horizontal level. He then lays them out on paper, to an appropriate scale, and can plot the position of any object inside his points by measuring from two or more of them. The system is simple and it works, but it takes time and patience.

That time can be considerably reduced if the surveyor uses a transit or a theodolite, instruments which can measure angles. As any veteran of a high school geometry course knows, you can do a lot with angles. The trouble is that optical surveying instruments do not work underwater.

Lamboglia, after much thought and consultation with divers, decided that photogrammetry was too theoretical and tape triangulation too time consuming. His idea was that a tape grid could be laid over a wreck, dividing the site into two-meter squares. The objects within each of these two-meter grids could then be photographed, numbered, and drawn in place before being raised.

The system was first tried on a Roman wreck off the island of Spargi, near Sardinia, in the summer of 1958. That year Lamboglia's divers worked for a month, putting in a total of 115 hours diving time. The system worked, but was not perfect. Although the wreck was less than sixty feet deep, divers got confused on the bottom and had a hard time drawing objects in the large six-foot squares, especially since the relationships shifted each time an object was moved.

Lamboglia's idea had been first to set up the whole grid, then photograph each square within it, and number the photographs. He then sent divers to the bottom with the numbered photographs attached to boards so that they could put tags, numbered to correspond to the photographs, on the objects. Then he removed the grid, replacing its key points with stakes, so that objects could be raised. Once the first layer was raised, the grid could be laid again and the whole process repeated.

In 1959 he returned to the site with an improved grid, and removed another layer of amphoras. He was startled to find that the 1959 grid could not be matched with the previous one. Furthermore, wood that had been uncovered in 1958 had completely disappeared by 1959. However, for the first time someone had determined the orientation and size of a shipwreck, and made a reasonable plan of the wooden parts exposed.

In 1961, ten years after his *Artiglio* expedition, Lamboglia, with the big research vessel *Daino* as a base, returned to Albenga with a much-improved grid made with steel instead of tapes. By 1962 he and his group had produced with this steel grid an accurate plan of the surface layer of amphoras on the Albenga wreck.

Elsewhere, other groups were beginning to build on the foundations laid by Cousteau, Taillez and Lamboglia. In the spring of 1960 the University of Pennsylvania Mu-

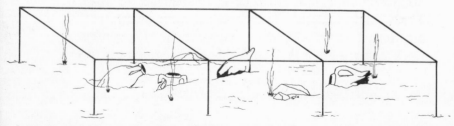

Lamboglia's frame.

seum sent an expedition to Turkey to work on the remains of the oldest shipwreck ever found, a small cargo carrier which sank at the end of the Bronze Age, between 1300 and 1200 B.C. The expedition was directed by a young American named George Bass, who had a good deal of experience in land excavations in both Greece and Turkey. Frederic Dumas was the expedition's chief diver. Bass was not a diver, and had never thought of being one till the Gelidonya job came up. He prepared himself by taking a YMCA course in Philadelphia. His first sea dive, with me on one side and Dumas on the other, took place at Gelidonya.

Bass had two ideas which were, and are, positively alarming to professional divers. The first was that an archaeologist was the only person who should direct an archaeological excavation, never mind where the excavation took place. The second, growing from the first, was that if anything could be done on land it could be done just as well underwater. He was backed by a heterogeneous crew, chosen because of qualifications other than diving, the theory being that anyone could learn to dive who was reasonably healthy and did not suffer from severe claustrophobia. (Most people feel a little claustrophobic when first set free in the sea; after a lifetime of moving in air, it wants a little practice to be comfortable while surrounded by water.) It takes years to train architects or engineers or archaeologists, but only days to teach someone to dive well enough to do his job in the sea.

We are still firm believers in this system, although we have had some interesting experiences with green divers. One of the best young archaeologists on Bass's staff was so shaky underwater that he was always sent down with a professional diver whose sole function was to keep him from getting drowned. I had a curious time with an epigraphist who couldn't swim but was so fascinated with a shallow-water wreck we were working on that he kept trying to snorkel down to it. The whole crew kept watch, we drained him out on deck every now and then, and after three days he asked for diving lessons.

The Gelidonya expedition attempted to use the working methods developed by Cousteau, Taillez, and Lamboglia, and to obviate the frills. We had an old fishing boat as a working base, moored every day over the wreck, but we camped on the beach a few miles away. We had a drafting frame which Dumas had developed. It was, we thought, the logical next step in the Lamboglia system.

The first thing we learned was that the frame was useless because the bottom was too rocky and irregular. We then experimented with mosaic photography, with mediocre results. Finally, driven by Bass, we used the standard tape triangulation method, and with it got a reasonably accurate plan. This was possible because the wreck was small, only thirty by ten feet, and little of the hull was left intact. Most of the objects were concreted together in huge lumps, which could be broken loose with an auto jack, triangulated, raised to the surface, then broken apart and drawn in detail on shore.

The wreck was only ninety feet deep, which meant that each diver could work for forty minutes during the first dive and thirty during the second, with only five minutes of decompression for each dive, provided the dives were six hours apart. Bass drove the professional divers mad. A professional diver learns very early that time on the bottom equals money, and accordingly works with an eerie speed and efficiency. Bass often spent his entire dive contemplating a bit of rotten wood, deciding what to do with it, while the experienced divers wondered how long it would be before he lost his mind completely.

It was soon obvious that Bass was correct and the divers wrong. The Cape Gelidonya wreck was, in the end, a reasonable technical success. We recovered about ninety-five percent of the material from the bottom, and knew exactly where about ninety percent of that had come from.

But we had not solved the problem of underwater drafting. Our plan, which was not as accurate as we had wanted it to be, had cost too much in terms of working time on the bottom. It was easy to raise the stuff. The hard job was drawing it in place. Although the excavation cost only $18,000, it would have cost a good deal less if we had not spent so much time in the primary task of recording what we found where we found it.

In 1961, with essentially the same crew, Bass set out to excavate the wreck of an early Byzantine ship at Yassi Ada, the small island off the coast of Turkey that we had explored years before and where we had found a whole series of ancient wrecks. The most interesting of these were two ships that had apparently struck the reef, then gotten off to sink in deep water.

The one Bass chose, Yassi Ada #3, lay on a gentle slope which began at 32 meters and ran for sixty feet to a depth of 36 to 38 meters. At the upper end, obviously the bow of the ship, were six iron anchors. The visible part of the wreck consisted of the anchors and the prosaic deck cargo of round amphoras which stuck out of the mud. In the middle, towards the lower end, was a mass of roof tiles and cooking pots, an area which we christened "the galley" the day we found it, and which afterwards proved to be indeed the galley.

Bass began by improvising a pair of transits in the blacksmith shop of the little Turkish village of Bodrum, the expedition's base. These were taken to the bottom and set up on fixed points. With them, divers could read angles

George Bass's "bedsprings" in place at Yassi Ada.

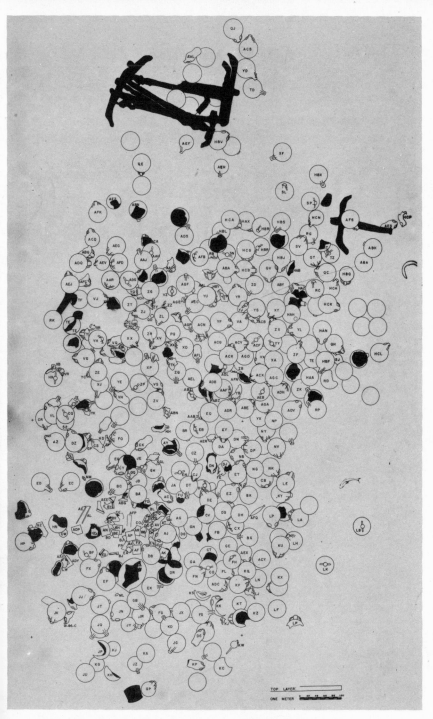

The top layer at Yassi Ada. The drawing took George Bass and his crew all summer.

which could be written down, then plotted on the surface. The method failed, because it required too much coordination between the three divers needed to work it, and because it was difficult to use when the water clouded from the movement of divers on the bottom.

Next he put down the Dumas-Lamboglia mapping frame, a square of pipe five meters on a side, which could be leveled on telescopic legs so as to be absolutely horizontal. Riding across two of the sides on little wheels was a horizontal bar to which a movable vertical pole was attached. This system proved inaccurate and too slow.

Bass then tried a series of wire grids — one, two, and

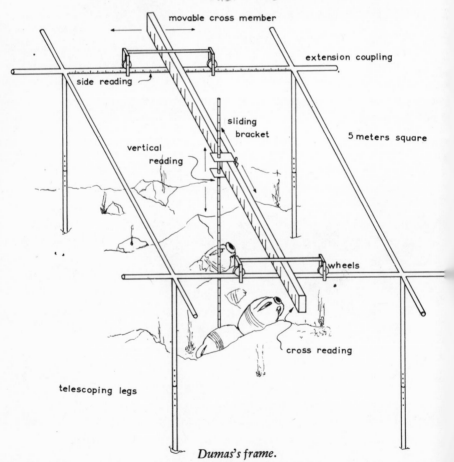

Dumas's frame.

three meters square — on which were strung wires ten centimeters apart like woven wire bedsprings. They were put into place and the four corners leveled and triangulated, then plotted on the master plan on the draftsman's board. Then relays of divers with plastic slates, ordinary carpenter's rules and pencils, drew the objects in the grids. Photographs taken through the grids served as a check on the drawings, and for filling in details.

Bass's crew spent most of the 1961 season experimenting with drawing methods and making an accurate plan of the top layer of the wreck. Little airlifting was done and few objects were recovered. But by the end of the year, Bass had the first really accurate plan of an amphora wreck ever made underwater. That fall they left the wreck, something that would have been impossible in either France or Italy where it would have been stripped by local divers as soon as the group left.

The next year they returned with an improved bedspring system. This was a steel grid like Lamboglia's which was assembled over the wreck. Its squares were two meters apart. It straddled the wreck area, with the squares stepped to accommodate the slope of the bottom, each square being leveled horizontally. Two portable towers, each four meters high, fitted onto the grids below. A camera mounted on a tower took photographs from the same angle for each photograph, so that the inherent distortion remained constant and could therefore be calculated out. These photographs, transferred to a 1:10 scale drawing, gave results accurate to the thickness of a pencil line.

They dug down into the wreck, photographing as they went, taking sections by dropping weighted meter tapes from the fixed grid. They found that the ship had tipped over onto one side, and were able to measure the angle at which the keel lay. The position of the fallen cabin's roof

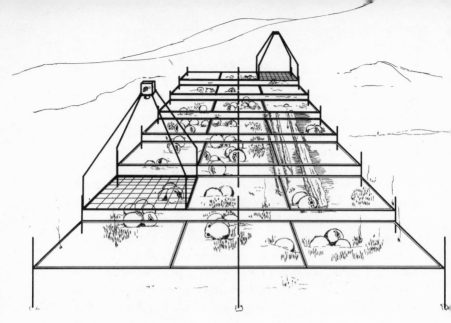

Bass's step frame with towers.

tiles enabled them to calculate the height of the cabin roof.

There was enough wood in place on the bottom so that it was possible to restore the ship on paper, timber by timber, to above the waterline. In places where ribs had rotted away, they could still trace them by the remaining nail holes. Most of the wood was so delicate that it could not be moved, floating away when disturbed by a movement nearby. Bass bought two thousand stainless steel bicycle spokes which, sharpened on one end, held the fragile wood in place until it could be drawn.

The cabin area was full of objects used by the crew. There were the usual roof and floor tiles, a big *pithos* or water jar, and the ship's kitchen pottery: plates, cups, cooking pots, and lamps. There was a copper kettle like the ones used in Bodrum today. There were two bronze steelyards for weighing cargo, again like those still used by peripatetic fruit- and vegetable-sellers all over the Levant. One had an arm nearly a meter and a half long on which was inscribed in Byzantine Greek *George the Elder, sen-*

ior sea officer. In the ruins of the cabin were copper and gold coins, apparently from the ship's cashbox. They had been minted in the reign of the Byzantine emperor Heraclius, who reigned from A.D. 610 to 641.

The Yassi Ada wreck produced the largest deposit of accurately dated Byzantine pottery ever found. It demonstrated that a complete excavation of an ancient shipwreck was technically feasible. Ships can be excavated to land standards, even when they lie in deep water.

However, diving is cruelly expensive. Bass had organized and administered his excavation as economically as possible. The expedition could not afford a research vessel, and in fact did not need one. An old eighty-ton barge was anchored over the wreck. The crew of about twenty slept on Yassi Ada itself, in a camp built on the island. The work still cost about $30,000 a year.

Whether or not underwater archaeology is a practical proposition depends in great part on whether it can compete, in terms of cost, with land archaeology. The first two years at Yassi Ada had shown that it was possible and extremely rewarding to work underwater to land standards. Yet over two-thirds of the diving time was taken up with problems of drawing the material on the bottom. At a clear-water site like Yassi Ada, the answer obviously lay in photography. Bass began looking into Dimitri Rebikoff's proposals of stereo photogrammetry, from ten years before.

This was a large problem. Stereo photomaps are a common surveying tool. An airplane flies in a straight line over the area to be mapped, while an automatic camera takes overlapping photographs at appropriate intervals. These form stereo pairs which, seen through the lenses of a stereo viewer, give the mapmaker a three-dimensional picture of the area. Stereo photomapping requires a large ma-

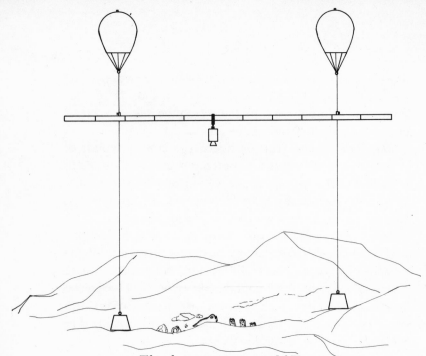

The photogrammetry model T system.

chine, and often a computer, and is rigged for photographs taken with long-focus lenses high in the air.

In the winter of 1963 Bass and Don Rosencrantz, a young engineer who had been working with him at Yassi Ada, discussed the problem with the architect and city planner Julian Whittlesey, an archaeology buff who gives much of his spare time to archaeological work. Whittlesey talked to various experts, and concluded that a simple system of underwater photogrammetry could be developed.

The stereo pairs would be taken from a bar which would hang, leveled, at a calculated distance over the wreck. The "flight" of the camera along the bar would be equivalent to the course of the photographic aircraft. The automatic camera would be replaced by an ordinary Rollei-Marine underwater camera, hung to the bar by an ingenious device which kept it constantly level. The divers would simply move the camera the correct distance along the bar between photographs. The bar was thirty feet long, and each run of the camera could cover a strip of bottom more than thirty by ten feet.

They tried the gadget during the summer of 1963, and to everyone's surprise, it worked. It was possible for a trained person to interpret the photographs and plot them on a plan with the aid of a fairly simple machine that could be used in camp at Yassi Ada. The cumbersome "bed-springs," at least for deep-water work, could be scrapped.

While Bass and his crew were experimenting with stereo photography at Yassi Ada, the search for the *Thresher*, the atomic submarine lost in the spring of 1963 in the Atlantic, was being carried out with all the deep-water searching equipment at the United States Navy's disposal. Those responsible for the search and the subsequent investigation of the remnants of the submarine realized that really accurate plans of small areas of the ocean floor could be valuable outside the specialized uses of archaeology. The Office of Naval Research and the National Science Foundation gave the University of Pennsylvania Museum grants for a small research submarine which could be used as an archaeological research vehicle, part of that function being to serve as a camera platform.

In 1964 Bass went back to Turkey with the submarine, which was the first civilian submersible built by the Electric Boat Company, builders of the unfortunate *Thresher*. Christened *Ashera* after the Phoenician sea goddess, she is designed to carry two men to six hundred feet at atmospheric pressure. Very maneuverable, she is able to move around almost as easily as a diver. She is equipped with viewing portholes, a fathometer, a gyro compass, and strong floodlights. Finally, she is mounted with two water-proofed aerial cameras designed for stereo photography.

That summer the *Ashera* made a photographic run over the second intact wreck at Yassi Ada, two hundred yards from Wreck #3. It is slightly deeper, deep enough so that we have never dared stay long enough to make a full plan of her cargo of jars, which are several hundred years older than those in Wreck #3. They are stacked in rows, seemingly undisturbed, although the upper parts of the hull have rotted away.

The little submarine's teardrop-shaped hull turned at the correct point and her operator, Yuksel Egdemir, steadied her on her course as Electric Boat Company engineer Don Rosencrantz gave him directions. Divers hanging in the water a hundred feet above saw the great strobe lights flash in rhythm as the *Ashera* passed over the wreck, then turned and passed again.

That night, when the pictures were developed, Rosencrantz reported to Bass that the stereo pairs taken from the *Ashera* were sufficient to make a completely accurate plan of the visible part of the wreck. The little submarine, with its special cameras, had proved itself capable of performing in a day the same job that had taken a team of nearly twenty people three months to do during that experimental summer two years before.

My own research went on in Greece and Italy. Where Bass concentrated on digging the very well preserved wreck in deep water at Yassi Ada, my group became involved in surveying cargoes in shallow water, which included rough cut granite and marble sarcophagi and granite and marble columns. They all lay on the Roman trade route that led past Cape Malea and Antikythera, around the Peloponnesus to Methone, up to Corfu, across the Adriatic to the south of Italy, and so down to the Strait of Messina and up the west coast of Italy to Ostia, the port of imperial Rome.

Methone: a third-century A.D. *wreck with sarcophagi.*

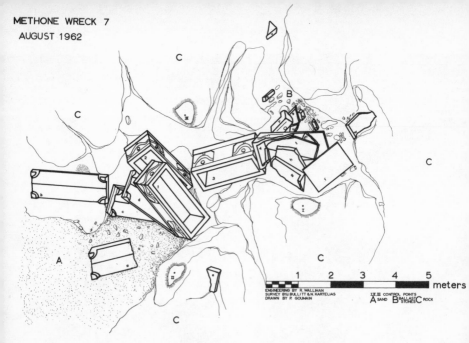

Methone: Wreck 7 from above.

These wrecks all lay in less than fifty feet of generally clear water. We found, after some trial and error, that such wrecks were easy to survey with the tape triangulation methods which had proven to be so time-consuming at Cape Gelidonya. The difference was in the depth, and in having a number of large objects to locate in plan rather than thousands of amphoras. We had no decompression problem; at thirty feet our time on the bottom was limited only by the cold. At depths over about sixty feet some kind of photogrammetry is more economical than triangulation. But it has been pretty well demonstrated that there are no horrendous technical problems in the path of the underwater excavator.

The experience of the archaeologists who worked with sponge divers at Antikythera and Mahdia, that of Taillez, Cousteau, and Bass, and the recent work done in various parts of the world by people like Robert Marx and me, makes a clear point. Underwater archaeology can be complicated and extremely expensive, but it need not be so, given crews of trained people who know what they are doing and are well led. As we have seen, the results of well-organized and well-executed excavations have justified the trouble and expense that went into them.

For all that, the general outlook for ship archaeology is not at all encouraging, because the wrecks are rapidly disappearing.

VII

∽∽∽∽∽

The Golden Pigs

> Sir, my grandfather knew the place, near the old stones.
> He told me. I will show you for a share. There was a
> golden sow, made by the ancients, and her seven piglets.
> . . . Gold, sir, gold. It's for a foreigner to find them . . .
>
> Greek village legend,
> commonly told to archaeologists

THE future of marine archaeology at the moment is
doubtful. There are said to be something close to three
million skin divers in America, and probably over a million
in Europe. In twenty years they have done more harm to
archaeological sites in the sea than all the forces of nature
together in three millenia. They have done some good,
too. Some we discussed in the last chapter; the rest we will
save till last, not to end on an entirely despairing note.

The problems seem to be more or less the same everywhere — the right authorities don't care, the wrong authorities do; people generally find it more fun to read
about and support groups that hunt gold than expeditions
which measure broken pots and draw nail holes; and
divers themselves think of looting wrecks as legitimate
sport. Or if they think it is wrong, it is just a little bit
wrong, like tearing up a parking ticket in a foreign city. A
brochure from a California travel agency for 1968 ad-

vertises a visit to the wreck of the *Matancero* (see pages 46-54), "an eighteenth-century Spanish galleon that usually yields artifacts . . . crosses, bottles, gems, spoons, cannon, cannonballs, etc." The divers who go on these trips are nice men, not criminals; if they cheat on their income tax at all, they probably don't cheat much.

The divers think of ship archaeology as an enormously complicated activity practiced by a very few specialists who are somehow never in the neighborhood when wrecks are found. In a way, but only in a way, they are right. The authorities, archaeological and otherwise, think of ship archaeology as an enormously complicated activity engaged in by exotic beefy types one step removed, if that, from the smuggling trade. And in a way, but only in a way, they are right too.

One might expect the useful cliché that northerners are more rational than their hotheaded southern cousins to apply here, but this is not necessarily so. In England, ordinary salvage laws apply to all wrecks alike, and anybody can buy a wreck from the navy. Taking 1650 as the date before which we must depend on wrecks for information about European shipbuilding, nothing disastrous seems yet to have occurred to the most valuable wrecks. But this is coincidence and probably only a matter of time, judging from what has happened with other extremely interesting ones. For example:

H.M.S. *Association* was a first-rate three-decker built in 1696 and wrecked with all hands on the Scilly Isles in 1707. Navy divers on leave found the wreck, which was then dynamited by Mr. Roland Morris, a professional salvage diver with an Admiralty contract for the *Association*.

De Liefde was a Dutch East Indiaman built in 1698 and wrecked in the Shetland Isles north of Scotland in 1711.

She was found and "excavated" with plastic explosive by Royal Navy amateur divers and by a commercial salvage team.

During the summer of 1967 a group of Swedish sport divers found the wreck of Peter the Great's flagship, the *Moskva*. She had been sunk in 1713 in a battle with the Swedes, her wreck lying on the Kalbådagrund shoal between Finland and Sweden in the gulf of Finland. The Swedes lifted some iron cannon and other objects, and sold them to private collectors in Sweden. The Finns have dived on the wreck but have not lifted cannon, since the guns must be chemically treated or they will fall apart after a few years' exposure to fresh air. The Finns are trying to get the cannon back for preservation, but both governments are now involved and the road is long.

The Mediterranean countries, having more ancient wrecks, more sunshine, and therefore very many more divers, are in much worse trouble. Lead anchor stocks had already vanished some years ago from the eastern Aegean, where helmet sponge divers sold them as scrap for good money. (There are about eight hundred members of the Greek divers' union, all helmet divers, and probably about four hundred more in Turkey.) Anchor stocks are still found in France and Italy, probably since professional divers there were very few until quite recently. Stocks discovered in the western Mediterranean are not necessarily melted down into scrap, since their souvenir or curiosity value begins to equal their scrap value. It has even been possible for a few devoted people, notably Gerhard Kapitän in Syracuse, to collect and study numbers of anchor stocks. This is in spite of enthusiasts like a man I know who says he has taken at least thirty tons of lead anchor stocks in the twenty-mile stretch of coast from Porto Cesáreo to Cape Santa Maria di Leuca at the extreme end

Kemal Arras on the wreck of a ship with a cargo of Rhodian amphoras of the first century A.D.

of the heel of Italy's boot, in the past ten years. He is probably telling the truth.

The possibilities of looting have expanded lately, and it is not any longer only scrap metal which is worth more than fish or sponges in terms of time and trouble on the bottom. A first century A.D. Rhodian jar, for example, was worth nothing fifty years ago, ten dollars ten years ago, and now perhaps thirty dollars at dealer price. It may be sold for twice that to a tourist, in spite of being worth very little in the commercial art markets of London or New York.

Every stretch of coast on the Mediterranean has its commercial diver or divers who make a living by spear or dynamite fishing, clearing trawlers' nets, raising anchors, and so forth. I've never seen one — that is, I've never drunk enough coffee, ouzo, or thick southern Italian wine (which Vergil's heroes sensibly cut with water) to arrive at a comfortable swapping of sea stories — who hadn't turned an ancient wreck to profit in one way or another. There is no reason at all to suppose this trend will reverse itself, and every reason to assume the contrary.

In the summer of 1967 there were two ship excavations done in the whole Mediterranean, both by marine archaeological groups of the University of Pennsylvania Museum, in Turkey and Italy; in 1966 only one; in 1965 and 1964 the same two groups were digging other ships. Meanwhile the opposition, so to speak, had traveled much faster and farther. A sample selection shows the general situation fairly well.

A Bronze Age ship near Arbatax in Sardinia carried copper ingots, many of which were salvaged by divers. Some of the ingots were sequestered by the Italian coast guard during the summer of 1967. Divers say some of the ingots were tin. The coast guard cannot guard the wreck continually, and it is still being robbed.

In Majorca a group of local divers found about six hundred amphoras off the northern end of the island on a bottom of sand and grass at thirty-five meters. Under the amphoras they found tin ingots. To salvage the tin, they dynamited the wreck and took about four hundred ingots. This yielded about four tons of metal, which brought a good price. There were inscriptions on some of the ingots, but when one of the divers asked permission of the wreck's "owners" to copy these inscriptions, it was too late. They had been melted down. In 1964 a few ingots remained, deep under the sand.

In Sicily, off the Lipari Islands, an amphora wreck of the third century B.C. lies at a depth of between two and three hundred feet. Mixed with amphoras were hundreds of beautiful Campagna black varnished bowls. The coast guard recovered over seven hundred objects from divers. The great quantity of Campagna-ware, unbroken and with its color preserved by the protective mud, attracted divers from all over Italy. Professor Luigi Bernabo Brea, archaeological superintendent of the region, reported to the government that he feared the wreck would not survive another year. The wreck is of great archaeological importance, since if it could be dated this would be remarkably helpful in dating Hellenistic sites all over the ancient Greek world.

The Italian authorities have offered a third of the finds to the institution which can excavate the wreck, a most unusual proposition among Mediterranean countries, yet it is difficult to hope that this splendid wreck will not vanish. Any diver can make "bounce" dives to recover objects. But the depth is so dangerous for extended work that responsible excavation of the wreck means diving with mixed gas, or underwater chambers with mixed gas systems, projects still experimental and expensive beyond the most optimistic hopes for an archaeological budget.

Elsewhere in Italy the situation varies from district to district. Our group has spent several seasons working near Taranto, much aided by the great courtesy, physical assistance, and moral encouragement from Professor Atillio Stazio of the Taranto Museum and all his staff. There are other districts perhaps equally hospitable to underwater research, but lack of funds or trained people or both has kept the preservers of history well outdistanced by its destroyers.

For some years the Italian government supported Professor Lamboglia's center of marine archaeology at Albenga. Working from the ex–German navy minesweeper *Daino*, manned with a crew of over a hundred men and officers, using divers recruited for two weeks each from government diving schools, Lamboglia worked for several years but the expense was prohibitive and the *Daino* is now laid up for lack of funds.

The French predicament, discussed in the previous chapter, is one of alienation between archaeological authorities and divers, though there are a few passionate researchers like Frederic Dumas who continue their solitary inquiries with a great deal of honor and next to no financial backing. For a while the coast guard watched those sites it was told by the state archaeological service to protect, but after many dozens of arrests and acquittals they simply gave up. There were too many sites, and the bottom of the sea is impractical to police. There are many diving clubs, some of them concerned with archaeology, but not one has yet carried out and published a technically correct excavation.

Likewise in Spain dozens of shipwrecks have been found, but none systematically excavated, none published. It is probably safe to say that there are no visible wrecks on the Spanish, French, or Italian coasts under less than one hundred fifty feet of water which have not been looted and fairly well destroyed.

In Turkey, while George Bass's group continues its work each season at Yassi Ada and elsewhere, sport divers in growing numbers join sponge divers in the general pillage. To make an arbitrary selection among many examples, there are, for instance, four known ingot wrecks in the Gulf of Antalya. Here is the story of one of them with a few names changed to protect the people and the wreck, should there be anything left of it to protect.

On a visit to Kalymnos in the spring of 1961, I met one of the oldest divers there. He remembered that when he was a small boy, at the turn of the century, he had seen some copper ingots from somewhere in south Turkey. About two tons of them had been salvaged by his father's boat. The ingots were of two types, one resembling the Cape Gelidonya ingots but with less pronounced legs, weighing about seventy pounds each. The second type was shaped like a turtle shell slightly pointed at each end. These weighed about eighty pounds apiece.

Some of the copper was sold to the local machinist, who used it to repair the copper parts of diving compressors and suits. He said that it was very soft pure copper, easier to work than the copper they ordinarily brought from Piraeus. The rest were sold for scrap, except for one of the turtle-shaped ones that was kept as a souvenir until finally, in 1958 or '59, only two years before I interviewed the diver, it too had been sold to a scrap merchant from Piraeus.

This account seemed to me to ring absolutely true. The

weights of the "oxhide" ingots were about right, and the fact that they were shorter-legged than the Gelidonya ingots indicated that they were probably of middle rather than late Bronze Age date. The purity of the copper rang true as well. I remembered noticing the seeming purity and softness of the copper when I had cut a sample of metal off one of the Gelidonya ingots.

Then, by a stroke of luck, the only survivor of the crew of the ship that had raised the ingots came to Kalymnos. He had been ship's boy, had tired of the sea and emigrated to America where he became an American citizen. It was the first time in fifty years that he had been home.

Yes, he remembered the ingots. There had been a depot ship and a diving boat, and they had been on a sponge diving trip down the Turkish coast like the ones I went on fifty years later and described in *Lost Ships*. They had anchored in a place I knew. The next morning they dragged a grapnel in the deep water half a mile offshore. The grapnel stuck.

A diver went down and found "three small hills which rose from the bottom to near the surface. On top of them and around them was a great mass of copper, mostly ingots, which lay in heaps several meters thick. The ingots were not much overgrown, and broke loose easily."

They worked the spot for two days, until both the depot boat and the diving boat were loaded as deep as was safe. The divers got only a small part of the copper; there were several meters of it still in place when they left. There were a few tiny golden beads, as big as the head of a pin, stuck to some of the ingots. Some of the divers got small blackened statues. They saw big copper cooking pots which were corroded and not worth saving. These they left on the bottom. There were also many bronze or copper objects like unsharpened knives with big handles, and some mysterious things like marbles, which exploded when they were raised to the surface and dried out.

That winter the owners sent a diving boat and a large schooner to pick up the cargo. Turkish soldiers, or bandits, fired on them from shore, and they abandoned the expedition.

The wreck is still there, if it was not robbed in the early 1900's by an expedition which my informant had not heard about. It is protected from archaeologists by the policy of the Turkish archaeological service, but not from casual skin divers in a yacht, or Turkish sponge divers, who could strip the site in a few days with no one the wiser.

Another cargo of ingots turned up in Greece in 1900. It was found by Captain Lucas Kalamakis, who contracted to do the underwater work when a breakwater was constructed in front of the harbor of Kyme, on the eastern side of Euboea. He found seventeen whole ingots and two fragmentary ones which are now in the Numismatic Museum in Athens. We searched for evidence of a wreck at Kyme in 1962 and found nothing. It seems likely that the breakwater was built over the site of the shipwreck.

The familiar pattern is repeated in Greece, with results as sad as elsewhere and considerably more absurd. Marine archaeology was administered by sportsmen again, in this case by an amateur spearfishing association directed by an admiral (retired), Theophilos Voutsaras. His impartiality derived from his being neither a diver nor an archaeologist.

Greek emotion runs strong about the defense of Neptune's treasure-house, and the police and military played sizable roles on the marine scene in Greece. A history of events would produce a volume the size of the New York telephone directory, and put the reader to sleep as well, but a look into that history here and there shows the trend of the whole.

In 1961 Edwin Link, inventor of the Link trainer for student pilots and internationally known researcher into problems involved in the exploration of the sea, came to Greece with his research boat *Sea Diver*. He had permission from the government, as represented by Admiral Voutsaras, to carry out a modest research program in southern Greece. He was arrested more or less by accident for stealing antiquities, and sentenced to two years in jail. This made headlines all over Greece, and was in fact the hit of the season among a populace which has long been a connoisseur of smuggling stories.

He paid the fine one is permitted to pay instead of going to prison, left Greece, appealed the sentence, and was eventually judged to be innocent. This second trial did not even make the second page of any of the papers.

A deputy of the French parliament, a friend of his, and their wives had hired a boat for an afternoon in Methone in 1963. They found some potsherds, showed them to one another on the boat, then proposed to drop them back in the sea where they had been found. Not on your life, said the boatman. They were taken to the harbormaster and arrested for stealing antiquities. More headlines were followed by an acquittal, which was not reported.

A lot of other people were arrested publicly and acquitted privately. Institutions sponsoring research began to abandon the beautiful blue waters of the Greek Aegean and send their people and their money elsewhere. Then in the summer of 1964 an incident occurred which reads like bad fiction but was typical enough to note in some detail.

Three friends were on their way back to America after a holiday in Greece. One had a cold, but the other two, divers and photographers, fishermen and general enthusiasts about life under the sea, wanted to go out on a sponge boat and have a dive before they left the Aegean. Neither of them was a professional diver. They were more or less ordinary "nice American tourists," the sort of men you would approach in the street to ask the correct time, except that one of them, Ed Cummins, had been head of the Air Force diving group in Greece a few years before and had inaugurated a stiff program to familiarize the Americans in his group with the common sense and Greek law of keeping hands off ancient objects in the sea. The other, Ed Zimbelman, is a landscape architect.

They went out with a Piraeus sponge boat on a Sunday morning, and had a good day photographing the helmet divers spearing fish. At the end of the day they agreed to meet the fishermen the next day and go out again.

The following morning they were waiting in the harbor for the Greek fishermen when they were arrested, interrogated, and taken to their hotel room which was searched. All their film was confiscated. On the film was a picture of one of them holding an amphora. They offered to go back at once and show the authorities where they had left the amphora in its place on the sea bottom, but no one was interested. Released pending trial, they flew back to the United States. The coast guard then released the photograph to the press. An accompanying article in *Eleftheria* of Sunday, May 31, 1964, is, in its depressing way, a little classic.

The caption read, "A foreign antiquities smuggler holding an amphora which he found on the bottom near Varkitsa. He was photographed by an accomplice who waited in a boat on the surface." The headlines were "ANTIQUITIES SMUGGLING BY NEW ELGINS" and "The Hidden Treasures of the Greek Seas." The reporter, Nasos Georgakolos, spared no effort to appall his readers.

Among the caravan of foreigners who come to visit our country, there exist various Elgins. They don't have the effrontery to remove the Acropolis whole, as did the British diplomat many years ago, with the help of the foreign conquerors, the Turks. They are **content** with little . . . They would prefer to take things **from** museums or from archaeological places, but there are too many eyes there that could see them. For this reason the Elgins go to the beaches, where there are many archaeological treasures, and where they can move freely.

Their appearance does not seem suspicious. They are like other tourists; only their talk and their "mugs" distinguish them. They usually wear shorts, and they have rucksacks on their backs, which contain useful things for long trips.

But they are equipped with two necessary aids. A photographic camera and a breathing apparatus. They dive very deep, make research, and take pictures. When they locate an archaeological bargain, they come to the surface and conspire about how they are going to take it out. . . .

A few days ago two foreign tourists were caught in action at the moment they were spearing an amphora. They were supposedly making a sea excursion with a small boat on the beach near Varkitsa. Their suspicious movements were noted by the coast guard. They were followed and allowed to dive. When they came to the surface embracing an amphora, they were arrested and sent to the prosecutor's office, with all the proofs of their purported underwater fishing.

The article goes on about how underwater smuggling has greatly increased lately, so that now the ministry of the merchant marine is obliged to take strict measures. A series of orders were given by Captain Andreas Valianas of the coast guard police, who listed nearly forty places where underwater fishing is prohibited and another dozen it is forbidden even to approach. "The suspicious and dangerous people . . . must be watched, not only by the coast guard but by individuals, especially the members of the nautical clubs of the Federation of Underwater Activity . . ." (This is the group headed by Admiral Voutsaras.) "The several Elgins who come to our country for special reasons must be kept out."

Here the cautious reader detects some carelessness with the facts, a carelessness with overtones of frame-up. The Americans weren't caught in the act of stealing; they were arrested with their shoes on in the harbor. They took each other's pictures; who was the accomplice waiting in the boat? (The fishermen were interrogated for some days following the article's publication, asked to act as witnesses of the crime. How successful the persuasion was we do not know, since the case has yet, in 1968, to come to trial.) They weren't on the beach. They weren't followed. They did not come to the surface embracing an amphora.

The list of forbidden archaeological sites is a list of places foreigners have been arrested. It has nothing to do with the sites of shipwrecks or scattered antiquities. In any case one cannot swim very many minutes in any direction in all of the Greek Aegean without turning up at least an ancient potsherd. To protect all the antiquities all the time the authorities have got to clear the beaches and persuade the Greeks to give up eating fish, a gargantuan task of infinite dimensions.

Was the case ever meant to come to trial? Where did the coast guard get their "information"? *Cui bono?* as detectives say.

First blood went to Admiral Voutsaras's association, to help it meet its new responsibilities. In 1965 the association received $15,000. *Ta Nea* said on August 18, under the heading "THE ABUNDANT TREASURES OF THE GREEK DEEP," that the first diver of the federation was a Greek, that they were beginning to work with experienced frogmen, and that they might find statues.

They worked for five days in Paros, found the water too deep and rough, announced that they had found archaeological treasures, and quit. In the following years the federation budget has done well, the last government infusion having occurred on January 1, 1968.

The summer of 1966 was a particularly busy one for journalists and divers. There was a bumper crop of sea treasure stories, including one about the likelihood of finding statues under the granite sarcophagi surveyed by the University of Pennsylvania Museum in 1962. (Our report had said that the sarcophagi lay on bedrock, but hope springs eternal.) The same Penn expedition had given the federation photographs, which still appear every now and then over various captions, one diver and one site looking much like many others when reproduced on fuzzy newsprint.

Arrest followed arrest. The nephew of a most distinguished lady from the American Agora excavations found his holiday interrupted by the police. Florent Ramauget and his wife, divers and owners of a charter yacht, lost a charter season and a good deal of money appealing his conviction on next to no evidence. Poorer, wiser, and considerably less enthusiastic about Greek charter cruises, they finally won a partial acquittal more than half a year later. To no one's surprise, they left Greece.

No incidents involving foreign divers occurred during the summer of 1967, partly because there were few tourists that summer, partly because the group of colonels who mutinied and established a new government in April of 1967 were anxious for good relations with the foreign press.

In the spring of 1967 Nikos Yialouris became director of the department of sculpture in the National Museum in Athens. Yialouris, himself a diver, had in 1963 visited the site of the only thorough survey of a shipwreck ever done in Greece. His intention was to support a workable plan of survey and protection of ancient sites in the sea. In February, 1968, he was fired for being "inspired with antinational ideas." A lot of water has flowed through the Aegean since Spiridon Stais set in motion the revolutionary excavation at Antikythera.

And a lot of the archaeological treasure in that sea has flowed out, just as the newspapers say, only the looters are not the ones whose names you see in the crime columns of the dailies. Most of the cases above involve a single amphora, not necessarily from a wreck, which could just as well have been bought in nearly any tourist shop. Hundreds of amphoras, nicely covered with seagrowth, find their way from the nets of local fishermen to these shops, with the permission of the antiquities service. Greek skin divers keep collections in their houses. Harbor gossip says that one foreign yacht got away with over a hundred amphoras. Greek divers have for a long time exploited a well-known Hellenistic wreck off the south end of Hydra. The Club Méditerranée in Corfu offered, as a final graduation exercise, a deep dive to a second century B.C. wreck. France is thus the richer for hundreds of diplomaed divers and their amphora souvenirs, and the wreck no longer exists.

All this, and more, is common knowledge among people who fish, dive, or just drink coffee along Greek waterfronts. But no diver will report finds to the antiquities service. The foreigner would lose his holiday, the Greek would lose days of work and therefore money, both risk the expense and embarrassment of prosecution, and anyhow, there is no organization in Greece with knowledge, staff, and money to cope with the problem.

It is a hard problem, but not insoluble. One way out is that taken by the Yugoslavs, who control yacht itineraries and prevent foreigners' diving anywhere at any time by sealing up not only compressors and bottles but masks and fins as soon as the yacht enters the country. This solution works, especially when the country is on a more or less wartime footing, but it is impractical in a place like Greece, which depends for over fourteen percent of its income on tourism. (In the summer of 1967 yachts were required to stop only at certain ports overnight, giving up all the pleasures of exploration and solitude, but there was such an uproar that the law was soon rescinded.)

There could, however, be an organization to which finds could be reported, small enough to keep its red tape under control, large enough to be able to send out an archaeologically trained diver to observe and record the site. Not many sites want constant watching. Many can be surveyed and left. Some can be photographed and left. Comparatively few are worth full-scale excavation.

The Israelis may have found part of the solution. After their archaeological finds are drawn and photographed, in place and individually, they are sometimes authorized to be sold and even exported. A thousand identical amphoras of a common type simply occupy storage space in the museum unfortunate enough to acquire them. One apiece for study purposes in all the museums of the country still leaves a lot left over. But the museums of cities and villages elsewhere in the world would be glad of such an amphora, perhaps, as would private people whose names and addresses would be known to the antiquities service for reference. Money from the sales could go back to the service, perhaps to help excavate other sites. This is not necessarily a universal solution, but an indication that solutions do exist and can be found.

There are many thumbs in the dike, trying to hold off the flood of ravenous scavengers. Perhaps the best of the organizations is the Committee for Nautical Archaeology at the Institute of Archaeology in London, which gives courses and seminars in marine archaeology as well as technical discussions and advice. The committee has not yet carried out an excavation, lacking funds and leadership to do so. But it has done excellent work in training students, and out of so many Indians a chief or two is bound to turn up before long.

In the United States, the Council of Underwater Archaeology has existed since 1958, but has yet to support a full-scale ship excavation. The council's interests are broad. At the third conference sponsored by the council, held in Miami in March, 1967, out of thirty-two papers delivered only two were reports of ship excavations. One was given by Anders Frantzen on that excellent, hardy perennial, the raising of the *Vasa*. The other was by Fred Van Doornick, giving an account of his restorations of the Yassi Ada wreck.

Smaller groups have done good work, such as the survey, done by the University of Acadia in Nova Scotia, of Louisbourg harbor and the ships destroyed by the British fleet there in 1758. This was done by a group of divers led by two young instructors who were not professional archaeologists but had done their archaeological homework thoroughly.

The Western Australian Museum in Perth has created a post for a curator of nautical and colonial history, who has been entrusted with the six known precolonial wrecks in western Australia. These include the wrecks of the *Batavia* and the *Golden Dragon,* both unfortunately dynamited before the creation of this position.

In Denmark Ole Crumlin Pedersen, a young naval architect, has gotten the government to finance a maritime museum and has started a true center of ship research. In Holland as well, the Dutch Archaeological Service has started a project to save shipwrecks that turn up in the lands reclaimed from the Zuider Zee. Directed by G. D. Van Der Heide, the meticulous Dutch have excavated dozens of shipwrecks dating from the early 1400's. Hundreds more have been located.

A number of individuals — Honor Frost, Frederic Dumas, Robert Marx and Gerhard Kapitän, among others — have worked singly or with small groups, digging and drawing history in the sea as fast as they can before it disappears. A group of divers from Cambridge University, including architects and engineers, have worked for several summers on their own or with other groups, training themselves and learning from others, as much as a summer's holiday will permit, about marine archaeology.

This last is perhaps particularly relevant. The growing groups of treasure divers whose principle tools are dynamite and metal detectors are not bad men. They are not scholars either. They dive for thrills, but are often susceptible to the other sort of thrill, that of learning about a ship's construction and journey from its careful excavation on the bottom.

The technology of marine archaeology is relatively simple, and can be mastered by most mechanically minded small-ship seamen. The only place in the world where a student can train to be a professional marine archaeologist is the University of Pennsylvania Museum, but not everyone wants to be a full-time professional. The urgent problem of the moment is turning looters into recorders, with some sort of organization to which finds can be reported without, as in Greece or France, drowning the diver in scandal and red tape.

There is a great deal of talent and goodwill available in museums, universities, navies and commercial organizations. The question is its organization for use. The barriers in the way of marine excavations are mainly the result of political bickering in city offices.

The problem is desperate. Soon the object of the bickering will have vanished like the American buffalo or the whooping crane; nor can we mate the last survivors, and hope against hope they will breed.

APPENDIX I

H.M.S. Nautilus

COURT-MARTIAL

WITH the kind permission of the Public Records Office, I quote PRO/ADM 5381 in full. It has never been published before and is a better account of the wreck than any of the watered-down versions, including mine, that have been published to date.

PRO/ADM 5381

Minutes of the Proceedings of a Court Martial Assembled and Held on Board His Majesty's Ship Atlas *off Cadiz on Friday the 15th Day of May 1807*

PRESENT
John Child Purvis Esquire, Rear Admiral of the White and Second Officer in the Command of His Majesty's Ships and vessels employed off Cadiz . . . . (President)

CAPTAINS

Wm. A. Ottway	Edwd Buller
Fra^s Fayerman	Rt. Honble Lord A. Beauclerke
Rt. Honble Lord H. Paulett	Wm. Shield
Ja^s Bissett	Sir In^o Gore
John Giffard	Saml Pym
Richard Thomas	. . . . .

Being all the Captains of the post ships that day in the Squadron off Cadiz except Captain Fra⁸ Pender of His Majesty's Ship *Queen*, whose Surgeon attended and Certified the Court of Captain Pender's inability to attend, through ill health.

The Persons to be examined being brought into Court and Audience admitted Read the order of the Commander in Chief of which the following is a Copy.

> By the Rt. Hon. Cuthbert Lord Collingwood
> Vice Adm. of the Red and Commander in
> Chief of H.M.s Ships and vessels employed
> and to be employed in the Mediterranean
> etc.

His Majesty's late Sloop the Nautilus having on the 5th day of January last, run on an Island at the entrance of the Archipelago, supposed to be that of Cerigotto, or on the rocks near it, where she was totally lost, when on her passage down with dispatches for me from Rear Admiral Sir Thomas Louis Bt.

I send you herewith a letter from Lieut. Alexr. Nesbitt the Senior surviving Officer dated the 19th January last, relating the circumstances of that unfortunate Event, and —

By virtue of the Power and Authority to me given, I do hereby require and direct you to Assemble a Court Martial as soon as Conveniently may be, which Court (you being president thereof) is hereby required and directed to investigate and enquire into the circumstances which led to this unfortunate Event — And to try Lieut. Alexr. Nesbitt and such of the surviving Officers and Ships Company of His Majesty's late Sloop Nautilus as are now in the Squadron for their Conduct on that occasion accordingly.

To: Jno. C. Purvis Esq. Rear Admiral of the White and Second Officer in the Command of H.M.s Ships and vessels employed,
    Off Cadiz
By Command of the Vice Admiral
    W. R. Cosway

Given under my hand on board His Majesty's Ship the Ocean off Cadiz this 13th day of May 1807.
[Signed] Collingwood

The Members of the Court and Judge Advocate then in Open Court and before they proceeded to trial, respectively took the Oath enjoined by Act of Parliament. Then the Letter from Lieut. Alexr. Nesbitt relating the circumstances of the Loss of His Majesty's late sloop the Nautilus was read, and the Court proceeded to Examine the said Lieut. Alexr. Nesbitt and such of the surviving Officers and Ship's Company as were then in the Squadron as follows — (Viz)

By the Court: Do any of You (meaning the Acting Master, the Gunner and rest of the Crew late belonging to His Majesty's late Sloop Nautilus at present on board), think, the loss of the Nautilus was occasioned by any misconduct on the part of Lieut. Nesbitt?

A: No.

All ordered to withdraw except Lieut. Nesbitt who was first sworn and examined as follows:

Q: Was Captain Palmer in the habit of Navigating the Sloop himself without consulting the Master?

A: No.

Q: Do you know whether the Master was Consulted respecting the Course to be steered from Anti-Milo?

A: He was.

Q: Do you know how Anti-Milo bore when you took your departure?

A: South-East by Compass about 5 or 6 Miles at Sun set.

Q: What course did you steer from the Island of Anti-Milo, after your departure and at what rate did you go?

A: A South-West Course, at the rate of 7 and 9 knots per hour.

Q: Did you work the Log-board at any time in the course of your Watch from Twelve to Four o'Clock?

A: No.

Q: What sail were you under at that time?

A: Double reef'd topsails on the Cap until Two o'Clock when we close reef'd and hoisted them.

Q: How had you the wind at that time?

A: At North-East until we made the Land.

Q: You mention in your Narrative that when you had the Island of Cerigotto on the Larboard beam there was a Rock on the Starboard beam. What distance was that rock from you?

A: About Six Miles.

Q: Describe what appearance that Rock had, if like an Island or otherwise?

A: It appeared to us, as a very high rock.

Q: What distance was the Sloop from Cerigotto at that time?

A: Between Eight and Nine Miles.

Q: Was it in your power to make any observation at any time respecting the place the Sloop was wreck'd upon?

A: Nothing more than by passing it.

Q: Do you think you ran between Cerigotto and the small Island of Pauri?

A: Certainly.

Q: Did Captain Palmer or any Officer work the board so as to ascertain the situation of the Sloop before the Land was seen?

A: The Captain consulted the Master at 2 o'Clock and perfectly ascertained the bearings and distance of the Island of Cerigotto.

Q: Do you know any reason why the Sloop was not brought too, after it had been once proposed in the course of the middle watch?

A: No other reason than the pressing nature of the dispatches on board.

Q: Was there any alteration in the course from seeing the Land till the time the Ship struck?

A: On Captain Palmer's coming on deck, we haul'd up W.S.W. afterwards to West, and at 4 o'Clock supposing ourselves clear of danger, shaped our Course W by N under Close reef'd topsail, the Courses, Jib and Driver.

Q: Was the night such as to see the land to bring the Sloop too at a proper distance?

A: No.

Q: What do you suppose the nearest distance between the Island of Cerigotto and Pauri?

A: About Nine Miles.   [Actually under five miles. P.T.]

Q: At what time did the Pilot give up the charge of the Sloop and for what reason?

A: At sun set, he having reach'd the limits of his experience and professing himself ignorant of the approaching coast.

Q: How far from the Rock of Pauri do you suppose the ship struck?

A: Between 5 and 6 miles.   [Actually under three miles. P.T.]

Q: Were there people properly stationed to keep a good look out during the middle watch?

A: There were.

Q: Had you any advantage from the Moon or was the night otherwise?

A: No advantage, the heaviness of the clouds preventing our experiencing any assistance from it.

Q: At what time of the Moon was it?

A: I do not recollect.

Q: You have mentioned in your Narrative that the boat pass'd with different people at different times, where did that boat go to?

A: To Cerigotto.

Q: Was it from Cerigotto that you had the Assistance of boats to take you and your people off the rock?

A: It was.

Q: Your narrative was dated from the Island of Cerago did you go there for the benefit of getting a passage to Malta?

A: For the purpose of expediting an Account of our loss and of providing for the distresses of the remaining part of the Crew at Cerigotto.

Q: Have you any reason to think that the *Nautilus* was lost owing to the want of Skill or Judgment in the Master?

A: No.

Q: Do you know if there was any difference of opinion between the Captain and Master in respect to the Courses the Sloop ought to be steered and the distance to be run?

A: None that I know of.

Q: Had you any Conversation with the Master during the night, relative to the safety of the Sloop?

A: None.

Q: Do you know of any blame that attaches to any of the surviving officers and Crew that respects the loss of the Sloop?

A: No.

Q: Did it appear to you as an Officer that there was a degree of danger in running for so narrow a passage in so bad a night as you have described?

A: Not knowing of any danger and being persuaded there was none by the Captain I apprehended nothing.

Q: Do you know of any Instance of Captain Palmer being advised by any Officer not to run for that passage during the night?

A: No, not officially. I had hinted the probability of danger but knowing of none, had been silenced by the persuasion of Captain Palmer.

Q: Do you know of any other officer in the Sloop having expressed to Captain Palmer any thing relating to the mode of conducting the Sloop, on the night she was lost?

A: I know of none.

The Court having no further Questions to ask Lieut. A. Nesbitt he withdrew, and Mr. Shillingsworth Acting Master next sworn.

Q: Relate to the Court all the Circumstances that led to the loss of His Majesty's late Sloop *Nautilus* from the time the Pilot gave up the charge of her off the Island of Anti-Milo.

A: After the Pilot had given up the charge, Captain Palmer desired me to shape a Course to go between Cerigotto and Candia. The Course I gave was SW. at 2. in the morning Captain Palmer sent for me in his Cabin and asked me my opinion what was best to do. I said that it would be most prudent to heave to till day light, he then close reef'd the topsails as I thought with an Idea of bringing too, but he afterwards determined to run and begg'd me to go below. When I came on deck to relieve the watch at 4 o'Clock I found the Land on each side of us nearly a-beam and the Sloop haul'd up W by N. without my ever being acquainted with the making the land or the time the course was altered, during the time I was taking the order from Lieut. Nesbitt the lookout Man cried out, "Breakers ahead" upon which

Lieut. Nesbitt ordered the Helm immediately to be put down when the Ship immediately struck on a sunken rock.

Q: Did you at 2 o'Clock ascertain the situation of the ship by the Log?

A: Yes, she had run the distance within 12 Miles by the Log.

Q: What was the Land you saw when you came on deck?

A: Cerigotto abaft the Larboard beam and the Island of Pauri a little before the Starboard beam.

Q: At what distance was each of them?

A: About 5 Miles to the Southward of Pauri and about Seven Miles to the Westward of Cerigotto.

Q: Describe what you mean by putting the helm down?

A: Putting the helm a-port.

Q: What was the size of the Rock you ran on and how high was it above water?

A: About a Cables length and about half the breadth the sea broke over the greatest part of it.

Q: Do you mean to say that Captain Palmer acted contrary to your advice and opinion in not bringing the Ship too, or shortening sail at 2 o'Clock?

A: Yes.

Q: By whose misconduct do you attribute the loss of the *Nautilus?*

A: Captain Palmer took the charge out of my hand at 2 o'Clock.

Q: Did you mention to any officer in the ship what might be the probable consequence of the Captain's perseverance of carrying sail and going on?

A: I believe not.

Q: Relate to the Court the whole of the Conversation that passed between you and Captain Palmer from the time you went into his cabin, to the time you went below as he desired you.

A: On my going into his Cabin Captain Palmer asked me my opinion of what was best to be done. I told him I thought it most prudent to heave to. The rest of the time we examined some Charts relative to the passage between Cerigotto and Candia, when the Captain told me to go below and that he was determined to run on, I then left him.

Q: Did you offer any further advice to the Captain?

A: I advised him to steer SW.

Q: How long were you Master of the *Nautilus?*

A: Two Days.

Q: Had you any knowledge of the Navigation previous to your being Master?

A: None.

Q: Do you know of any reason why you were not called when they first saw the Land?

A: No.

Q: How was the wind at the time you came upon deck?

A: N.N.East.

Q: Are there any soundings at any distance from the Island of Cerigotto?

A: I believe not.

Q: Can you state to the Court any further circumstances relative to the loss of the *Nautilus* beyond what you have already mentioned.

A: No.

Q: Do you know of any blame that attaches to Lieut. A. Nesbitt or Mr. Drummond the Gunner or the other men now on board this ship relative to the loss of His Majesty's late Sloop the *Nautilus?*

A: Certainly not.

The Court having no other questions to put to Mr. Shillingsworth, he withdrew and, Mr. Charles Drummond (Gunner) Sworn.

Q: Relate to the Court all the Circumstances that you know of relative to the loss of H.M.s late Sloop *Nautilus?*

A: I know nothing about it, being in my Cot at the time she struck.

The Court having no other question to ask Mr. Drummond he withdrew, and George Smith (2nd Master and Coxswain) Sworn.

Q: Relate to the Court all the Circumstances that you know of relative to the loss of His Majesty's late Sloop *Nautilus.*

A: I took the com at 2 o'Clock, my orders were a S.W. course which continued till 3. The look out man forward call'd out "Land a head" the Captain immediately said to Lieut. Nesbitt haul your wind on the Starboard tack and make sail — this continued till 4. often asking me how high she laid, my reply to him was N.W. by N. At 4. the Captain was on deck again, Lt. Nesbitt told me to keep her W. by N. At ¼ past 4 I was relieved by the other 2nd Master telling him to keep her W. by N. and be very particular who you have at the helm. The Captain called me down in his Cabin where I found him and the pilot holding a Chart in his left hand, his dividers in his right — he asked the pilot if he knew this Land the pilot said he did not, as he had never been thro' this way before — The Captain then asked me if his bed was made. I told him yes — he said Go, and tell the Officer of the Watch I want him — When on deck I saw Mr. Shillingsworth taking the charge from Lt. Nesbitt. I told Mr. S. the Captain wanted him; he went down and I after him, and just as I got to the foot of the ladder I heard some one forward, cry out, "Port, hard a lee, Breakers a-head." Lt. Nesbitt ran aft ordered the helm to be put a-lee, which we had scarcely done when she struck — the people ran on deck crying out, and Mr. Nesbitt ran fore and aft pacifying the men, saying "if you are Britons, behave like Britons," until he saw the Sloop bilged when he said it was of no use, Get the yard tackles down. The people ran to the Captain's Gig and I ran round the deck to find the Captain to tell him of it. I found him in his Cabin putting some papers in the fire and the private signal box by him — I shut the door, went on deck, and saw they had lowered the Gig halfway down. Conceiving nothing but Death before my eyes I jumped into the Gig, pulled her clear of the Quarter, laid on our Oars and divided our Clothes amongst many that were naked — all telling me to command the boat as I was so well used to her. We pulled up to the Island of Pauri; got there at 8 o'clock, all went on shore except myself and another. They soon came back saying they could see nothing of the ship nor any person on the rock, that no water was to be found, and that one part of the Island was overrun with wild leeks on the other part were hundreds of Goats and pigs, but no Men to be seen on it.

I

We rested in the boat all that day thinking the weather would moderate, for to pull over to Cerago as we could see a fortification there. Between 12 and 1 in the night one of us discovered a light and we certainly thought some of the *Nautilus*'s men were on the rock. Finding the weather moderated very fast I asked who would volunteer to go down with me in the boat to see who was living. Four and myself went — when we found them very numerous telling them we could take 10 in the boat and no more — We took the pilot to talk the language he came in the 5th person and desired I would not take in any more. We then pulled away to Cerigotto. The Natives came down armed and much alarmed at seeing us; When the pilot went and spoke to them they behaved with the greatest humanity, trying day after day to get the boat off the beach which was not accomplished till Saturday morning at 2 o'Clock. We then returned to the rock at 10 or 11 o'Clock and took the remainder of our people back to Cerigotto, I could perceive only 10 of our number that were likely to survive that night.

Q: Did you hear any Conversation between the Captain and any Officer in the Sloop respecting the bringing to, rather than running down to the Islands?

A: No.

Q: Did you see the breakers a head on which the ship ran afterwards?

A: I never discovered them till she struck.

Q: In your opinion was the whole of the conduct of the surviving officers and Crew during the perilous situation the *Nautilus* was placed in, becoming their situations?

A: In my opinion they all behaved with the very best Conduct.

The Court having no further questions to ask, George Smith withdrew, the Court was Cleared, and the Members proceeded to deliberate on the Sentence which being done the Court was again opened, and Audience admitted, and the Sentence read accordingly — which was,

That the Court is of opinion the loss of His Majesty's late Sloop the Nautilus was occasioned by the Captain's Zeal to forward the public dispatches, which induced him to run in a dark tempestuous night for the passage between the Islands of Cerigotto and Candia, but that the Sloop passed between Cerigotto and Pauri and was lost on a Rock in the SW. part of that passage, which Rock does not appear to have been laid down in Heather's Chart by which it is said the said Sloop was navigated, it being the only one of those seas on board.

That no blame attaches to the Conduct of Lieut. Alex. Nesbitt, or such of the surviving Officers and Ship's company, at present in the Squadron on this occasion, but, that it appears to the Court, that Lieut. Alex. Nesbitt and the other surviving Officers and Crew did use every exertion that circumstances could admit. The Court therefore adjudged the said Lieut. Alex. Nesbitt and the other surviving Officers and Crew of His Majesty's late Sloop Nautilus to be acquitted and they were acquitted accordingly.

And it appearing to the Court that the Conduct of George Smith (the Coxswain) who was ultimately the means of saving so many Men was such, as induced the Court to recommend him to the Commander in Chief, and the said George Smith was thereby recommended accordingly.

———————

I George Hayward Deputy Judge Advocate at this Trial do hereby Certify, that the within contains a Correct Copy of the Minutes taken by me at this Court Martial.

[Signed] Geo. Hayward.

NAUTILUSES OF THE ROYAL NAVY

There have been several *Nautilus*es in the Royal Navy.

1. Sloop built 1784. Wrecked off Flamborough Head, 1799.

2. Our *Nautilus*. Built 1804 at Milford Haven.

Dimensions		
	112.0	Gun deck
	94.8¼	Keel
	29.8	Breadth
	9.0	Depth
	438.0	Tons

Light draught Afore, 10; abaft, 11.3
Number of men 121
Guns   18 9-pounders
Carronades   6 12-pounders, quarterdeck
        2 12-pounders, forecastle
Draught   Mr. Barralies

Classified as a sloop rigged as a ship and *not* rigged as a brig. Captured Spanish Giganta, nine guns, May 3, 1806, in company with H.M.S. *Renommee*. See ADM 51/1590 and *St. James Chronicle for May 17, 1807.*

3. Standard Columbine-class brig. Built 1807 at Mistley Thorn. In commission by October, 1808.

Dimensions 100.0 Gun deck
       77¾ Keel
       30.6 Breadth
       12.9 Depth
      302.0 Tons
Guns   16 32-pounders
       2 6-pounders

Sir Wm. Rules, Columbine Class.
Broken up, 1827.

4. 14: captured from Americans, July 16, 1812. Added as *Emulous*.

5. 10: brig sloop. Built at Woolwich, 1830.

6. Training brig launched at Pembroke, May 2, 1879.

7. Destroyer: built 1910. Renamed *Grampus* in 1913. In Dardanelles. Sold in 1920.

8. Also two submarines, a drifter and a trawler.

APPENDIX II

∿∿∿∿∿

Antikythera Wreck

SEQUENCE OF EVENTS, 1900–1901

*(reconstructed from the published
material available to me)*

1900 November 6   Kondos and Economou arrive in Athens

24   R.H.N. Steamship *Michaeli* arrives at Antikythera, commanded by Commander (?) Sotiriades. Economou on board. Dives from sponge boat by Kondos and crew. Bad weather.

27   *Michaeli* returns to Piraeus. Complaints that she is too large.

December 4   Steam-schooner *Syros* arrives. J. Boumboulis in charge. Byzantinos on board. Bad weather.

11   Returned to Piraeus.

26   *Syros* arrives at Antikythera.

27   Raised Ephebe.

1901 January 10   *Syros* loaded statues.

22   Exhibit in Athens.

23   Trouble with divers. They demand more money.

24   Complaints that divers are smashing things.

28   Iron anchor raised. (Later research showed it to be modern.)

[243]

	February	8	*Michaeli* arrives from Piraeus with VIPs on board. Divers very discouraged.
		9	Raising statues with *Michaeli's* big winch.
		12	*Michaeli* returns to Athens.
		16	Diving begins again.
		17	Colossal statues dumped. Some raised.
		18	Three statues raised. Divers very tired.
1901	February	19	Divers refuse to work.
		20	Divers persuaded to work a couple of days more.
		21	Dives.
		23	Divers stop work again.
		26	Divers returned Athens to have a one-month rest. Talk of hiring new divers.
	March	17	Left Piraeus with partly new crew, four divers added.
		18	Bad weather begins and lasts into March 24.
		24	Begin diving.
		29	Quit diving for Easter.
	April	9	Begin diving.
		15	Kritikos dies.
		16	Talk of hiring Italian divers.
	May	20	Dives.
		25	Month of June doubtful. No references.
	July		Bad weather sets in (*melteme*).
	August		Work during some days, but very little because of *melteme* (seasonal wind).
	September	20	The last dives.
		22	Project called off.

In going over the above schedule, which is admittedly incomplete, it is difficult to extract more than eighty days of actual diving. During many of these days, such as when they were lifting stone blocks and colossal statues, the divers can have worked for only a part of the available time.

At the rate of two dives per day per diver, the six divers can have spent only one hour per day on the bottom, and even at three dives per day, they would have been able to work only one and a half hours per day.

A tabulation of the published accounts in Greek leads me to make an approximate estimate of about one hundred working hours of actual bottom time. The preceding table showing the sequence of events was the basis for this estimate.

COST

This is difficult to calculate because the cost of the naval vessels involved was probably written off as "training" or "special services" or something similar. It is possible to arrive at a figure of something (in terms of today's dollars) like a quarter to a half a million dollars, if one counts the gross cost of the whole expedition to the Greek government.

This sum is excessive in terms of the time worked on the bottom; however, in terms of the value of the statues recovered, it is probably reasonable. An art dealer acquaintance of mine says: "A bronze like the Antikythera Ephebe has not appeared on the market for generations, so there is no comparative yardstick: such a bronze might well fetch one hundred thousand dollars, and might be worth more if circumstances were right."

So one cannot blame Stais for organizing what was essentially a salvage job rather than an archaeological excavation.

Chapter Notes and References

CHAPTER I: THE SEA CHANGE

11 Great Basses wreck, off Ceylon
   Arthur Clarke's *Treasure of the Great Reef* (New York: Harper & Row, 1964); and Peter Throckmorton, "The Great Basses Wreck" in *Expedition*, vol. 6, no. 3 (1964).

12 Borstö Islands wreck
   Abo Underrättelser, August 13, 1961; *Sveriges Flotta*, vol. 60 (1964); Henrik Rosenius, *Marine Arkeologi i Finland;* and Ora Patoharju's report to CMAS on underwater archaeology in Finland to 1962.

13 *Vasa*
   Anders Franzen, *The Warship Vasa* (Stockholm, 1959).
   Commodore Edward Glason, "The Raising of the Royal Swedish Ship *Vasa,*" *Mariners Mirror*, vol. 48, no. 3 (1962). A solid technical report of the *Vasa*, written for the specialist.
   Captain (E) Gunnar Schoerner, *Regalskeppet* (Stockholm, 1966). In Swedish with English summary.

16 Deep-water conditions
   Harald U. Sverdrup, *The Oceans* (New York: Prentice-Hall, 1942), pp. 647 ff.

19 Bay of Navarino wrecks
   C. M. Woodhouse, *The Battle of Navarino* (London: Hodder and Stoughton, 1965).

20 *Columbine, Heraclea*, etc.
   Peter Throckmorton, "Ships Wrecked in the Aegean Sea," *Archaelogy*, vol. 17, no. 4 (1964); and "Wrecks at Methone," *Mariners Mirror*, vol. 51, no. 4 (1965).

CHAPTER II: REEFS, ARCHIVES, AND THE AGE OF EXPLORATION

33 Shipwreck literature
   See *Shipwreck and Empire* by James Duffy (Cambridge, Mass.: Harvard University Press, 1955). William O. S. Gilley's *Narra-*

tives of Shipwrecks of the Royal Navy Between 1793 and 1849
(London, 1851) is the best of a good many examples of such
literature. A more typical example is *The* MARINERS CHRON-
ICLE — *or Authentic and Complete History of* POPULAR
SHIPWRECKS *recording the Most Remarkable disasters which
have happened on the ocean to people of all Nations, Particularly
the adventures and* SUFFERINGS OF BRITISH SEAMEN, *by*
WRECK, FIRE, FAMINE *and other calamities incident to a life
of Marine enterprise,* by Archibald Duncan, Esq. In six volumes,
with suitably dramatic illustrations, it went through various editions in the early 1800's.

Compilations of shipwrecks are still being published: for ex-
ample, *Shipwrecks and New Zealand Disasters 1795–1950* by
Charles W. N. Ingram and P. Owen Wheatley (Wellington,
N.Z., 1951); *Wrecks Around Nantucket* compiled by Arthur H.
Gardner (New Bedford, Mass., 1915 and 1943); *A Guide to
Sunken Ships in American Waters* by Adrian L. Lonsdale and
H. R. Kaplan (Arlington, Va., 1964); *The Vanishing Fleet* by
B. W. Luther (Boston: privately printed, 1965).

For statistics of the British Merchant Navy, see *Why Wrecks
Happen, How Wrecks Happen, and How to Prevent Them* by
Thomas Gray(?), reprinted from *Nautical Magazine* (London,
1873).

35 Brigs of the Columbine Class
The statistics on losses of these brigs are taken from Gilley's
Narratives of Shipwrecks of the Royal Navy; they were compared with the notes on copies of plans made for construction
of brigs as given on H.M.S. *Columbine*'s original drafts. They
are in the main accurate, but I have not been able to obtain the
material here in Athens to double-check the fate of every brig
in the Columbine series. I have assumed that brigs named on the
H.M.S. *Columbine* drafts are the same ones given in Gilley,
which is not necessarily so, as the normal practice in both the
British and American navies is to keep names. Thus one can
sometimes find that many ships have borne the same name.

In any case, these 18-gun brigs were all quite similar because
they were built after the lines of Sir William Rule's *Cruizer* of
1797, a model so successful that it was used for this class of ship
until the end of the days of the sailing navy.

37 Coral reefs on trade routes
Mendel L. Peterson, *History Under the Sea* (Washington, D.C.:
Smithsonian Institution, 1965), p. 3.

38 H.M.S. *Daedalus* court-martial
Public Records Office document PRO/ADM/1/05437.
See also William O. S. Gilley, *Narratives of Shipwrecks of the
Royal Navy* (London, 1851). The source for the Maxwell quotes
is also Gilley, pp. 208 ff.

44 H.M.S. *Loo* wreck and the Crile dives off Florida
George and Jane Crile, *Treasure-diving Holidays* (New York: Viking, 1954), p. 183.
Mendel Peterson's paper, "The Last Cruise of H.M.S. *Loo*," is in the Smithsonian Miscellaneous Collections, vol. 131, no. 2.

48 Blair and Marx off Yucatán
Clay Blair, *Diving for Pleasure and Treasure* (New York: World, 1960).

55 Great Basses reef, off Ceylon
See notes for Chapter 1.

73 Wrecks off Australia
Hugh Edwards, *Gods and Little Fishes* (London, 1962) and *Islands of Angry Ghosts* (New York: Morrow, 1966).
Henrietta Drake Brockman's *Voyage to Disaster* (London and Sydney, 1963) gives a translation by E. D. Drock of Pelsaert's journal and tells the whole chilling story of the *Batavia* mutiny. The story of the actual survey of the wreck is told by C. H. Halls in the annual *Dog Watch*, no. 21 (1964). Halls has written about the *Golden Dragon* in *Westerly*, nos. 2 (1963) and 1 (1964), published in Perth.

CHAPTER III: THE WRECK OF THE *NAUTILUS*

79 Battle of Matapan
Ronald Seth, *Two Fleets Surprised* (London: Geoffrey Bles, 1960). Seth gives a bibliography on Matapan from both sides.

80 Inscription in Rhodes
Lionel Casson, *The Ancient Mariners* (New York: Macmillan, 1959), pp. 155, 156.

80 H.M.S. *Nautilus*
There are two groups of documents concerning the *Nautilus*. First, contemporary accounts of the wreck, which seem to have been mostly drawn from a single source which has now disappeared, probably Lieutenant Nesbitt's original letter to Admiral Collingwood describing the loss of the ship. Although some accounts give more details than others, they are all more or less identical: Marshall's *Naval Biography*, vol. III, pt. 2, pp. 371 ff.; *Naval Chronicle*, vol. 22 (1807), pp. 89 ff.; *Tales of Shipwrecks*, edited by James Lindridge, 2d ser., vol. II (1835), pp. 217 ff.; and Thomas Bingley's *Shipwrecks and Disasters at Sea*, vol. III (Boston, 1812), pp. 441 ff.; and pp. 258 ff. of the 2d series (Boston, 1835). Gilley's version of the *Nautilus* incident in *Narratives of Shipwrecks of the Royal Navy* . . . (London, 1851) has been recently paraphrased, without attribution, by Edward Rowe Snowe in *The Fury of the Seas* (New York: Dodd, Mead, 1964).
Several of the accounts, notably Gilley's, seem to be quoting survivors' accounts which are not now attributable to any particular person. The disaster did not arouse much interest at the time. The first and only news that Joan Saunders was able to find was recorded on April 18, 1807, in *The Times*, briefly and

inaccurately: "One half of the crew took to the boats and were fortunately picked up by a Russian Frigate . . ."

The second group of documents comprises primary sources: The minutes of the proceedings of the court martial in which Lieutenant Nesbitt was tried (ADM 5381, printed in the Appendix, page 231); *Nautilus*'s last muster roll, on November 24, 1806 (ADM 37/17146), a page of which is reproduced on page 89; and the plans, which are in the Maritime Museum, Greenwich.

Nautilus missed being famous by a few hours when she was beaten into Falmouth by H.M.S. *Pickle* with news of the Battle of Trafalgar. See *England Expects* by Dudley Pope (London: Weidenfeld, 1959) for a description of the race and of life on *Nautilus* under John Sykes, the captain that Palmer replaced two years after Trafalgar.

For further information about tonnage and construction, see John Edye London's *On the Equipment and Displacement of Ships of War* (London, 1832) and the notes for Chapter II under the heading "Columbine brigs."

83   "Twelve or fourteen families"
        Thomas Bingley, *Shipwrecks and Disaster at Sea*, vol. III, p. 455.

101   The fate of Lieutenant Nesbitt.
        Marshall's *Naval Biography*, vol. 3, pt. 2, pp. 371 ff.

CHAPTER IV: THE ANTIKYTHERA WRECK

In Greece, the gap between educated and uneducated, between villager and city man, is nowhere so apparent as in the language. Schools teach what is called *Katharevousa* (clean language), in which government decrees are made and textbooks written. It is a made language, created out of ancient Greek by a dedicated group of early nineteenth-century schoolteachers who felt that Greece's long division and the Turkish occupation had created dialects that could not be reconciled. The languages are as different as Chaucer and modern slang. Even today, the language differences lead to bad breakdowns in communication between groups.

In reading over the different reports on Antikythera in the contemporary Greek papers, one finds nowhere a detailed description of the sea bottom by a diver. There is no evidence that any of the people responsible for the excavation ever made an attempt to get an accurate description of how objects lay on the bottom. The archaeologists at Antikythera were, except for Economou, Katharevousa speakers trained in art history, philology, or philosophy, and they were as lost in the company of the dialect-speaking divers as the divers must have been in theirs.

Conversations in the text are either those I actually heard on the spot, or those I heard in similar sponge boats in similar situations.

I have put in details such as "a gray dawn" (because dawn on Antikythera would be gray during a southeast gale) or "socks his wife had knitted for him" (this is true for all the married Greek helmet divers I know who are on good terms with their wives). I have not put in conversations which directly concern the work without having evidence that they occurred and a good idea of what was said. It is obviously impossible to document everything in the chapter, as there is simply insufficient space. The interested reader will, however, find what he requires in the sources listed.

Although between twenty thousand and fifty thousand Greeks have been directly concerned with the sponge industry every year for the past hundred years, the first diving manual in Greek was published only in 1965, by an American-trained Greek navy U.D.T. officer, Manolis Papagrigorakis (*O Ipobrikios Anthropos*, Athens, 1965).

Remarkably little has been published about Antikythera in any language; the primary sources are all in Greek. The young archaeologists Kourouniotes and Valerio Stais, who had interested themselves in the wreck, were shuffled out of the job of publication by John Svoronos, who published, at the Greek government's expense, a long and rather uninformed and inaccurate account of the wreck and the finds. (This was republished in German, and is the source of most of the information in Professor Karo's article in *Archaeology*.)

It is easy to be critical of Svoronos, who leveled sharp attacks on Valerio Stais and Kourouniotes, but it should be remembered that he was a fine scholar as well as an antiquarian of the old school. When he worked on purely antiquarian problems such as numismatics, he produced work which is still very valuable.

What follows is a limited bibliography and explanation of the sources I consulted. The reader who wants to go farther should see notes in Mrs. Weinberg's introduction to the American Philosophical Society's transactions of Antikythera.

Ephemeris Arkaeologiki (Athens: The Archaeological Society, 1902), pp. 146-171. This appears to have been the combined effort of several people, Kourouniotes among them, and is not signed. It gives photographs of the statues before cleaning and restoration, and a good short account of the project. The author or authors were not familiar with the problems of diving.

J. N. Svoronos, *To en Athenais Ethnikon Mouseion* (Athens, 1903), pp. 1-86. (German translation published in 1908.) Svoronos theorized that the wreck was of the fourth century A.D. His analysis of the finds has been made for the most part obsolete by later research. He does not seem to have visited Antikythera, and bases much of his account of the actual work on accounts in the daily newspapers. He gives a list of these, which is useful but incomplete.

Valerio Stais, in *Ta Ex Antikitheron Evrimata* (Athens, 1905), attacks Svoronos and dates the wreck, correctly, in the first century B.C.

George Karo, "Art Salvaged from the Sea," in *Archaeology* (no. 1, 1948). The chief source in English and remarkable for the number of factual errors it contains. These arise from Karo's attempt to dramatize information taken from the original *Ephemeris* article and the German version of Svoronos's *Ethnikon Mouseion*. Unfortu-

nately, he does not use the more accurate information given in the
Ephemeris article, but prefers Svoronos, who got much of his information from an uncritical reading of the popular press.

Marine Archaeology, edited by Joan du Plat Taylor for CMAS (New
York: Crowell, 1966), pp. 35 ff. Extracts from Karo's article, including an eyewitness description of the site by Frederic Dumas, the
only trained observer who has dived on the site and written about it.

"The Antikythera Shipwreck Reconsidered," *Transactions of the
American Philosophical Society*, new ser., vol. 55, pt. 3 (1967); 48
pages of articles by Gladys Davison Weinberg, Virginia Grace, G.
Roger Edwards, Henry S. Robinson, Peter Throckmorton, and
Elizabeth K. Ralph, in which are discussed the commercial amphoras, glass, Hellenistic and Roman pottery, the ship and the C-14
dates of the wood. Their conclusion is that the ship went down
in the first quarter of the first century B.C. Notes in the publication
give additional Greek references.

Derek J. de Solla Price, "An Ancient Greek Computer," *Scientific
American* (June 1959). Price discusses the clock or computer found
at Antikythera and concludes that it was last set in 80 B.C. and
that it was probably made in 82 B.C. He says that it is the only
surviving evidence of a current of thought in ancient Greek civil-
ization which has been lost to us and that it shows the Greeks to
have been further ahead in their technology than anyone had imagined. Dr. Price is working on a book about the computer, which
is eagerly awaited.

The newspapers of the time which Svoronos referred to in *Ethnikon
Mouseion* were hunted down and microfilmed by Michael Valtinos.
We are grateful to the director of the National Library, Mr. Andreas
Papandreou, for his kind permission to do this. We think we found
almost everything published in the Athens press during the nine
months that the work went on at Antikythera, although several papers
cannot be found. Valtinos and the writer translated the articles that
seemed to be significant, and looked at the rest. The articles translated
included those in *Asty*, March 2, 5, 6, 7, and 10, 1901 and February 8,
1901; *Panathenaia*, vol. I, December, 1900 (this eyewitness account by
George Byzantinos is the most readable and sensible of those that
appeared); *Naftiki Hellas*, July 26, 1950 (an article by Hermopoulitis,
which gives an eyewitness account of the work — he was a navy PO
at the time — and a valuable account of the group of amphoras found
in the sand; I am indebted to Miss Virginia Grace for calling this to
my attention).

I am aware that I have only scratched the surface of the Antikythera story. I believe I have consulted most of the available public
sources, but certain that I've missed some and that I have made mistakes. There is still much work to be done, and a more extensive
reconstruction of the excavation could be a worthwhile thesis project
for an archaeological student who knows modern Greek well. I have
not been able to consult the files of the antiquities service, nor the

logbooks of the *Syros* or the *Aegelia,* if they still exist. Stais's personal papers appear to be lost, but it might be possible to find other documents of the time that were kept by people who were there. Such a project would render my account obsolete and would form the basis for a continuation of the excavation. The future excavator at Antikythera can be sure of finding a wealth of material in the smashed hull, under the sand.

132   Quotation from Lucian
      See Lucian, *Works,* translated by K. Kilburn (Cambridge, Mass.: Harvard University Press, 1960), vol. 6, p. 159. (Loeb Classical Library)

133   Quotations from George Byzantinos
      See *Panatheaia,* vol. I (December, 1900). The free translations are mine.

138   Diving and decompression methods
      Those used by Greek helmet sponge divers who work in the same tradition as Kondos's men are described in my "It's a Wonder They're Alive" in *Men Underwater,* edited by James Dugan and Richard Vaughn (Philadelphia, 1965).

141   Decompression tables
      J. B. S. Haldane, *Report of a Committee Appointed by the Lords Commissioners of the Admiralty to Consider and Report upon the Conditions of Deep Water Diving* (London, 1907).

143   Divers' efficiency
      A. D. Baddely, "Nitrogen Narcosis and the Free Diver," *Triton* (February, 1966).

153   The ancient computer
      Derek de Solla Price, "An Ancient Greek Computer," *Scientific American* (June, 1959), and a forthcoming book by the same author.

163   The salvage of the *Mentor*
      A. H. Smith, in "Lord Elgin and His Marbles," *Journal of Hellenic Studies,* vol. 36 (1916).

CHAPTER V: TRIAL AND ERROR

171   The Albenga wreck
      Nino Lamboglia, "La Nave Romana di Albenga," *Revue d'Etudes Ligures,* vol. 18, no. 3 (July, 1952) and no. 4 (December, 1952). The basic account of the first work done. For Lamboglia's preliminary report of work done from the *Artiglio,* see "Diario di scavo a dorbo dell'*Artiglio,*" *Inguana e Intemelia,* new ser., vol. 5, no. 1 (January-March, 1950), pp. 1–8. See also Francisca Pallares Salvador, *Dos Años de Campana Arqueológica con la Nave* Daino (1950), a pamphlet on the first work at Albenga. It gives an account of the first experience with drafting frames and shows them in place.

CHAPTER VII: THE GOLDEN PIGS

      Mr. Morris, as this book goes to print, has brought out his
      version of the *Association* story, in which he eloquently defends
      his interest in wreck and his working method. He puts a strong
      case, and his book is the only sensible report to date on the
      much-publicized Scilly wrecks. See Roland Morris, *Island Trea-
      ure* (London: Huchinson, 1929).

      Unsigned *Report* of January, 1969, issued by the Bureau of
      Marine Archaeology (Meriarkeologian toimisto). Muinaistiet
      toimikunta Hallituskatu 3 Helsinki Finland.

      International Herald Tribune (Paris), February 27, 1968.

      Eric S. Hansen and J. Sherman Bleakney, *Underwater Survey
      of Louisbourg Harbor for Relics of the Siege of 1758* (Wolfville,
      Nova Scotia: Acadia University Institute, 1962).

      Olaf Olsen and Ole Crumlin Pedersen, *The Skuldev Ships*, vol.
      38 of *Acta Archaeologica* (Copenhagen, 1967).

      See G. D. Van Der Heide in *Antiquity and Survival* (The
      Hague, n.d.). P.O.B. 2030.

      Honor Frost, *Under The Mediterranean* (New York: Prentice-
      Hall, 1963). This is Miss Frost's account of her underwater in-
      vestigations. It is full of information of anchors, harbors, and
      wrecks she has seen or heard about and the early days of wreck
      diving in the south of France. The book is a mine of information.
      Robert Marx's major work has not yet been properly published
      as a bound book, although several impressive mimeographed
      reports are circulating. These include: 1. "Glass Bottles Recov-
      ered from the Sunken City of Port Royal, Jamaica, May 1, 1966–
      March 31, 1968," issued by the Caribbean Research Institute of
      the College of the Virgin Islands, St. Thomas (January, 1969);
      39 pp. of text and drawings of glass bottles, invaluable to the
      student of seventeenth-century shipwreck material. 2. Five mas-
      sive papers on clay smoking pipes, wine glasses, and brass and
      copper items from Port Royal, attached to Marx's Preliminary
      Report. The five papers total about 450 pages of text and draw-

ings, and are presumably available from the Jamaica National Trust Commission, Kingston, Jamaica.

Frederic Dumas's account of his lonely struggle to save something from the Chrétienne A wreck is in his *Épaves Antiques* (Paris: Maisonneuve et Larose, 1964). The Introduction, by Professor Michael Mollat of the Sorbonne, is in part an appeal to the consciences of divers and to the interest of archaeologists. As we have seen, there has been little response.

Selected Bibliography

$\sim\sim\sim\sim$

As I have said in another place, bibliographies of underwater material, especially European underwater material, are fairly useless, because the average reader has not got access to the sources. It has been my experience that after a long hunt for what sounds like a wonderful article in an obscure French or Italian periodical, I more often than not end up with just another skin diver item.

The interested reader can find the basic material on Mediterranean marine archaeology in any good classical library. In including European books below, I give only those which are, in my opinion, worth looking up.

Atti del II Congresso Internazionale di Archeologia Sottemarina, Albenga 1958. Bordighera: Museo Bicknell, 1961. Like Benoit's *Épave*, this massive collection pretty well describes all work done in Italy to 1958, and makes most of the publications mentioned in the numerous articles superfluous.

Bass, George. *Archaeology Under Water.* London: Thames and Hudson, 1966. (Ancient Peoples and Places Series)

Benoit, Fernand. *L'Épave du Grand Congloué à Marseille.* XIV Supplement to *Gallia.* Paris: Centre National de la Recherche Scientifique, 1961. This book contains a bibliography of nearly everything written in France and Italy on Mediterranean marine archaeology to 1961; it renders most previous articles in *Gallia* superfluous.

Bert, Paul. *La Pression Barométrique.* Paris: Masson, 1873.

Blair, Clay. *Diving for Treasure.* London: Arthur Barker, 1960.

Clarke, Arthur. *Treasure of the Great Reef.* New York: Thames and Hudson, 1966. (Ancient Peoples and Places Series)

Dugan, James. *Man Under the Sea.* New York: Harper, 1956.

Edwards, Hugh. *Islands of Angry Ghosts.* New York: Morrow, 1966.

Frost, Honor. *Under the Mediterranean.* New York: Prentice-Hall, 1963.

McKee, Alexander. *History Under the Sea*. London: Huchinson, 1968. This has a wonderful account of the beginnings of helmet diving in England, Mary Rose, etc., etc.

Peterson, Mendel. *History Under the Sea*. Washington: Smithsonian Institution, 1965.

Taillez, Phillippe. *Nouvelles Plongées sans Câble*. Paris: Arthaud, 1957.

———. *To Hidden Depths*. London: William Kimber, 1954.

Taylor, Joan du Plat, ed. *Marine Archaeology*. New York: Crowell, 1966. A translated selection of material published in Europe to 1964; very useful because it makes the material available in English and contains articles with many useful notes for the student wishing to look up primary references.

Ucelli, Guido. *Le Navi di Nemi*. Rome, 1950. This large, beautifully done book is the final report of the first good excavation of Roman shipwrecks. These were two pleasure barges, sunk in a freshwater lake near Rome. Ucelli gives, in his notes and bibliography, almost all of the significant publications on ship archaeology up to the time of writing.

Woodhouse, C. M. *The Battle of Navarino*. London: Hodder and Stoughton, 1965.

Index

~~~~~

British East India Company, 71
British navy. *See* Royal Navy
Brockman, Henriette Drake, 74
bronze: preservation underwater, 22, 131; objects found in wrecks, 55, 61, 64, 69, 75, 107, 130, 173, 202. *See also* Antikythera wreck
Bronze Age wreck. *See* Gelidonya, Cape
Broussard, Henri, 182
Byzantinos, George: and Antikythera wreck, 131–132, 133–135, 143, 162

Cannon and cannonballs. *See* brass; bronze; iron; Great Basses wreck; *Nautilus* wreck
C.A.S.M. (Club Alpin Sous-Marine de Cannes), 182
Cagnes-sur-Mer, wrecks at, 188
Calucci, Emmanuel, 100, 168
Calypso (research ship), 84, 175–176, 179
Cambrian, H.M.S. (wreck), 80, 163–164
Cambridge University, 228
Cameras, underwater. *See* photography
Campagna ware, 176, 215
Canopus, H.M.S., 103
Cap Roux, wrecks at, 188
Cape of Good Hope, 42, 54
Cape of the Swallows. *See* Gelidonya, Cape
Carbon 14 dating, 159
Carducci (Italian destroyer), 79
CEDAM (Club de Exploraciones y Departes Aquáticos de México), 50–52
Centa River, 170
Cerigo Island (Kythera), 92, 94
Cerigotto Island (Antikythera), 88
Ceylon, 42, 54, 55, 56, 58, 65
Ceylon Department of Antiquities, 55
Chamois, (sunken destroyer), 141

Champlain, Lake, 12
charts, navigation (19th-century), 85–86
chemical reactions in ancient wrecks, 22–23, 31, 71–72
chemistry, modern: and preservation of wrecks, 30–31
China, early trade with, 54
china and porcelain: recovered from wrecks, 45, 69. *See also* amphoras; pottery
Chrétienne A wreck, 182–183, 184
Christianinni, Gaston, 175, 179, 184
Clarke, Arthur C., 55–58, 64, 65, 72–73
"closed groups," 32, 178, 191–192
Club Alpin Sous-Marine de Cannes, 181, 182
Club de Exploraciones y Deportes Aquáticos de México, 50–52
Club de la Mer, Antibes, 184
Club Méditerranée, Corfu, 225
coconut fibers, preserved underwater, 69–70
Codrington, Admiral, 19
coins: found in wrecks, 45, 55ff., 73, 75, 183, 203
Colbert, Jean Baptiste, 181
Collingwood, Admiral Cuthbert, S., 85, 86, 101, 103
Colombo, 56, 59, 64ff.
Columbine, H.M.S. (wreck), 21
Columbine class sloops of war, 35–36
Committee for Nautical Archaeology, Institute of Archaeology, London, 227
"computer," ancient, 153–155, 160, 161
Conference of Undersea Archaeology, 1958, 186
Constantinople, 103, 127, 152
Cook, Captain James, 58
copper: preservation underwater, 6, 19, 22, 64, 108; corrosion of, 31, 65; objects found in wrecks,

copper (*cont.*)
69, 202, 218; use in shipbuilding, 158
coral reefs, wrecks on, 37–38, 44–45, 47, 75. *See also Alceste, Daedalus,* Great Basses reef, *Loo, Nautilus,* Titan Reef
Corfu, island of, 101, 160, 206
Corinth, Greece, archaeology at, 127
Corning Glass Institute, 30
Council of Underwater Archaeology, 227
Cousteau, Jacques-Yves: visits Antikythera site, 84, 152; work at Grand Congloué, 175–178, 179; co-inventor of Aqua-lung, 173, 174; pioneer work in undersea research, 175–176, 180, 190; mentioned, 183, 194, 196, 208
Cozumel Island, 47–53 *passim*
Cranborne Chase, excavations at, 174
Creamer, M., 74
Crete, 88, 113, 135, 163
Crile, George, 44–46
Crile, Jane, 44–46
Cuba, 46, 50
Cummins, Ed, 221
Cyprus, 135, 136
Cyrenaica, 125

Daedalus, H.M.S. (wreck), 38–42
Daino (research vessel), 194, 216
Dardanelles, 77, 88, 90, 103
De Liefde (wreck), 211
decompression: tables, 138–139, 141; schedules, 175
Delos, island of, 161, 179
Delphi, excavation at, 127
Denham, Capt. Henry, 79
Diamond, H.M.S. (destroyer), 79
diving and divers: helmet diving techniques and equipment, 118–119, 121, 139–141, 145, 174; naked divers, 129, 166–167, 168; physiological effects, 136–145;

diving and divers (*cont.*)
mortality rate, 141; record depths, 141, 167; revolutionized by Aqua-lung, 143, 173, 174; and destruction of archaeological sites, 212–219. *See also* bends; marine archaeology: difficulties with salvage divers; narcosis; sponge boats; sponge diving
diving boats, 114, 116–117
Dodecanese Islands, 114, 116, 124, 126, 127, 139
drafting, underwater, 197–201, 203. *See also* photogrammetry
drafting frame. *See* mapping frame
Dramont wreck, the, 188
drawing, underwater. *See* drafting; photogrammetry
Duckworth, Admiral, 103
Dugan, James, 84
Dumas, Frederic: and the Grand Congloué wreck, 175, 179; and the Chrétienne A wreck, 182, 183; on 1960 Gelidonya expedition, 195, 196; later work, 216, 228
Dumas-Lamboglia mapping frame, 196, 200
Dutch Archaeological Service, 228
Dutch East India Company, 54, 56, 70, 71, 72, 73

Economou, A., 127, 128, 130, 131, 136, 146, 148, 149
Edwards, G. Roger, 156–157
Edwards, H. Milne, 180
Edwards, Hugh, 74
Egdemir, Yuksel, 206
Egypt (sunken liner), 170, 171
Electric Boat Company, 205, 206
Eleftheria, (newspaper), 221
Elgin, Lord, 76, 128, 163, 167, 168
Elgin marbles, 76, 101, 128, 163, 167, 168
L'Épave du Grand Congloué (Benoit), 179

Piroux, Dr., 184
pitons, use of, 68
Pitt-Rivers, General, 174, 178
Planier Islands, wrecks at, 188
plate fleet, wreck of Mexican, 75
Plutarch, 160
Plymouth, England, 71
Pola (Italian heavy cruiser), 79
porcelain. *See* China and porcelain
Porguerelles, wrecks at, 188
Pori Island, 79, 87, 88, 91, 94
Port Calypso, 179
Port Royal, 44
Porto Cesáreo, Italy, 212
Porto Longo, Greece, 20
Potamos Bay (Antikythera), 82, 96, 113, 114, 117, 124, 130
Potamos (village and harbor), 83, 97, 149, 150, 151
pottery: preservation underwater, 30, 70; objects found in wrecks, 130, 149, 173, 176, 202, 203; as signpost of wreck, 169–170; commercial vs. archaeological value, 190–191; importance for dating, 191. *See also* amphoras; China and porcelain
Pozzouli, Italy, 159
Pression Barométrique, La (Bert), 141
pressure jets, underwater, 45, 178
Price, Dr. Derek de Solla, 154, 155, 160, 161
profits from expeditions, 72–73, 151
Public Records Office, London, 33, 54
Purvis, Admiral John Child, 85
Pylos, Greece, 19, 21

Quaglia, Commendatore, 171

Raccoon, H.M.S. (destroyer), 79
radiocarbon dating, 159
Ralph, Elizabeth, 159
Ramauget, Florent, 224
Rebikoff, Dimitri, 192, 203

Red Sea, 54
reefs, coral. *See* coral reefs
Regulations and Instructions Relating to His Majesties Service at Sea, 87, 88
Rhodes, island of, 34, 80, 113, 155, 156, 160, 161
Rhodian jars, 164
Riviera, 168, 170, 191
Robinson, Henry, 157
Roessingh, M. P. H., 71
Roman wrecks: in Sicilian salt marsh, 15–16; near Taranto, 22; in Greece (1962), 54; Spargi, island of, 193; San Nikolo Bay, 164. *See also* Albenga wreck; Antikythera wreck; Grand Congloué wreck; Titan Reef wreck
Rome, 8, 128, 133, 160, 206
Rosencrantz, Don, 204, 206
Royal Navy, 33, 34, 35, 38, 45, 80, 101, 105, 107, 109
Russell, Richard, 11, 71, 72

Saint Helena, 43
Saint-Tropez, wrecks at, 188
salt water vs. brackish or fresh water in preservation of wrecks, 11–14
San Nikolo Bay, 101, 131, 135, 148, 163, 164, 166
Sankte Nikolai (wreck), 13
Santa Maria di Leuca, Cape, 160, 212
sarcophagi from wrecks, 22, 206
Sardinia, 193, 214
Schliemann, Heinrich, 127, 174, 180
Scilly Isles, 75, 211
scorpion fish, 60
sculpture. *See* Antikythera wreck; Elgin marbles
Sea Diver (research boat), 220
Servienti, Jean Pierre, 178
Sezen, Tosun, 138, 142
Shakespeare, William, 8
sharks, 60, 77, 80, 81
Shetland Isles, 211

Shillingsworth (master of *Nautilus*), 86, 87, 91, 101
ship archaeology. *See* marine archaeology; wrecks
shipbuilding: Greek and Roman, 8, 17; medieval, 17
shipworm. *See* teredo
shipwrecks. *See* wrecks
Shovell, Sir Cloudesley, 75
Sicily, 15, 90, 160, 179, 180, 215
Siebe, Augustus, 166
silver: preservation underwater, 22–23; objects found in wrecks, 45, 69, 107. *See also* coins
skin divers: and destruction of archaeological sites, 210–219 *passim*
Slamat H.M.S. (troopship), 79
Smith, George, 88–97 *passim*, 100, 101, 109
Smith, Jon, 77, 81, 82, 107, 108, 109, 113, 114, 162, 163, 166
Smith, Logan, 7
Smithsonian Institution, 22
soap sponge, 118
Sorima Company, 171
Spain, wrecks off, 217
Spargi, island of, 193
sponge boats. *See* diving boats
sponge divers, 114–117, 124, 138, 139, 166–167
Stadiatis, Elias, 116–129 *passim*
Stafford, Joan, 107
Stafford, Roger, 107, 109, 114
Stais, Spiridion, 128, 131, 136, 142–150 *passim*, 153, 225
Stais, Valerio, 153
Standard, H.M.S., 103
statues. *See* Antikythera wreck; Elgin marbles
Stazio, Atillio, 216
stereo photomapping. *See* photogrammetry
Stockholm harbor, 13
stone objects found in wrecks, 75, 206. *See also* marble
Stotti, George (Stotto Georgios), 167
Strait of Messina, 159, 206

Straits of Bonifaccio, Corsica, wrecks at, 188
submarine for undersea research, 205, 206
sulfur on rotting wrecks, 22, 71–72
Sulla (Roman commander), 132, 133, 160, 161
Sumatra, 54
Surat, 54, 55, 56, 66, 71, 73
surveying, underwater, 178, 192–194, 196–201, 206, 208
Svoronos, J. N., 152
Syme, island of, 114, 115, 116, 124, 126, 127, 129, 139, 140, 141, 152, 166, 167
Syracuse, Sicily, 212
Syros (research ship), 131, 134, 135, 146

Ta Nea (newspaper), 223
Taillez, Philippe: work at Mahdia, 195; work at Titan Reef, 183–187; makes photo mosaics, 192; mentioned, 190, 194, 196, 208
Tangalla, Ceylon, 57, 58, 60
Taprobane, Ceylon, 57
Tasman, Abel, 58
Taranto, Italy, 10, 22, 125, 156, 160
Taranto Museum, 216
Tasman, Abel, 58
television, closed-circuit, in underwater exploration, 176
temperature of water: relation to corrosion, 11
Tempest, The (Shakespeare), 8
teredo worm, 11, 16, 18, 19, 30
Terplane, Suez, 152
textiles, found in wrecks, 13
theodolite, 193
Theoharis, Dimitrios, 145, 147
Thompson, Bill, 44
Thresher (atomic submarine), 205
Throckmorton, Joan, 80, 81, 107
Thunderer, H.M.S., 103
Titan Reef wreck, 185–187, 192